IMAGES
of America

Jewish Family and Children's Service of Greater Philadelphia

On the cover: The Jewish Foster Home, America's oldest institution of its kind, celebrated its 70th anniversary in 1925 with a celebration of its wards. The children pictured here are in front of its magnificent facility at 700 East Church Lane, in the Germantown section of Philadelphia. (Courtesy of the Philadelphia Jewish Archives Center.)

IMAGES
of America

JEWISH FAMILY AND CHILDREN'S SERVICE OF GREATER PHILADELPHIA

Allen Meyers

ARCADIA
PUBLISHING

ISBN 978-0-7385-3828-0

Published by Arcadia Publishing
Charleston, South Carolina

Printed in the United States of America

Library of Congress Catalog Card Number: 2005924381

For all general information contact Arcadia Publishing at:
Telephone 843-853-2070
Fax 843-853-0044
E-mail sales@arcadiapublishing.com
For customer service and orders:
Toll-Free 1-888-313-2665

Visit us on the Internet at www.arcadiapublishing.com

Welcome!
At Jewish Family and Children's Service of Greater Philadelphia,
our doors are always open
so that whatever challenges individuals or families may face,
they do not have to face them alone.

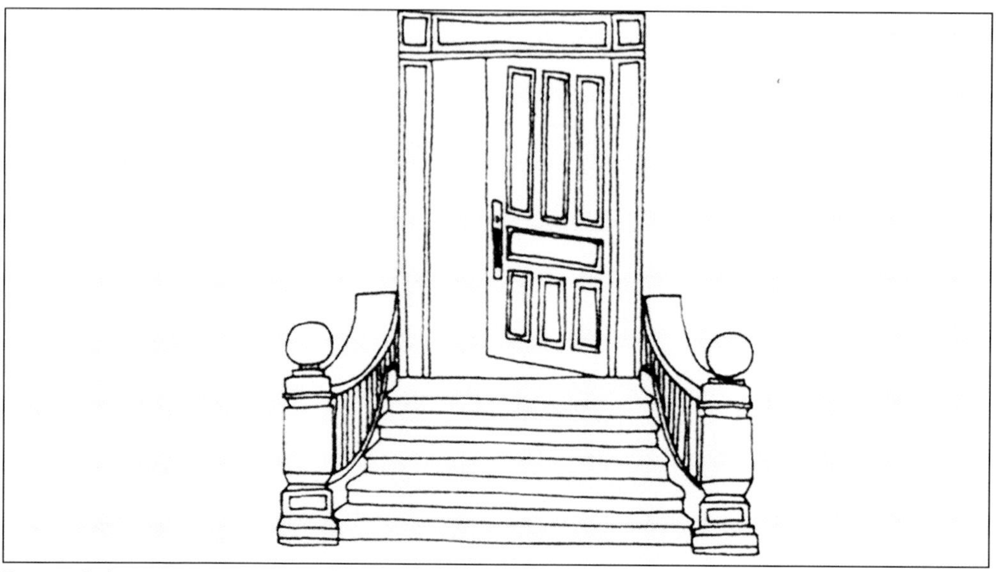

Pictured above is an artist's rendering of the doorway at 1610 Spruce Street in Center City, the home of Jewish Family and Children's Service of Greater Philadelphia and predecessor agencies, the Jewish Welfare Society of Philadelphia and the Jewish Family Service of Philadelphia, from 1944 to 2001. (Courtesy of JFCS.)

Contents

FOREWORD

When Jews of Philadelphia came together, 150 years ago, to take care of those in the community who were not able to make it without help, they were following two essential statements that reflect the systems of value that lie at the roots of the Jewish community in the United States. The often-quoted words of Emma Lazarus's well-known poem "The New Collossus" are the embodiment of our forerunners' pledge to those seeking refuge: "Give me . . . your poor, your . . . wretched." A biblical verse found in Leviticus sounds the pedal tone for the work of individuals forming themselves into a community. "And you shall love your neighbor as yourself" requires that we translate that love into caring for each other. It is not sufficient that we care about one another. To create and sustain community, it is necessary that we transform that caring into concrete acts of loving kindness.

When the first predecessors of Jewish Family Service and the Association for Jewish Children organized themselves in the mid-1800s as agencies of the Jewish community to provide a lifeline for those who needed it, Jewish values stood as the foundation for these Jewish communal institutions.

Who were the people, who were our first clients? They were our ancestors who arrived at these shores and needed assistance in providing for their families until they found work and became self-sustaining. They were in need of financial and emotional support and basic vocational guidance. They needed to learn how to negotiate the city via its streetcars and how to provide guidance to their children in a culture new to them. Like the children in Henry Roth's masterpiece *Call It Sleep*, their children were in a universe alien to our parent-clients. These families needed guidance. Sometimes the gap between the generations was so great that it required providing services to children, temporarily living in quarters separate from one another. Husbands and wives, born here or having migrated from other lands, sometimes were finding themselves at an impasse with one another. The protagonists of *Call It Sleep* did not know of such resources in their community. One wonders, had they known, would they have made the trip uptown?

Boards of governors broadly shaped the aims and scope of services developed and provided by professional social workers. The larger organized Jewish community assisted with funds and partnerships that were formed to provide the services and financial assistance necessary to keep our clients out of poverty.

Over the course of ensuing generations, Jewish families became part of the Philadelphia body politic, as the earlier new Americans, who had come from the German-speaking states, had done. It was during the interbellum years of 1918 to 1939, and even during the years of World War II, that the Jewish community turned inward, looking after the needs of those who comprised the Jewish community of Philadelphia. The community helped individuals and families with precious papers of sponsorship. They were lifesavers for those few. Unprepared for the personal histories of those who later reached the community from the indescribable experience of World War II, the Jewish community reached out with traditional assistance and the well-intentioned but painful advice to "forget the past and build a new future." It took years for us as a community to reeducate ourselves. We took our first steps with the refusenik refuges from the Soviet Union in the 1970s, offering services to individuals and families, much as the American Jewish community had done in the 1880s, offering services to "them" but not integrating them into "our" homes and lives. When the second wave of Soviet Jewish emigrants came to Philadelphia and its environs in the early 1990s, we were, in fact, ready for them, inviting many into our homes and becoming the communal families that they needed, even if only for a short time. Our work with former refuseniks and subsequent Russian émigrés comprised one of our finest hours. Some are part of our staff today! We celebrate together as part of the same community.

I am grateful to have been asked to write these words of historical background. My encounter with Jewish Family and Children's Service started almost 50 years ago as a first-year student at the University of Pennsylvania School of Social Work. I was assigned and trained in the Services for Older Persons program. That exposure to the community and social work imprinted on me a professional identity of respect and responsibility, sensitivity, clear-eyed study and critique, and teamwork that grew with ensuing years of practice. As a current member of the board of trustees of Jewish Family and Children's Service, I value the rigorous and respectful guidance that brought me fully into the world of social work and the maturing of the Jewish community.

—Adena Potok

Our Predecessor Agencies and Past Presidents

ASSOCIATION FOR JEWISH CHILDREN

JEWISH FOSTER HOME, 1855

Mrs. Anna Allen — *Mr. L. J. Leberman* — *Mr. Henry Cohen*

JEWISH FOSTER HOME AND ORPHAN ASYLUM

Abraham Hart — *Mason Hirsh* — *Clinton Mayer*
Isadore Binswanger — *Leo Loeb* — *Harry Nusbaum*

HEBREW ORPHANS HOME

Morris Haber — *Max S. Apt*
Harry J. Cohen — *Max Markovitz*

FOSTER HOME FOR HEBREW ORPHANS

Benjamin L. Rubinsohn — *Leo H. Heimerdinger* — *Laurence Brunswick*

JUVENILE AID SOCIETY

Mrs. Sol Selig — *Mrs. Arthur Loeb*
Mrs. I. A. Liveright — *Mrs. B. I. DeYoung*

HOMEWOOD SCHOOL (HEBREW SHELTERING HOME)

L. B. Levinson — *Harry Sax* — *Henry W. Schorr* — *Lester Hano*
J. I. Burnstine — *Joseph Herbach* — *Henry W. Braude* — *George Schorr*

NORTHEASTERN HEBREW ORPHANS HOME

Mrs. Frannie Ziserman — *Mrs. Lois Sabaroff* — *Mrs. Louis Tobin*
Mrs. Bertha Reidenberg — *Mrs. Louis E. Myers*

ASSOCIATION FOR JEWISH CHILDREN

Jacob C. Gutman — *Alfred J. Goldsmith* — *Irving Schwartz*
George M. Kohn — *Lester Miller* — *Seymour Kurland*
Samuel E. Feldgoise — *Dr. Earl S. Scott* — *Joseph Smukler*
Samuel H. Levy — *Mrs. Anita Langsfeld* — *Richard J. Braemer*

JEWISH FAMILY SERVICE, 1869

Simon W. Arnold — *Morris Kind* — *Mrs. Alice Gouley*
Moses Simon — *Albert H. Lieberman* — *Ralph Huberman*
Solomon Gans — *Abram S. Berg, Jr.* — *William E. McKenna*
Edward Rothschild — *Robert D. Abrahams* — *Arnold M. Kessler*
Simon Loeb — *Samuel A. Goldberg* — *Mark K. Kessler*
Max Herzberg — *Robert H. Fleisher*

Predecessor agencies of today's Jewish Family and Children's Service of Greater Philadelphia reflect a long line of distinguished leaders, as named above. (Courtesy of JFCS.)

Introduction

Now celebrating more than 150 years of service to thousands, Jewish Family and Children's Service of Greater Philadelphia (JFCS) began as an orphanage—and with a dream.

Founded in 1855 under the leadership of Rebecca Gratz, JFCS's original predecessor, the Jewish Foster Home, began with the dream of a better life for orphaned, impoverished Jewish children. Rebecca Gratz, the foremost Jewish woman leader of the 19th century, had already founded the Female Hebrew Benevolent Society and the Hebrew Sunday School Society to aid those less fortunate in the community. Moved by the sight of homeless Jewish children selling matches on the street to sustain themselves, she led other influential and compassionate women of her day to establish America's first Jewish orphanage. The Jewish Foster Home opened at 799 North Eleventh Street with five children and gave rise to a new era of Jewish caregiving in America.

In 1869, JFCS's second-earliest predecessor agency took root with the founding of the United Hebrew Charities of Philadelphia. Housed in a single rented room at 30 North Seventh Street, it coordinated the Jewish community's charitable work and use of charitable dollars and provided a host of direct services. The dream of a better life for those in need inspired its creation as well. United Hebrew Charities's mission was a broad one: to provide food, clothing, fuel, and medical assistance, grant loans, nurse the sick, aid in obtaining employment, and cover the funeral expenses of Jewish families who could not do so alone.

These two powerful organizations in Jewish communal life and their successor agencies evolved and grew over generations, continuing to adapt their services to meet the changing needs of Philadelphia's Jewish community. They responded with vision and strength to unforeseen events of human history—world wars, mass immigration and refugee crises, economic panics and the Great Depression, tuberculosis and other health threats—and they helped families deal with everyday issues and the overwhelming stresses that place children and adults at risk. Together they were blessed by the dedication of community volunteers, who enabled them to stretch limited resources and who did so much to enhance the agencies' quality of care. Inspired by a tradition of caring rooted in Jewish values of *tikkun olam* (repairing the world), *gemilut chasadim* (acts of loving kindness), *mitzvot* (good deeds), and *tzedakah* (justice), these agencies persisted in reaching out to members of the community in crisis and in need. In doing so, they also reflected the increasing professionalism of social work.

The birth of the Federation of Jewish Charities in 1901 (now the Jewish Federation of Greater Philadelphia) to oversee communal fund-raising and planning gave new strength and support to their efforts.

By the end of the 19th century, the Foster Home for Hebrew Orphans, heir to the original Jewish Foster Home founded by Rebecca Gratz, occupied a large stone mansion in Germantown. It housed as many as 200 children in its heyday. In 1941, it joined with other Jewish children's service organizations to form the Association for Jewish Children of Philadelphia (AJC). The home closed its doors in the early 1950s as the emphasis in child welfare services shifted away from institutional settings and toward more homelike settings of group homes, in-home services, and foster care.

Jewish Family Service of Philadelphia (JFS), which had originated as the United Hebrew Charities and developed out of a broader service tradition, grew to include offices throughout Philadelphia and beyond and increasingly to emphasize counseling and casework. It continued to provide resettlement and emergency assistance and created far-reaching new programs, including senior services, Jewish family life education, and consultation.

The merger of these two great agencies in 1983 combined their strengths and enabled them to serve children and families alike, from birth through old age. The new agency became known as Jewish Family and Children's Service of Greater Philadelphia (JFCS) and was housed at the office of the former JFS at 1610 Spruce Street.

Today's JFCS, headquartered at 2100 Arch Street, serves more than 44,000 individuals and households throughout Greater Philadelphia each year with a wide variety of counseling, support, and education services. It also reaches out with spiritual support through its chaplaincy program. The agency's sense of community, of "reaching out . . . touching lives," has gone forth for more than 150 years, giving aid and comfort to thousands of people of all ages, helping them sustain their lives with dignity and strength. It is the daily work of translating Jewish values into action.

Allen Meyers, a noted community historian, author, and graduate of Gratz College, along with JFCS and Marcia Zoslaw Siegal, former JFCS director of marketing and communications and consultant to the history book project, present a snapshot of Jewish Family and Children's Service of Greater Philadelphia's collective history.

One

The Jewish Foster Home

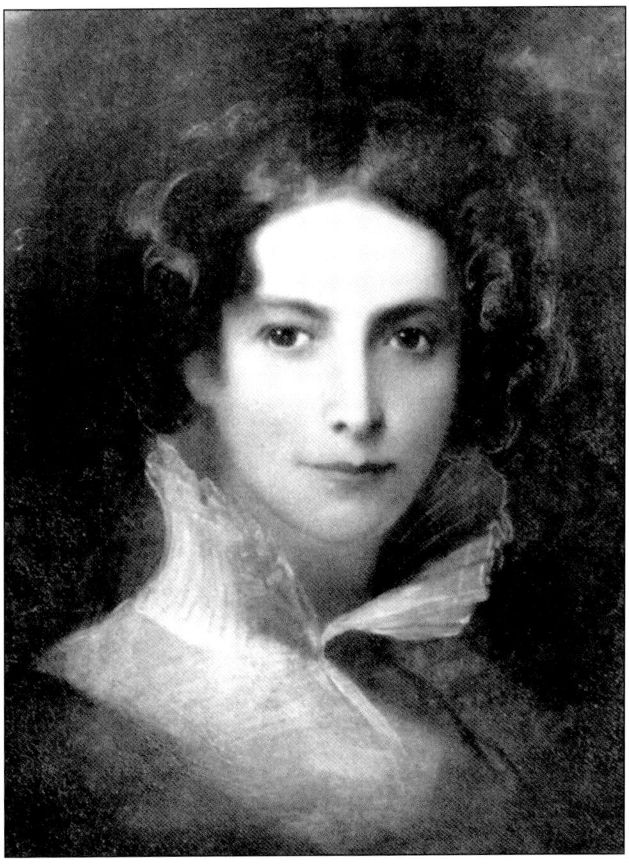

Local Jewish women in the mid-19th century banded together to create organizations to assist the poor and the vulnerable in the Philadelphia Jewish community. Rebecca Gratz (1781–1869), the daughter of prominent Philadelphia businessman Michael Gratz and his wife, Miriam, provided great leadership in these endeavors. She led in the founding of a number of important Jewish communal institutions, including the Female Hebrew Benevolent Society (1819), the Hebrew Sunday Society (1838), and the Jewish Foster Home, America's first Jewish orphanage (1855). (Portrait by Thomas Sully; courtesy of the Philadelphia Jewish Archives Center.)

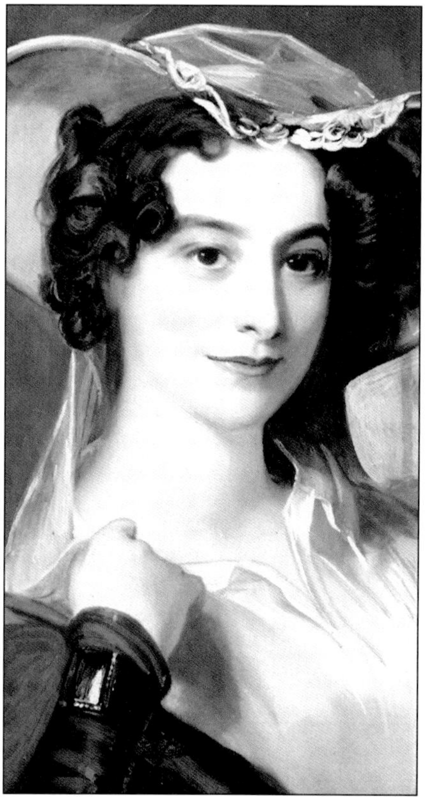

Painted by different artists of her day, Rebecca Gratz was portrayed in varying ways and even became the subject of legend, said to be the inspiration for the Rebecca of Sir Walter Scott's *Ivanhoe*. Her dedication as a social activist and her indefatigable energy improving lives in her community were constant throughout her life. Seventy-four years old when she established the Jewish Foster Home, she is considered to be the "founding mother" of today's Jewish Family and Children's Service of Greater Philadelphia (JFCS) since the home was JFCS's original predecessor agency. (Portrait by Thomas Sully; courtesy of Temple University Libraries, Urban Archives, Philadelphia, Pennsylvania.)

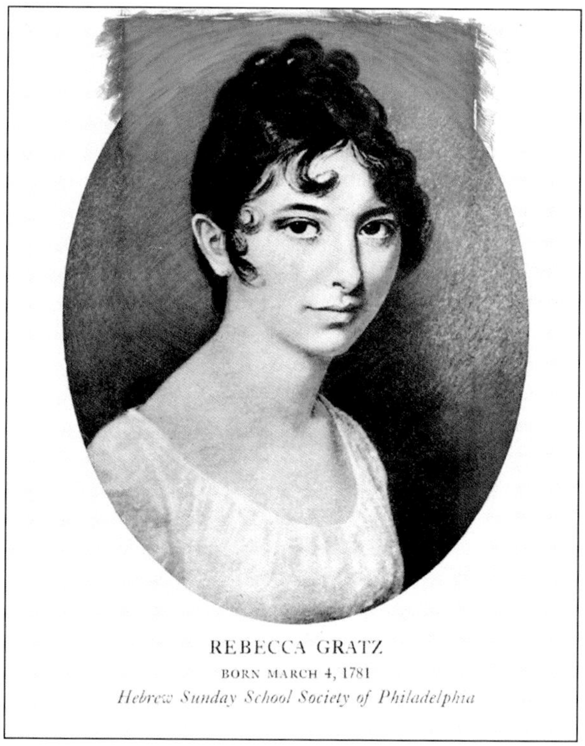

Among the artists to portray Rebecca Gratz, pioneering philanthropist and social worker, was the painter Edward Greene Malbone. (Courtesy of Temple University Libraries, Urban Archives, Philadelphia, Pennsylvania.)

This statue of Rebecca Gratz, housed in the State Museum of Pennsylvania in Harrisburg, honors her as a famous Pennsylvanian and leading citizen of her time. In addition to her role in the Jewish community, she helped establish and served on the boards of nonsectarian institutions devoted to assisting underprivileged women and children, including the Philadelphia Orphan Asylum. She drew inspiration to establish the Jewish Foster Home in part based on that experience and her belief that orphaned Jewish children would best be served by an institution where they could observe Jewish religious traditions. (Courtesy of Temple University Libraries, Urban Archives, Philadelphia, Pennsylvania.)

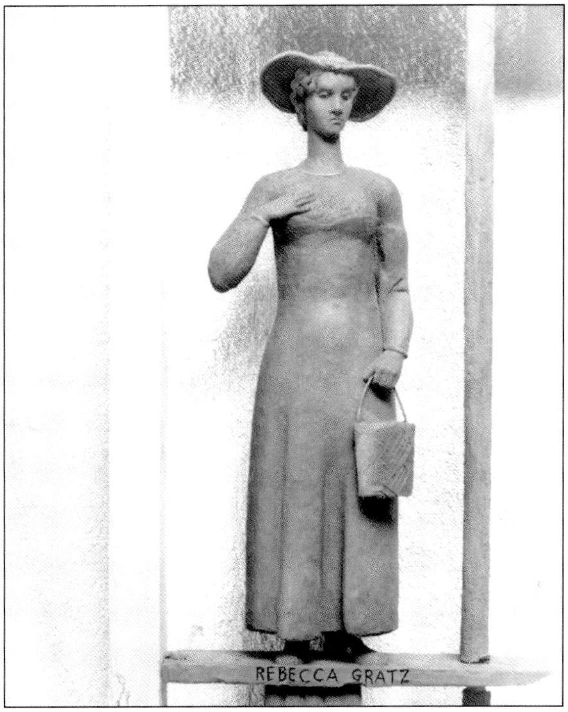

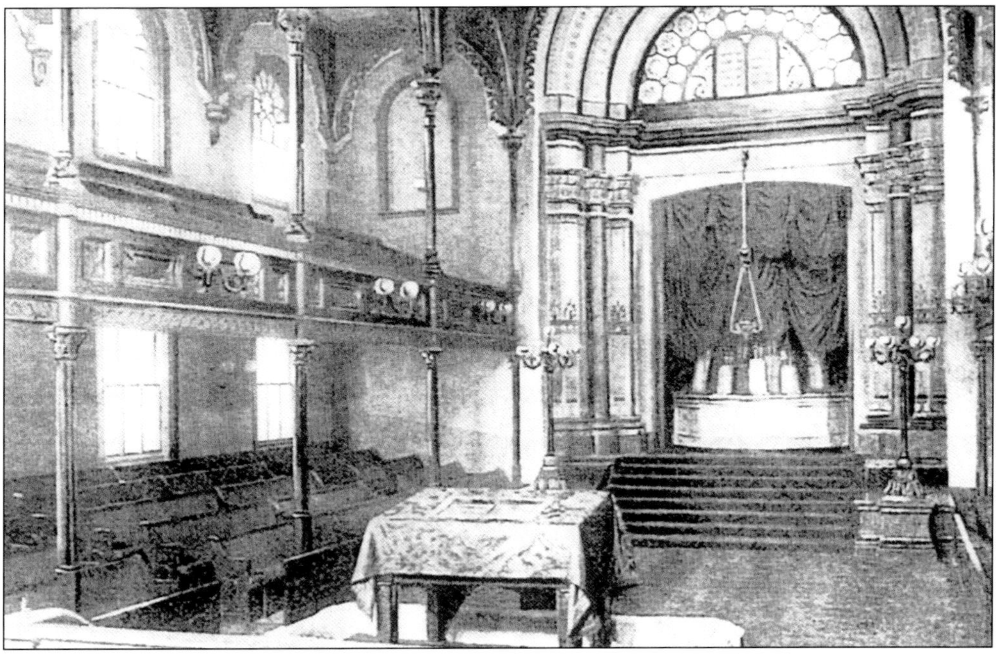

Congregation Mikveh Israel, Philadelphia's first synagogue, included many prominent members of the Philadelphia Jewish community and was a hub of Jewish charitable activity. Rev. Dr. Sabato Morais, spiritual leader of the synagogue, helped inspire congregant Rebecca Gratz in her lifelong work in the local Jewish community. He consecrated the Jewish Foster Home when it was dedicated May 1, 1855. Pictured above is the synagogue sanctuary. (Courtesy of the Allen Meyers collection.)

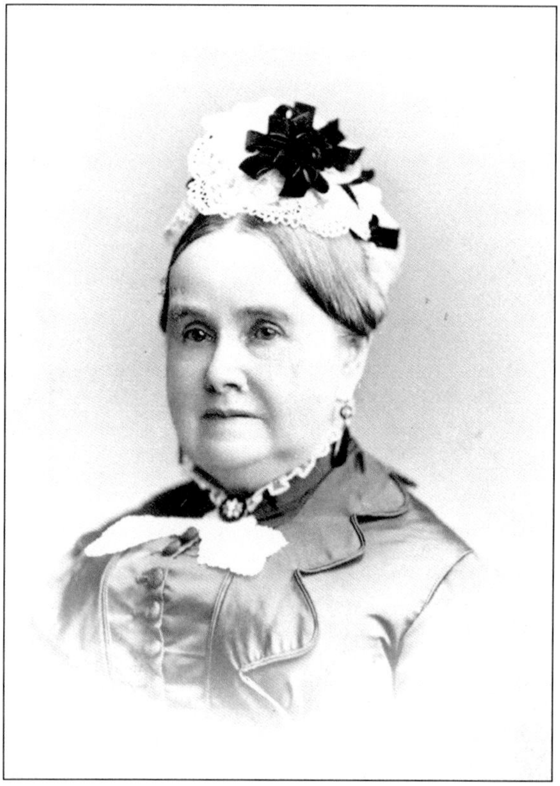

Women played a vital role in the development of the Jewish Foster Home. That commitment was exemplified by its first directress, Anna Allen (1855–1867), who oversaw day-to-day life at the facility. (Courtesy of the Philadelphia Jewish Archives Center.)

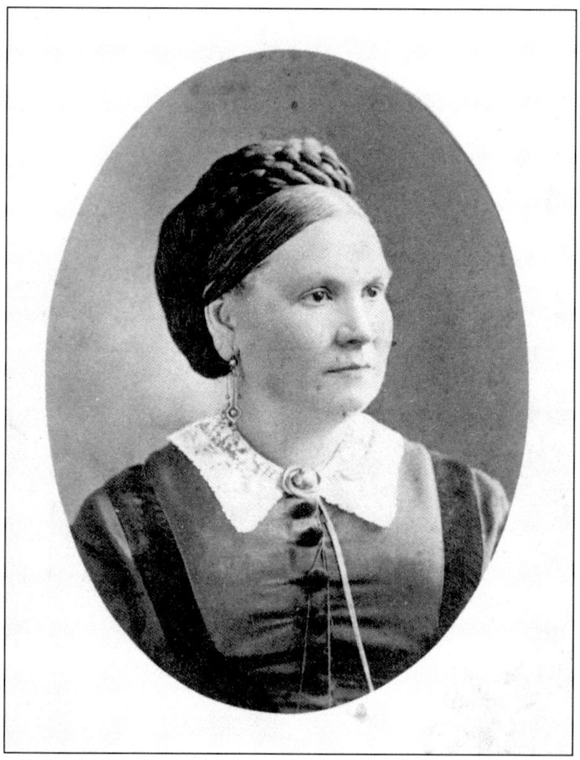

Mrs. L. J. Lederman, another directress of the Jewish Foster Home, came on board in the post–Civil War era when the home gave sanctuary to a growing number of orphan children. She was celebrated as a "virtuous woman, far above pearls is her value" when she was introduced at the 1869 Purim Ball sponsored by the United Hebrew Charities. (Courtesy of the Philadelphia Jewish Archives Center.)

Religious leaders in Philadelphia's Jewish community banded together to urge congregants to join in raising funds for community projects, motivated by the tradition that "all Jews are responsible for one another." Arriving in Philadelphia in the 1870s, Rev. Dr. Marcus Jastrow encouraged this philanthropic spirit in his own congregation by influencing individuals at Rodeph Shalom to join in communal support of the Jewish Foster Home. (Courtesy of the Philadelphia Jewish Archives Center.)

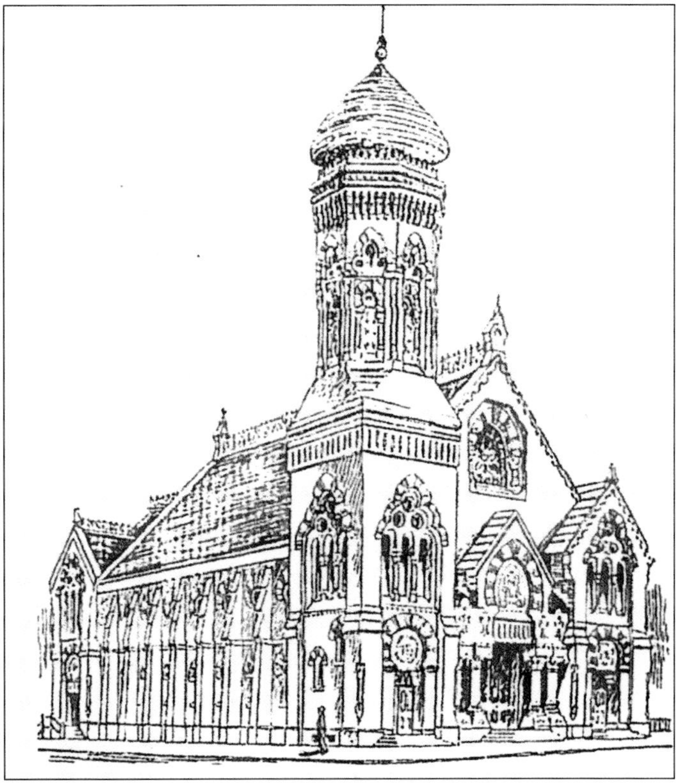

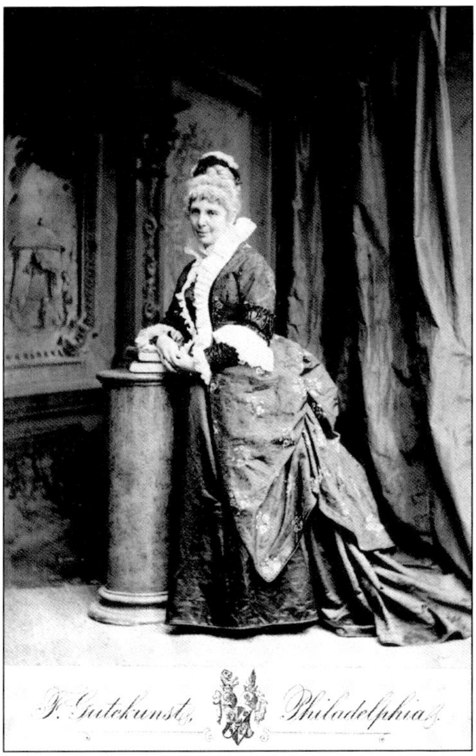

Mrs. Henry Cohen served as first president of the Ladies Associate Board for the Jewish Foster Home and as a directress in the 1870s. The home had relocated in 1860 to expanded quarters at 1431 North Fifteenth Street. The economic panic in 1873 increased poverty nationwide, and in Philadelphia, more Jewish children were in need of help. By 1874, the Jewish Foster Home had cared for 112 children in its 19 years of existence. (Courtesy of the Philadelphia Jewish Archives Center.)

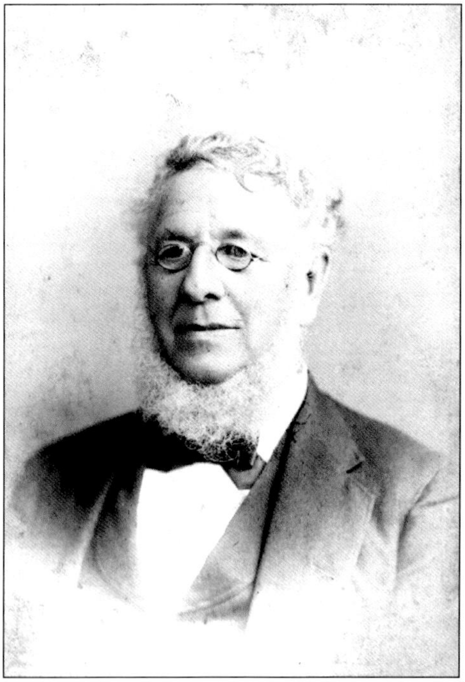

Abraham Hart, a leader of Jewish communal affairs, took the helm of the Jewish Foster Home as president from 1874 to 1875. He had been instrumental in raising funds for the institution since its earliest days. (Courtesy of the Philadelphia Jewish Archives Center.)

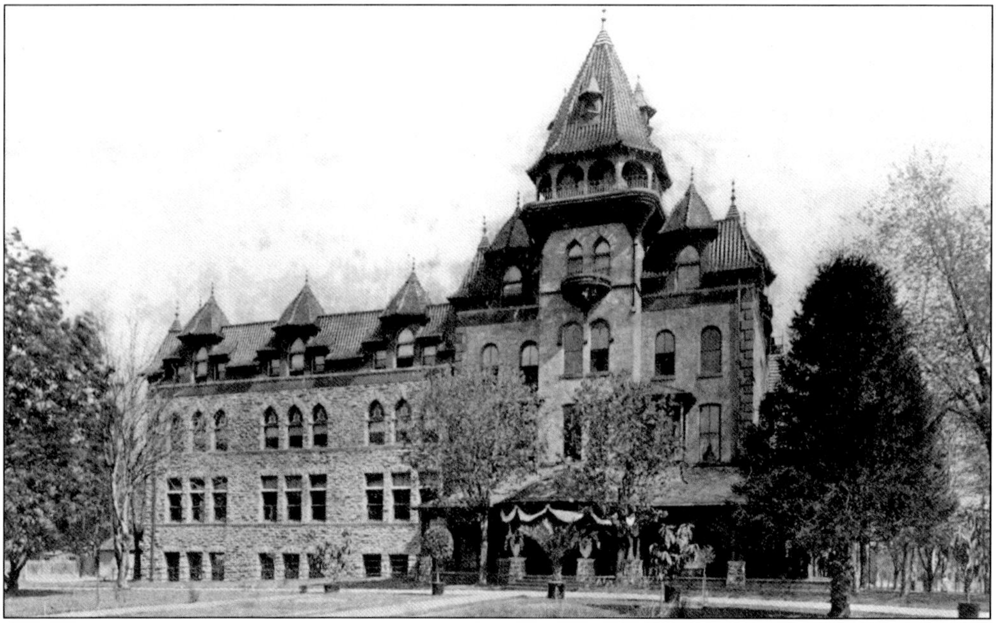

The Jewish Foster Home had become a national model for Jewish and non-Jewish orphanages in its quality of care. As the organization expanded, there was a demand for greater Jewish community support. Isidore Binswanger, a prominent communal leader, served as president of the home (now formally renamed the Jewish Foster Home and Orphan Asylum of Philadelphia) from 1875 to 1890. He played a leading role in its 1881 move to larger quarters at 700 East Church Lane in Germantown in what was then a suburban-like section of the city. The new facility opened with 39 children. It would remain a haven for Jewish children in crisis and in need for 70 years. (Courtesy of the Philadelphia Jewish Archives Center.)

Isidore Binswanger, president of the home when it relocated to its final quarters in Germantown, knew each ward by name. He was beloved by the children for the personal interest he took in their welfare. The Binswanger name would be prominent throughout successive generations of agency history. (Courtesy of the Free Library of Philadelphia, Print and Picture Collection, John F. Lewis Portrait Collection.)

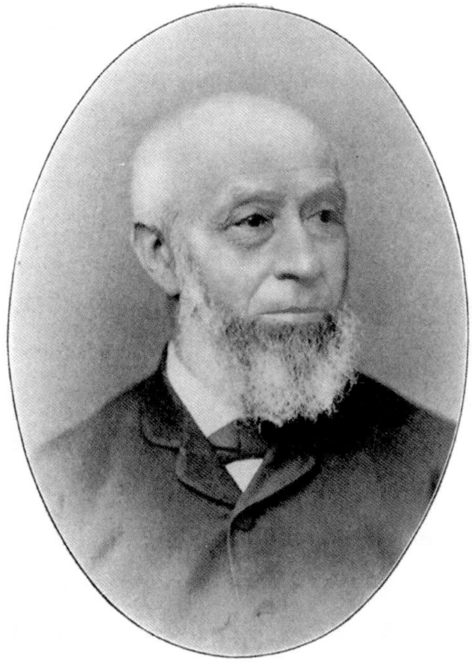

ISIDORE BINSWANGER
President 1875–90

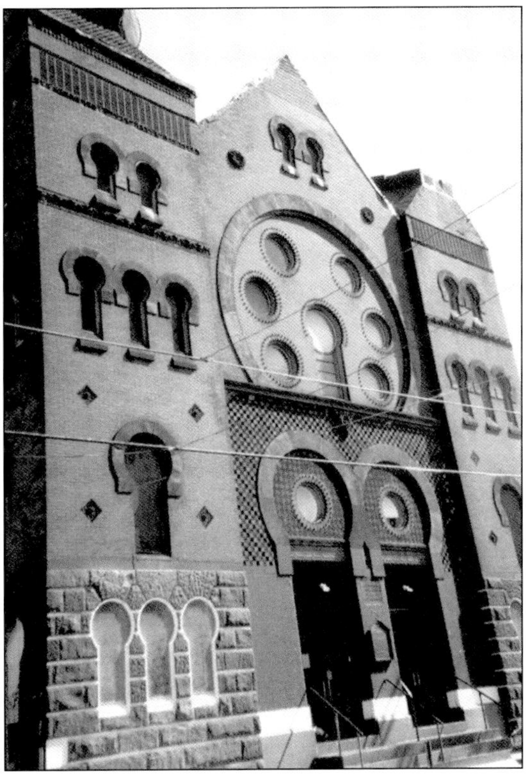

The growth of Jewish congregations in Philadelphia in the late 19th century allowed for the continuous development of Jewish philanthropy. This was of great help at the same time the community was facing a huge influx of Eastern European immigrants that began in the 1880s. At Congregation Adath Jeshurun, located at Seventh and Columbia Avenues, for instance, many congregants had dual affiliations with the synagogue and the Jewish Foster Home and Orphan Asylum. (Courtesy of the Allen Meyers collection.)

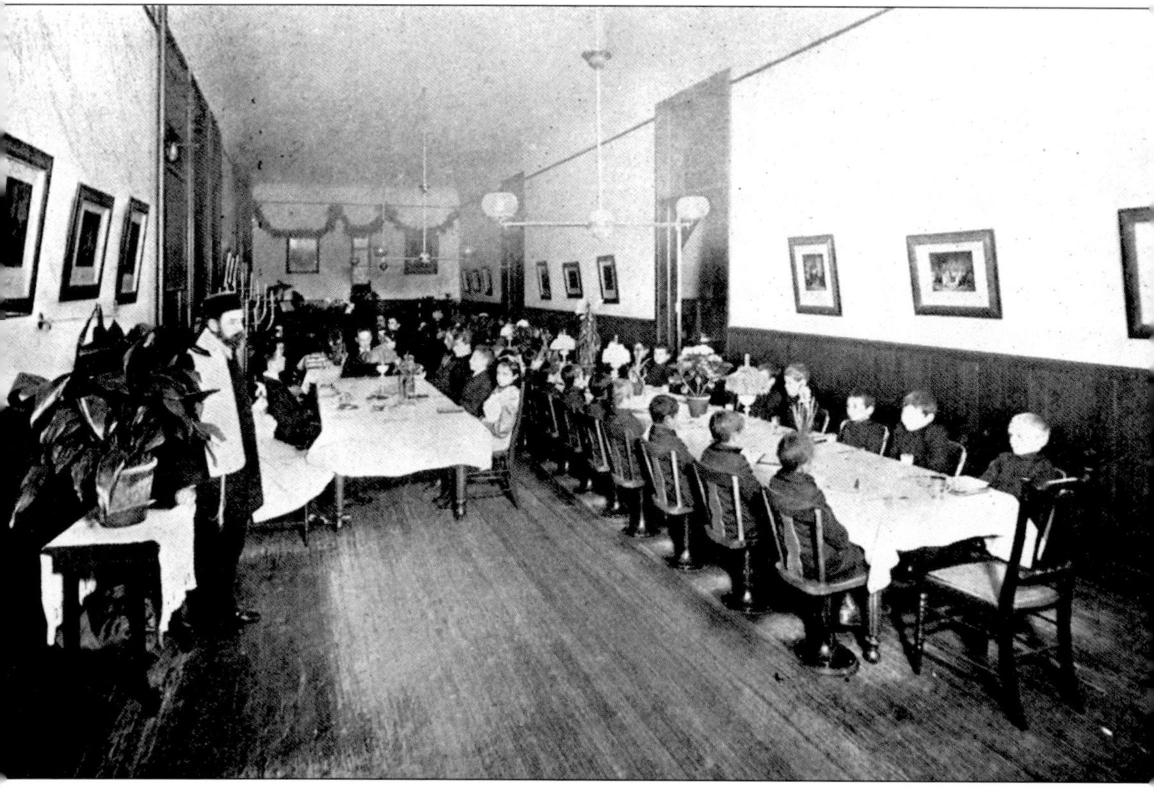

The sense of family and community permeated the institution founded by Rebecca Gratz. The Jewish Foster Home and Orphan Asylum, supported by prominent Jewish families, welcomed and observed Jewish holidays and festivals, as in this celebration of a Passover seder. (Courtesy of the Philadelphia Jewish Archives Center.)

As the Philadelphia Jewish community grew throughout the 19th century, so did the orphanage and its ability to support a growing number of new wards. Reform Congregation Keneseth Israel (1847) built its new building at Broad Street and Columbia Avenue in 1892. Additions were planned for the Jewish Foster Home and Orphan Asylum in the same year—funded after an appeal from Keneseth Israel's pulpit by its leader, Rabbi Joseph Kraskopf. (Courtesy of the Dropsie College Archives.)

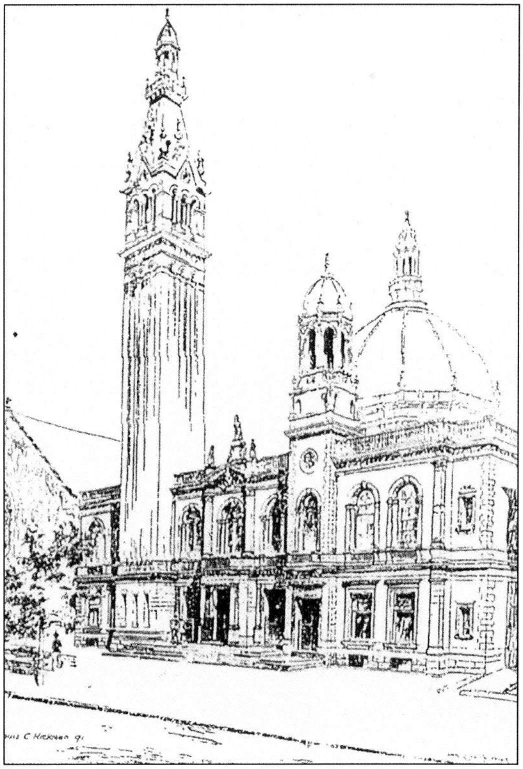

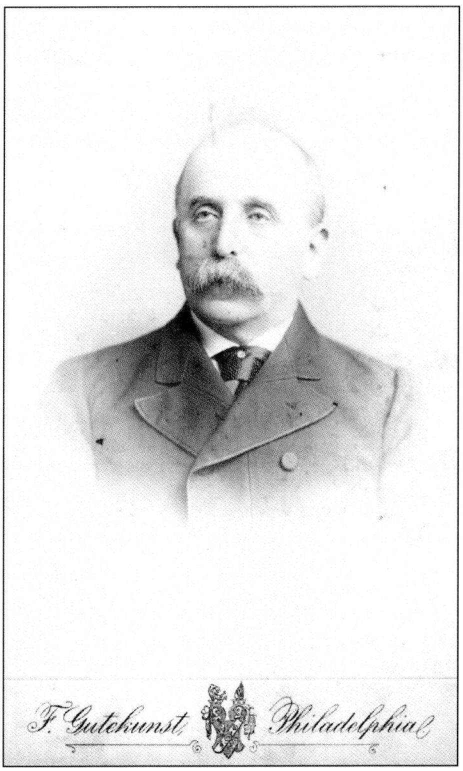

The leadership of the Jewish Foster Home passed to Mason Hirsh (left) from 1890 to 1892. He would be succeeded by Leo Loeb, who helped lead the orphanage forward into the 20th century despite many obstacles, including the nationwide economic depression of 1893 and the challenges of the massive wave of Jewish immigration. (Courtesy of the Philadelphia Jewish Archives Center.)

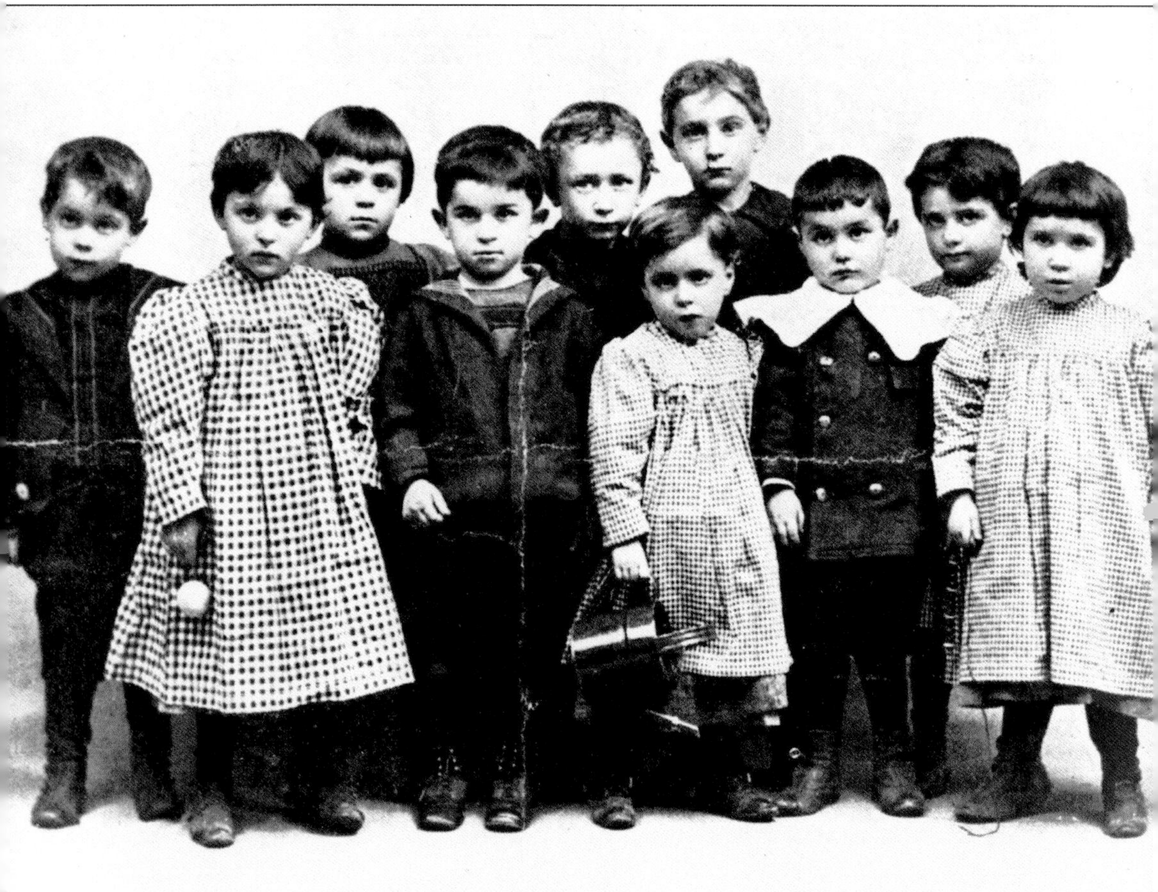

From the 1880s to the 1920s, thousands of Jewish immigrants from Russia and Poland flocked to Philadelphia seeking refuge from religious persecution. Immigrant children of that era are portrayed above. The home had admitted its first child of Eastern European origin in 1882. Now, joined by new Jewish orphanages and child welfare organizations that had arisen to meet rising demands of these "new immigrants," it would continue to serve Jewish children—immigrants and others—in need of shelter and care well into the 20th century. (Courtesy of the Philadelphia Jewish Archives Center.)

Two

Predecessors and Partners

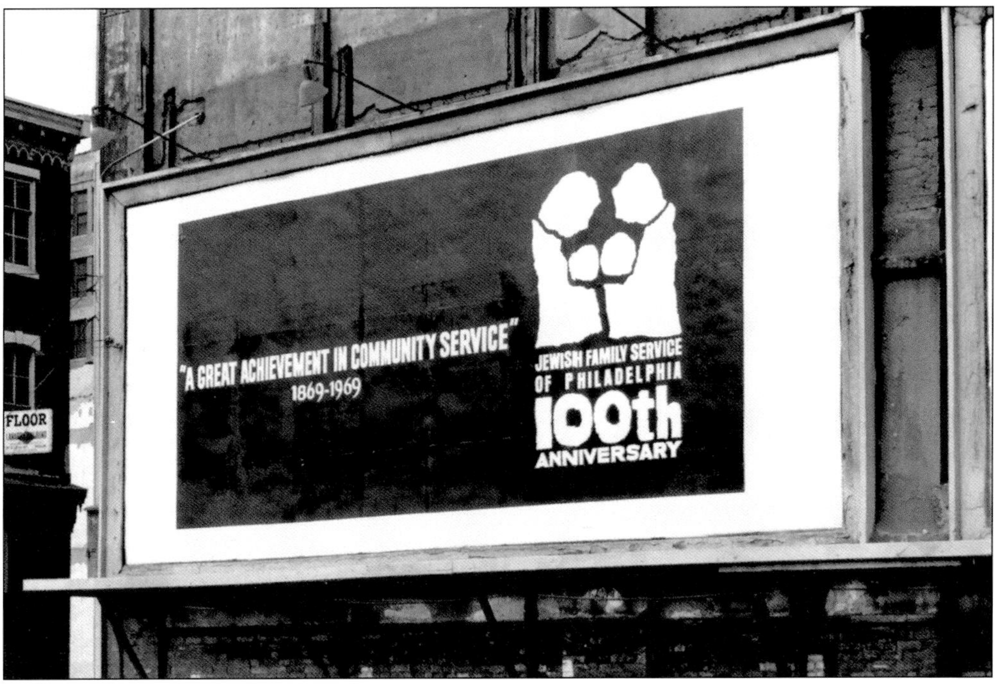

The dream of a single formal agency to merge many of Philadelphia's existing Jewish charitable organizations and better coordinate their fund-raising and resources became a reality in 1869 with the creation of the United Hebrew Charities of Philadelphia. United Hebrew Charities was the original predecessor of Jewish Family Service of Philadelphia (JFS) and the second-earliest predecessor agency of today's JFCS. A century of service was the theme for this billboard that highlighted the 100th anniversary of JFS in 1969. (Courtesy of the Philadelphia Jewish Archives Center.)

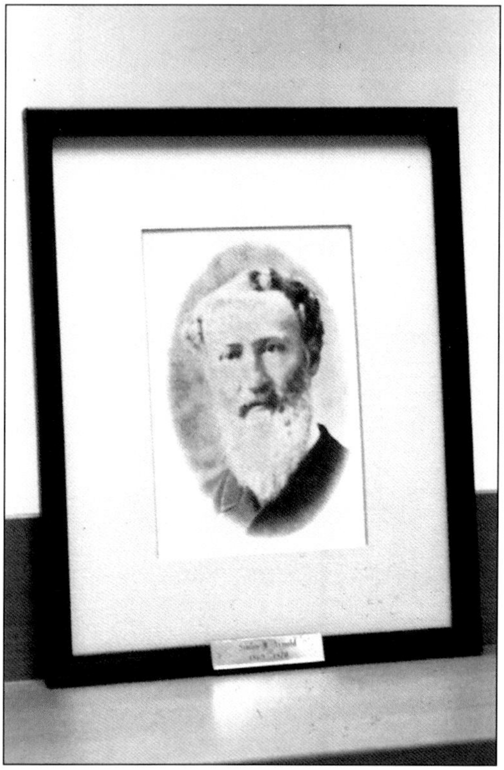

Simon Arnold was the first president of United Hebrew Charities. Its first office was a single rented room on 30 North Seventh Street. Within its first 130 days, the agency served 117 families and 114 single persons with 1,031 yards of goods, 661 garments, 237 pairs of hosiery, 125 pairs of shoes, 78 pieces of bed linen, 22 blankets, 110 tons of coal, and 29 loans totaling $700. Applicants for relief came to the office on Sundays when the board met to give final approval. (Courtesy of JFCS.)

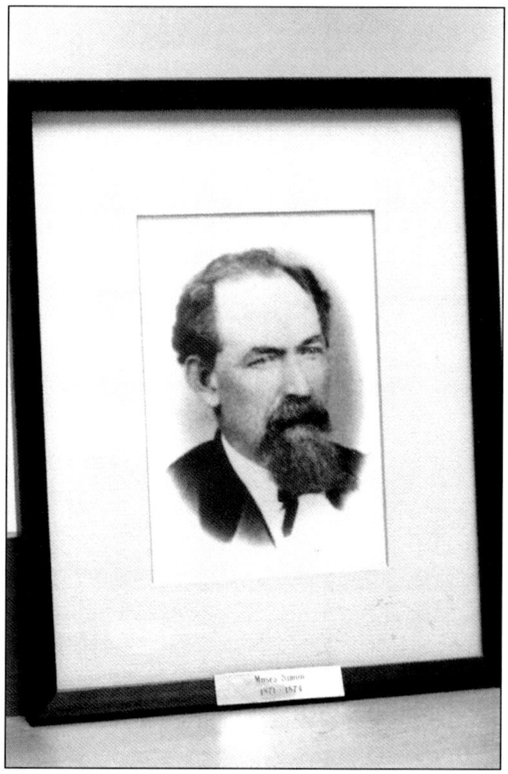

Simon Arnold was succeeded by Moses Simon (1871–1875), who led the United Hebrew Charities during the panic of 1873 when demands for relief for food, shelter, fuel, and other critical necessities of daily life rose sharply. (Courtesy of JFCS.)

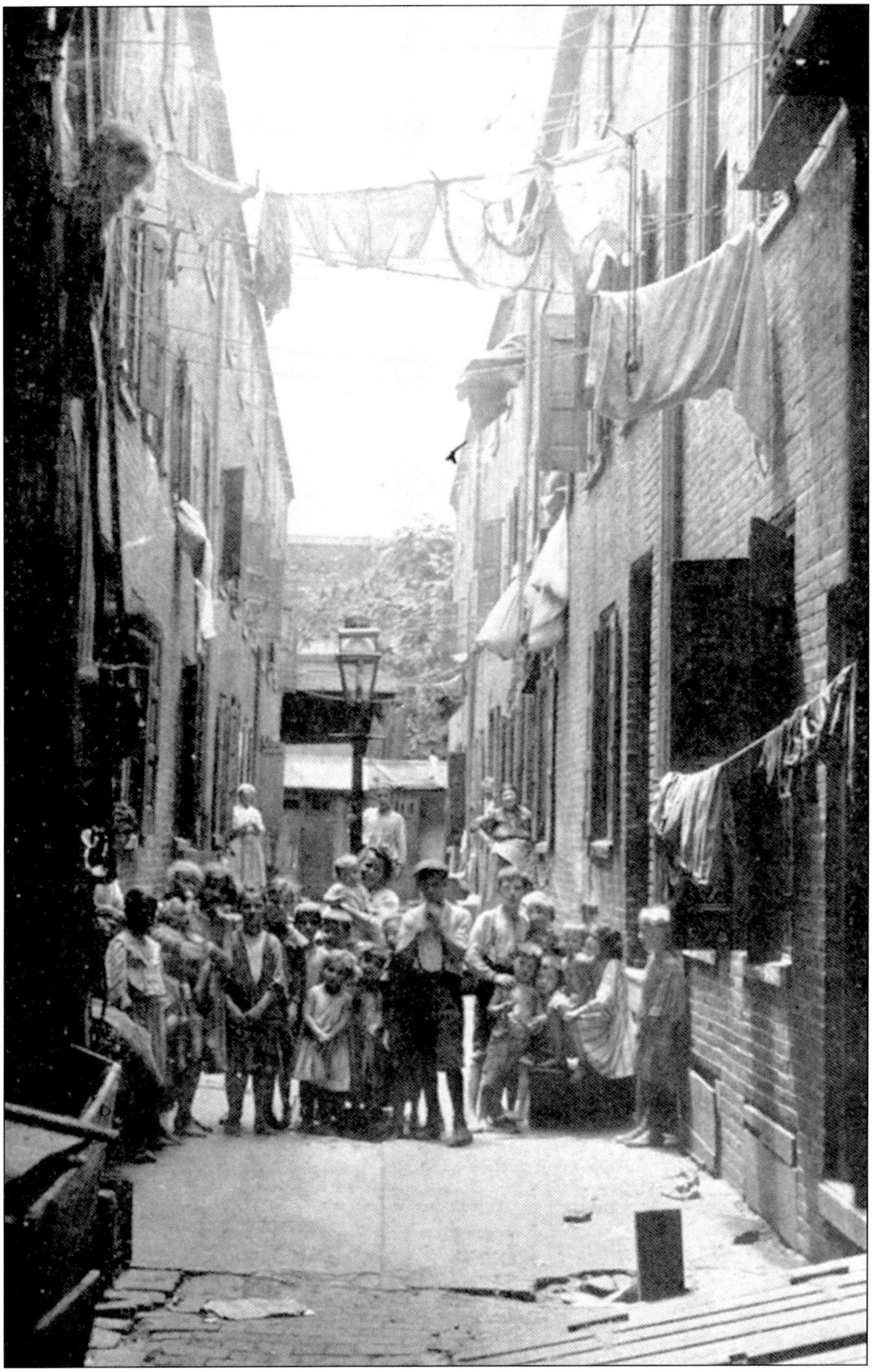

Slum living conditions were of great concern to the United Hebrew Charities and its successor agencies. Members of the ladies' committee were assigned responsibility for individual families, whom they visited on a regular basis. Visitors provided food and clothing allotments and taught mothers better housekeeping methods when needed. (Courtesy of the Philadelphia Jewish Archives Center.)

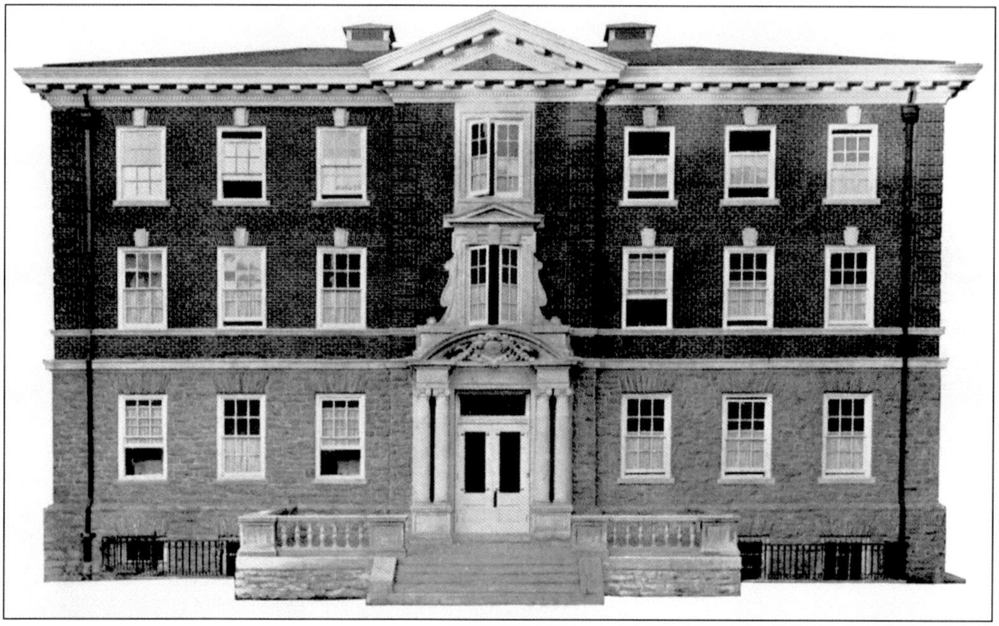

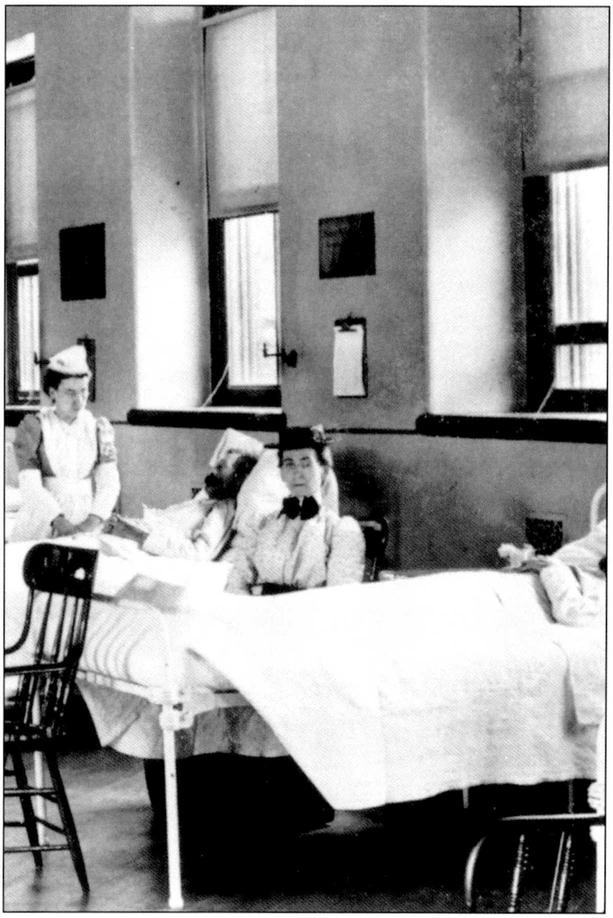

Tuberculosis was a scourge throughout the 19th and into the 20th centuries in Philadelphia. It often reached epidemic proportions, especially in overcrowded and impoverished slum neighborhoods. This escalated demands on the United Hebrew Charities for financial assistance and on local orphanages for shelter for orphaned children. Jewish Hospital, founded in 1865, and Mount Sinai Hospital, founded in 1925, became important allies in treating this disease that devastated families and children. In the early 1900s, the United Hebrew Charities also had its own staff physicians to care for clients with tuberculosis. The agency joined with other Jewish social service organizations to promote the formation of Eagleville Sanitarium in 1909 to care for the growing number of tuberculosis patients in the community. Pictured here is the facade of Jewish Hospital and a ward with nurse, visitor, and patients. (Courtesy of the Philadelphia Jewish Archives Center.)

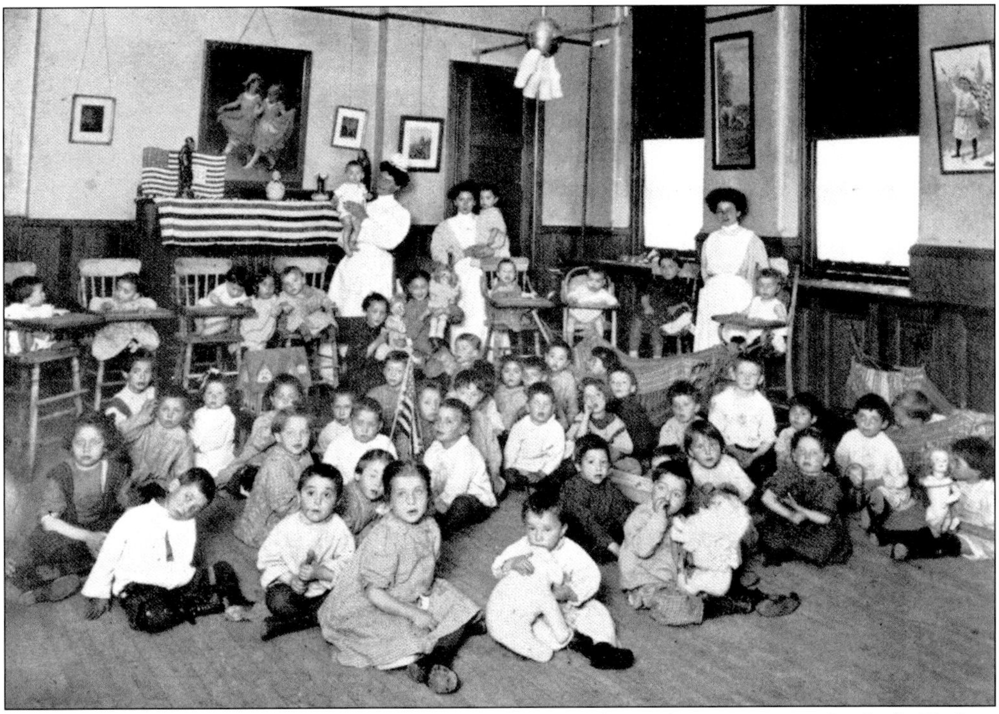

The Young Women's Union was formed in 1885 by members of Congregation Rodeph Shalom under the leadership of Fanny Binswanger. It aided immigrant children of Jewish origin. The union operated a kindergarten and a nursery school to assist in the Americanization of these newcomers. The United Hebrew Charities also reached out to many of the same immigrant families with financial aid, employment assistance, and social work services. (Courtesy of the Philadelphia Jewish Archives Center.)

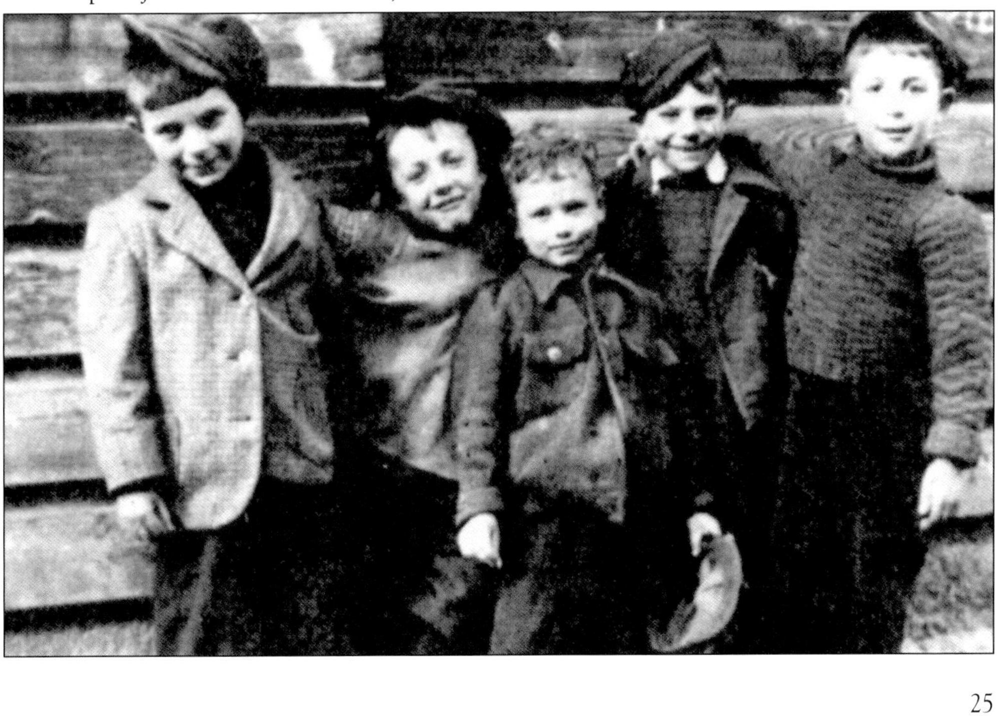

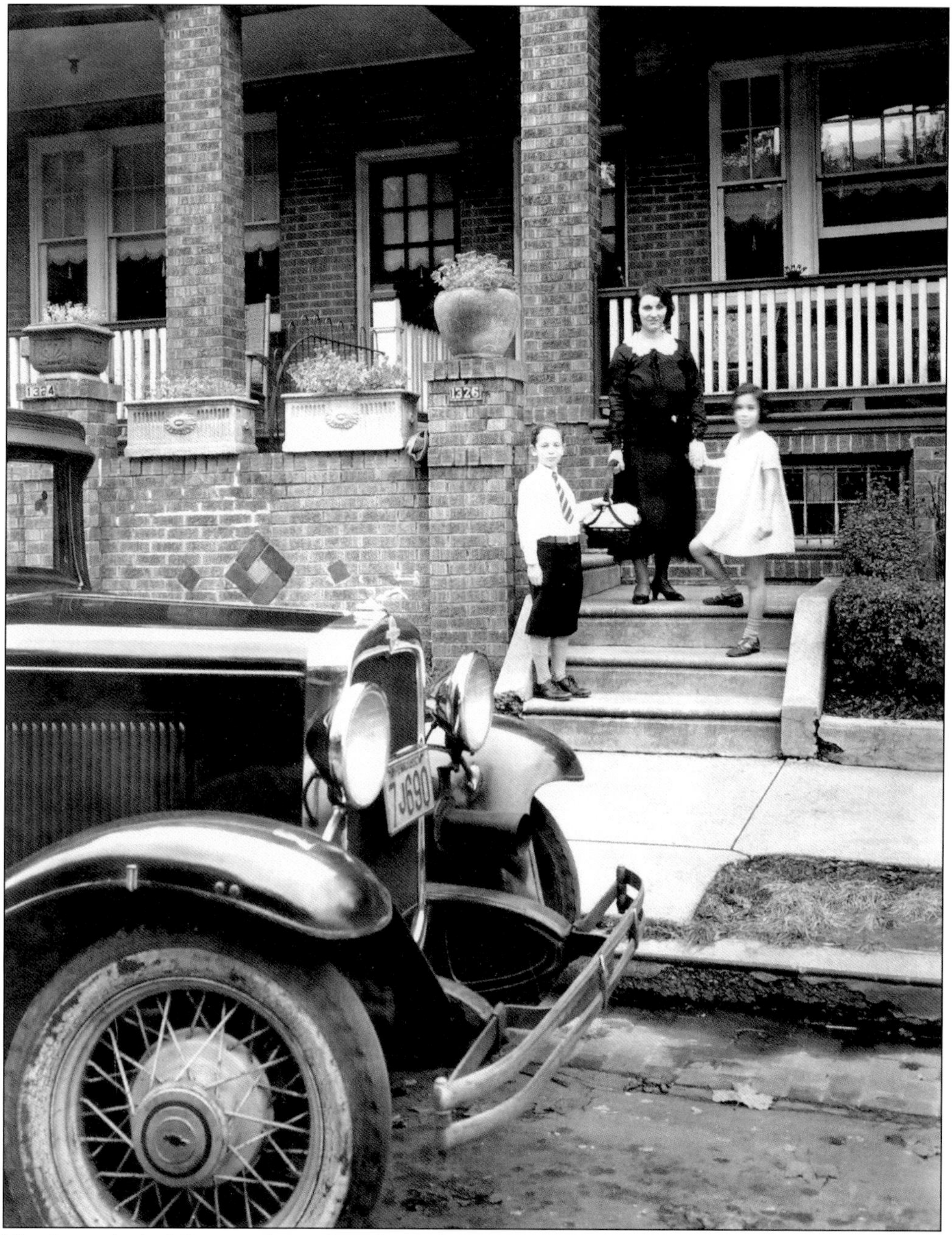

The Juvenile Aid Society, formed in the early 1900s, was an outgrowth of the Young Women's Union, and later became part of the Association for Jewish Children (AJC). It was founded by Mrs. Sol Selig of Philadelphia "to prevent young people from entering into a life of crime and despair." This group placed and supervised Jewish children in foster homes and assumed responsibility for youths referred to it by juvenile court. At the suggestion of the Philadelphia Board of Education, it would later provide home and school counseling to a number of predominantly Jewish public schools. (Courtesy of the Philadelphia Jewish Archives Center.)

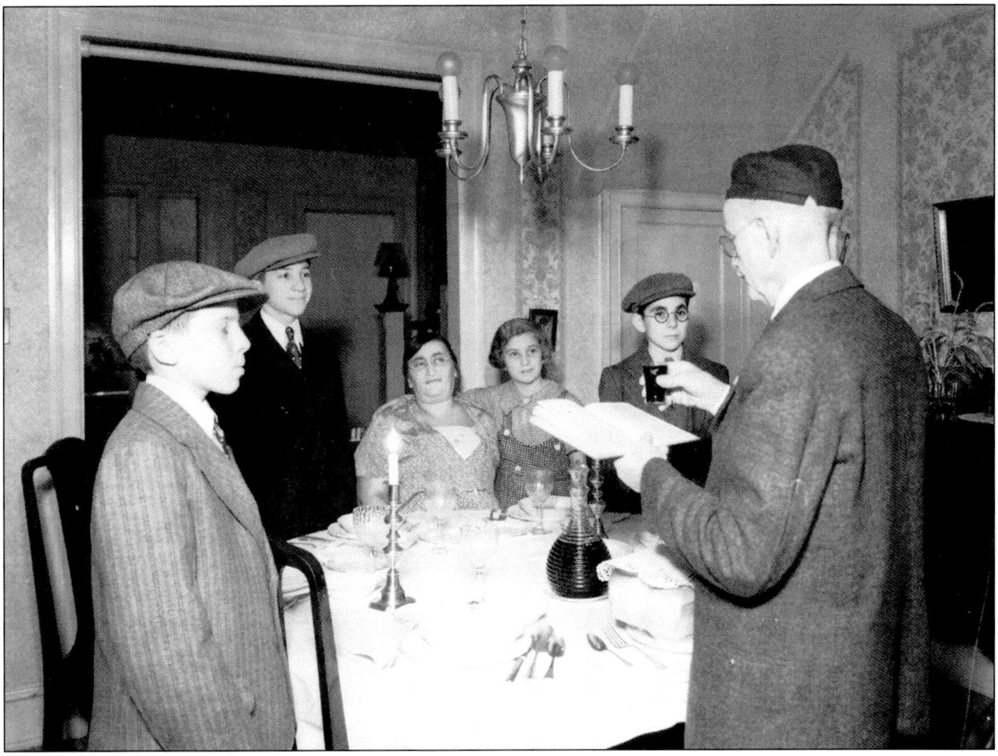

Religion was a central part of life in many of the foster homes that were under the auspices of the Juvenile Aid Society. (Courtesy of the Philadelphia Jewish Archives Center.)

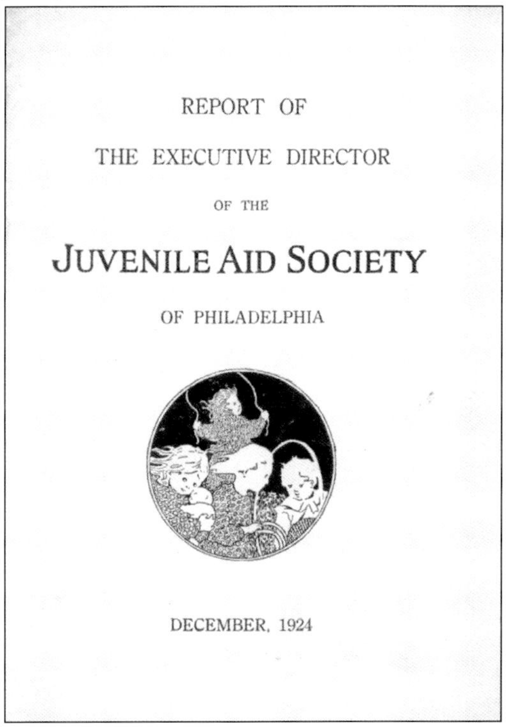

REPORT OF

THE EXECUTIVE DIRECTOR

OF THE

JUVENILE AID SOCIETY

OF PHILADELPHIA

DECEMBER, 1924

By 1924, the year this report was issued, the Juvenile Aid Society placed most of the children in the Jewish community requiring foster care—124 in all that year. These were children who, for emotional or physical reasons, could not be accommodated in other Jewish institutions of the day but who did not require placement in what were thought of as "special institutions." The Juvenile Aid Society joined in the AJC in 1941 as the Jewish community moved to consolidate child welfare services and streamline costs. (Courtesy of the Philadelphia Jewish Archives Center.)

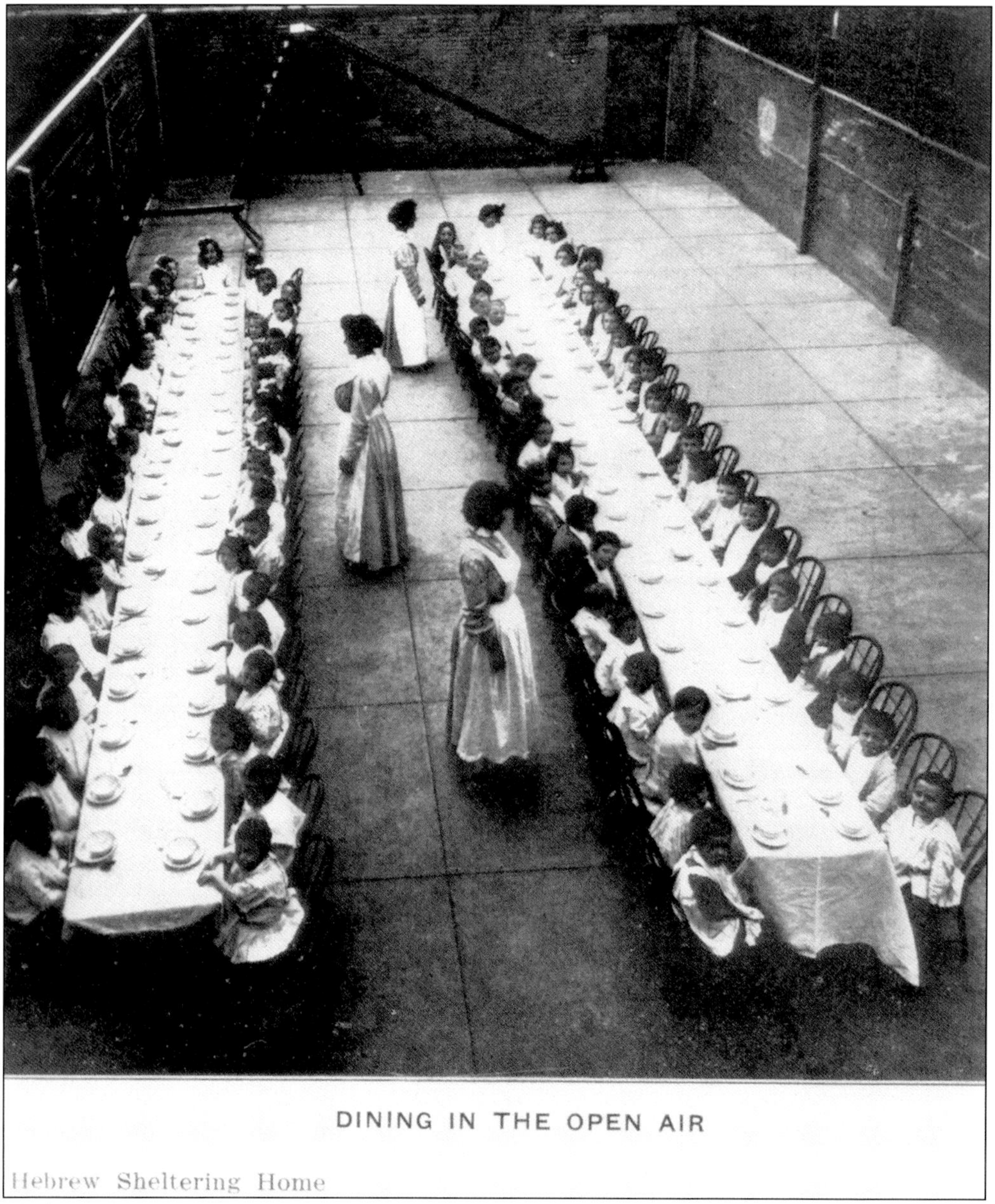

Children dine in the open air at the Hebrew Sheltering Home, one of the Philadelphia Jewish communal institutions that arose during the peak period of immigration to deal with the growing number of children who were orphans or whose families could not care for them. The Hebrew Sheltering Home housed Jewish children from infancy to age seven and created a department to care for unwed mothers and educate them in basic child care and household skills. Many orphaned children transferred to the Jewish Foster Home and Orphan Asylum as they grew older. The Hebrew Sheltering Home later became the Homewood School, which joined with other Jewish children's service organizations to form the AJC in 1941. (Courtesy of the Philadelphia Jewish Archives Center.)

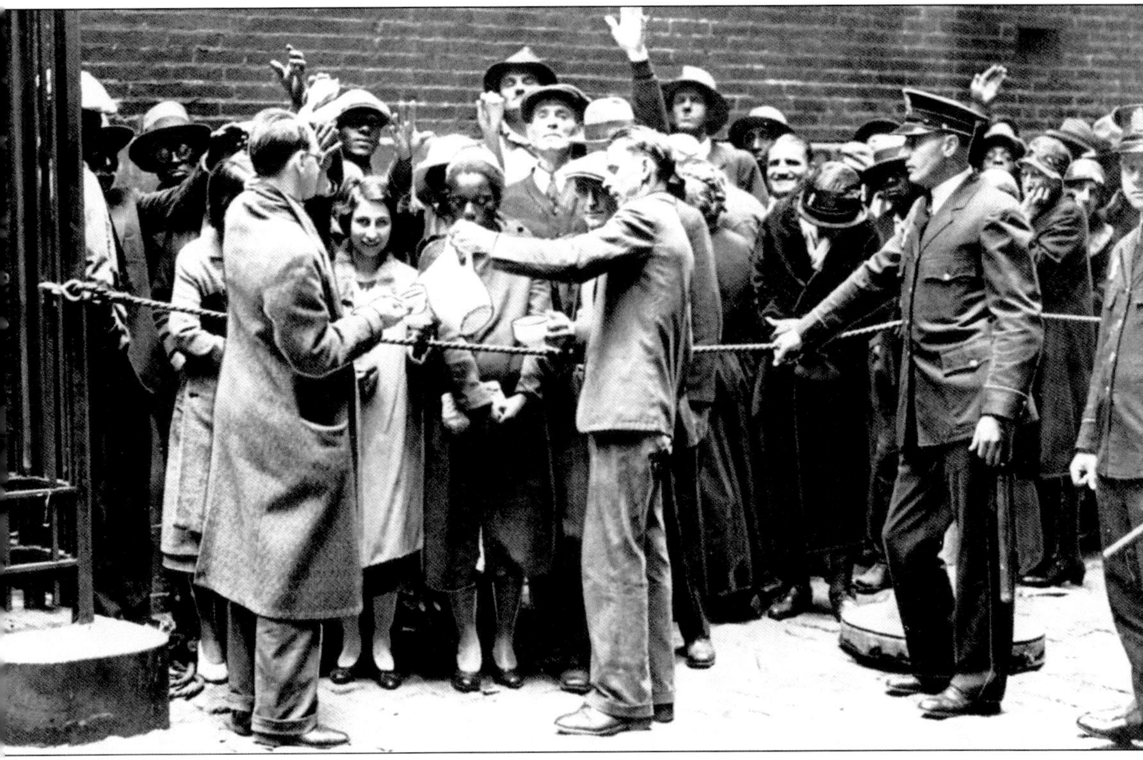

Nationally the unemployment rate reached 25 percent during the Great Depression, from 1930 to 1939. In Philadelphia, thousands in the local Jewish community were affected. The federal government stepped in with public relief programs to address the enormous financial needs that could not be met by local agencies. During this period, JFCS's predecessor agency, the Jewish Welfare Society of Philadelphia (as the United Hebrew Charities was now called), expanded its focus on counseling and casework, becoming increasingly a service rather than a relief agency. In this image, people wait in a public relief line. (Courtesy of the Philadelphia Evening Bulletin, Photojournalism Collection, Temple University Libraries, Urban Archives, Philadelphia, Pennsylvania.)

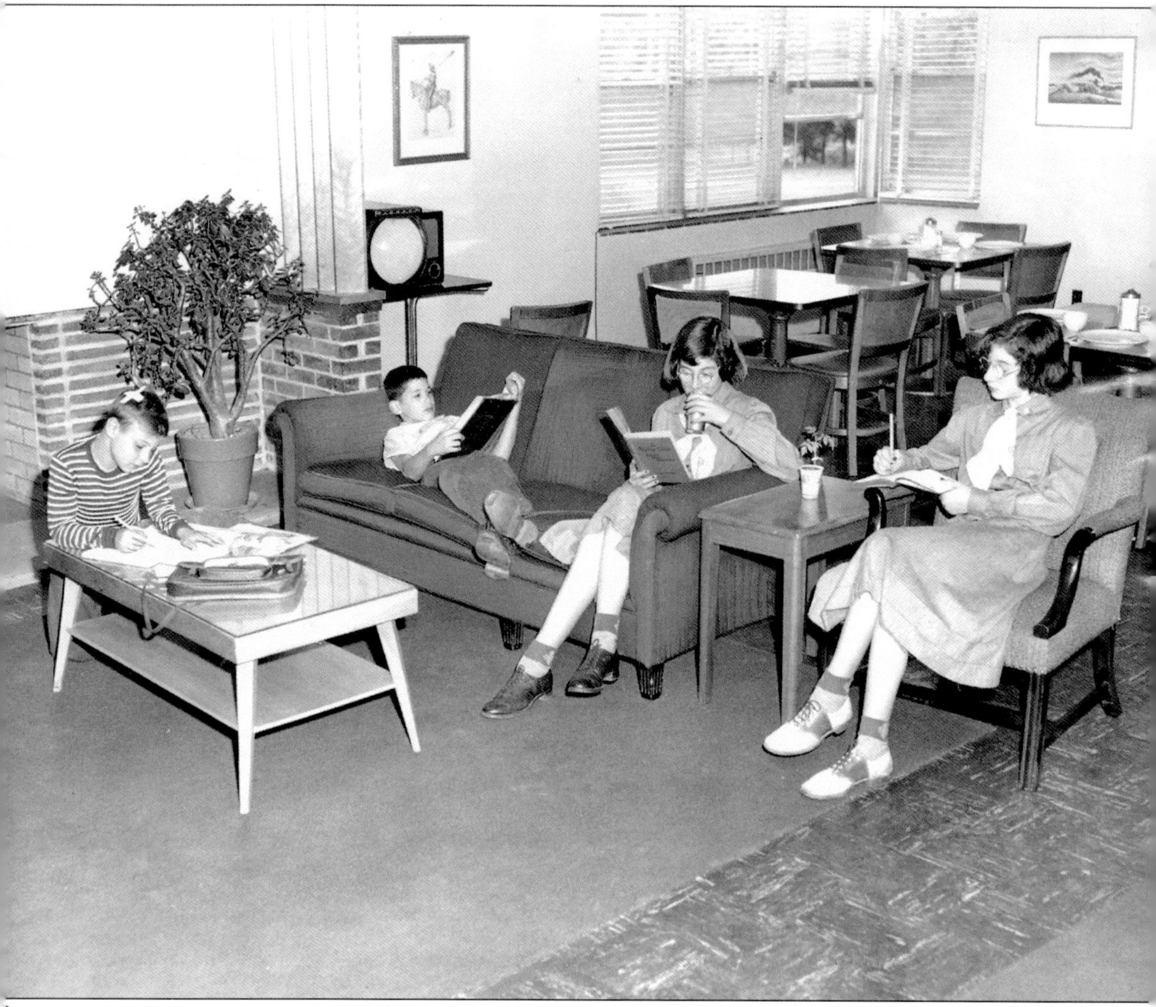

In 1951, the Association for Jewish Children of Philadelphia opened new headquarters at Thirteenth and Spencer Streets. (The reception area is featured in this photograph.) The AJC, an immediate predecessor to today's JFCS, was heir to the child welfare tradition that began with the Jewish Foster Home. It provided foster care and adoption services, services to children in their own homes, Project PRIDE (a substance abuse prevention program for public schools), and operated group homes for children. Volunteers provided additional emotional support. They helped sponsor Jewish holiday programs in the residences and served as shoppers, tutors, Jewish "big brothers and big sisters," and much more. (This photograph may not be of actual clients.) (Courtesy of the Philadelphia Evening Bulletin, Photojournalism Collection, Temple University Libraries, Urban Archives, Philadelphia, Pennsylvania.)

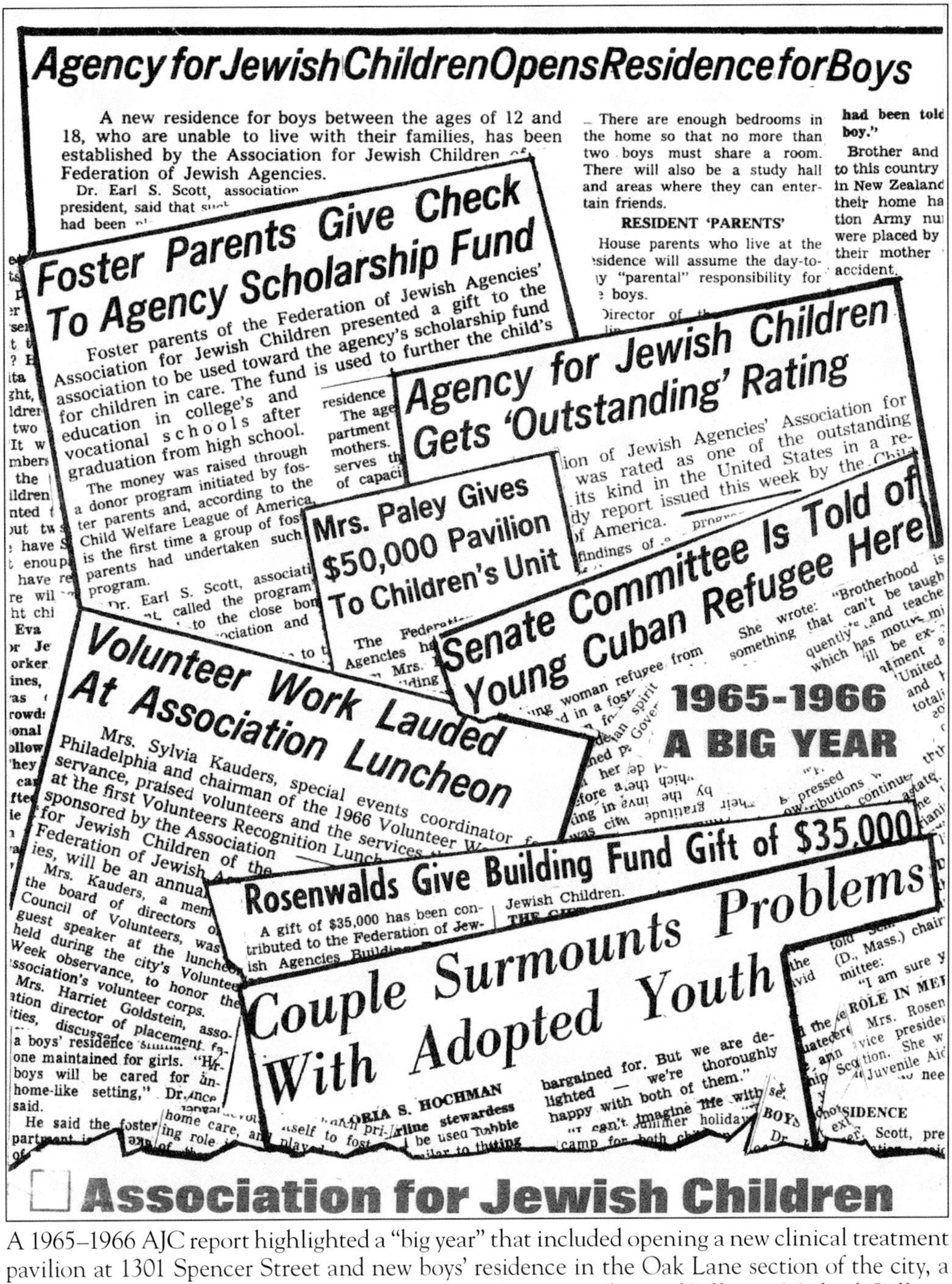

Agency for Jewish Children Opens Residence for Boys

A new residence for boys between the ages of 12 and 18, who are unable to live with their families, has been established by the Association for Jewish Children of Federation of Jewish Agencies.

Dr. Earl S. Scott, association president, said that ...

There are enough bedrooms in the home so that no more than two boys must share a room. There will also be a study hall and areas where they can entertain friends.

RESIDENT 'PARENTS'

House parents who live at the residence will assume the day-to-day "parental" responsibility for the boys.

Foster Parents Give Check To Agency Scholarship Fund

Foster parents of the Federation of Jewish Agencies' Association for Jewish Children presented a gift to the association to be used toward the agency's scholarship fund for children in care. The fund is used to further the child's education in college's and vocational schools after graduation from high school.

The money was raised through a donor program initiated by foster parents and, according to the Child Welfare League of America, is the first time a group of foster parents had undertaken such program.

Agency for Jewish Children Gets 'Outstanding' Rating

Mrs. Paley Gives $50,000 Pavilion To Children's Unit

Senate Committee Is Told of Young Cuban Refugee Here

Volunteer Work Lauded At Association Luncheon

Mrs. Sylvia Kauders, special events coordinator of Philadelphia and chairman of the 1966 Volunteer ... servance, praised volunteers and the services ... at the first Volunteers Recognition Luncheon sponsored by the Association for Jewish Children of the Federation of Jewish Agencies, will be an annual ...

Mrs. Kauders, a member of the board of directors of the Council of Volunteers, was guest speaker at the luncheon held during the city's Volunteer Week observance, to honor the Association's volunteer corps.

1965-1966 A BIG YEAR

Rosenwalds Give Building Fund Gift of $35,000

A gift of $35,000 has been contributed to the Federation of Jewish Agencies ... Jewish Children.

Couple Surmounts Problems With Adopted Youth

Association for Jewish Children

A 1965–1966 AJC report highlighted a "big year" that included opening a new clinical treatment pavilion at 1301 Spencer Street and new boys' residence in the Oak Lane section of the city, a volunteer corps of 68, a training program for psychiatry residents of Jefferson Medical College, and a long-distance adoption by a Philadelphia family of two children from New Zealand. (Courtesy of the Philadelphia Jewish Archives Center.)

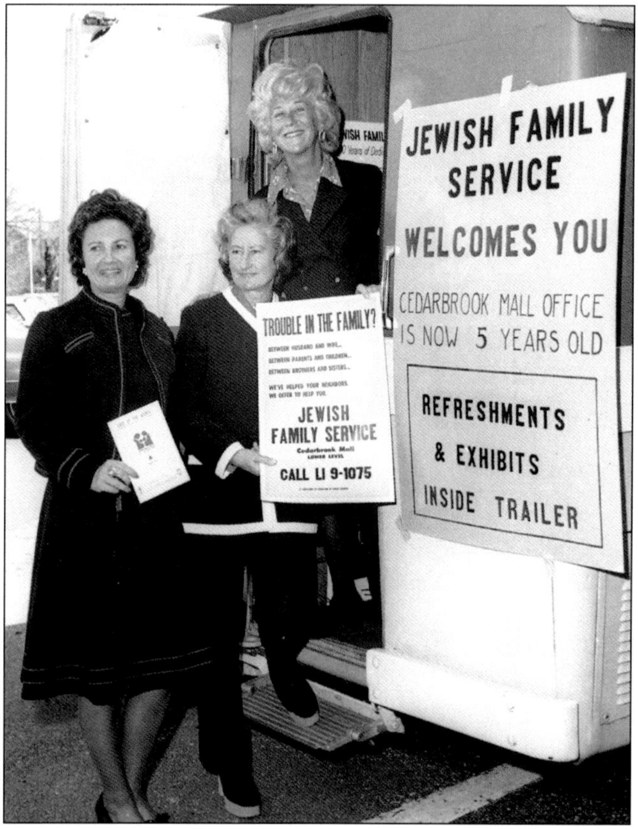

Jewish Family Service of Philadelphia (JFS), an immediate predecessor agency to today's JFCS, celebrated the anniversary of its Northwest District Office at Cedarbrook Mall in Wyncote, which opened in 1968. JFS was a pioneer in opening a social service office in a shopping center—a move designed to ensure high visibility and convenience as the Jewish population spread out from the city to the suburbs. Pictured here are JFS board leaders (from left) Janet Ginns and Carol Gerstley. (The person at far right is unidentified.) (Courtesy of the Philadelphia Jewish Archives Center)

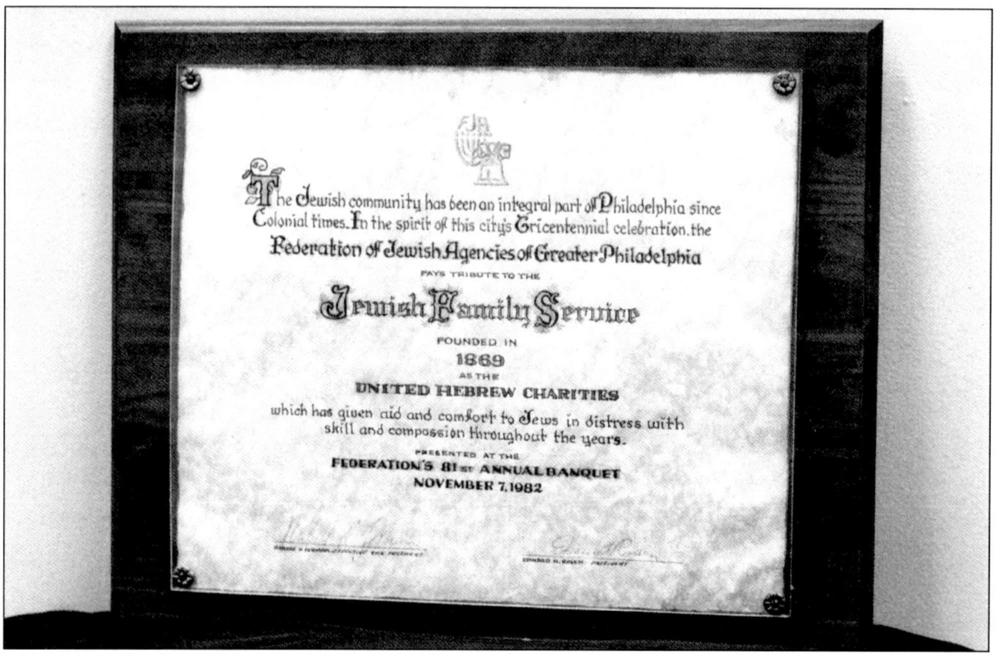

This 1969 plaque, recognizing the JFS's 100 years of vital and compassionate service to Jews in distress, hangs in the Center City Office of today's JFCS. (Courtesy of JFCS)

Three

The Home Kids

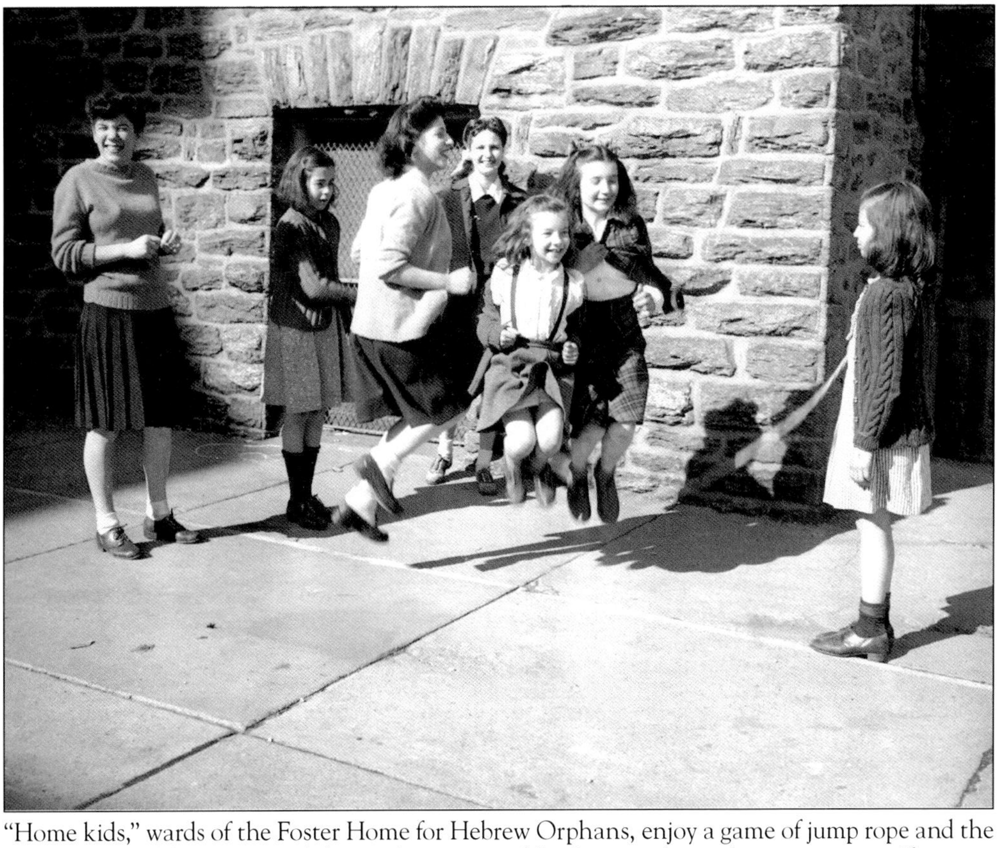

"Home kids," wards of the Foster Home for Hebrew Orphans, enjoy a game of jump rope and the bonds of friendship. As an adult, an alumnus would reflect on the orphanage years as "for some of us . . . the best years of our lives" and "for a lot us, the first real home we ever had." (Courtesy of the Philadelphia Jewish Archives Center.)

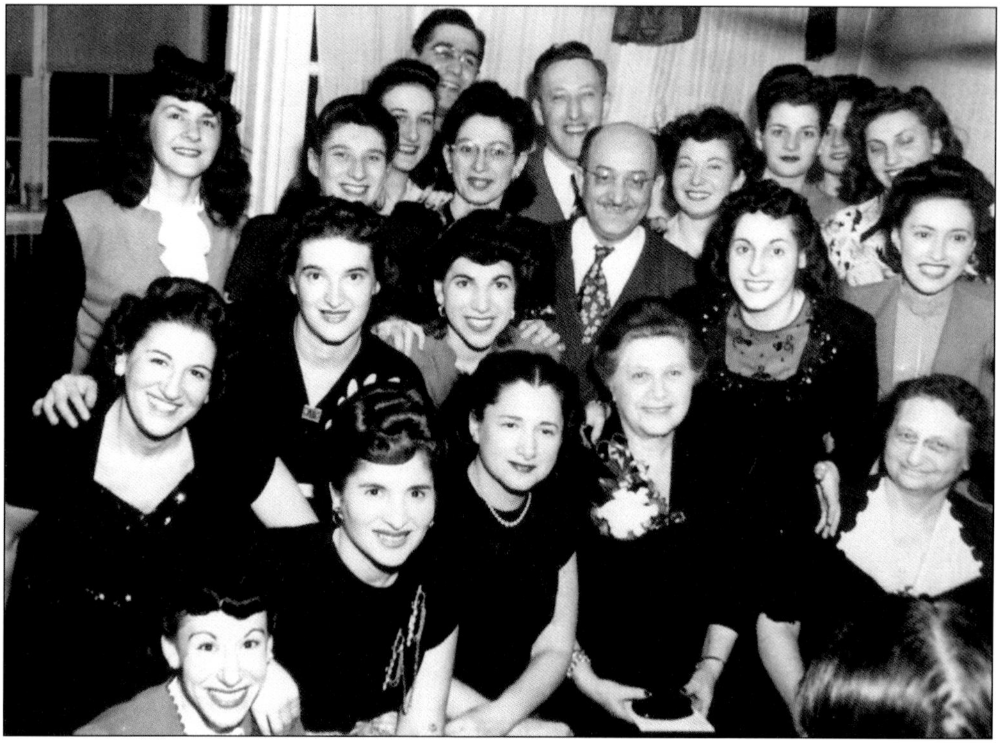

The Jewish Foster Home and Orphan Asylum, at 700 East Church Lane in the Germantown section of Philadelphia, became home to thousands of Jewish children facing circumstances beyond their control from the 1880s through the first half of the 20th century. Shown here are some of the resident children grouped around Herman Gumnit, superintendent of the home, and loyal benefactor Blanche Kohn. (Courtesy of Pearl Clavner.)

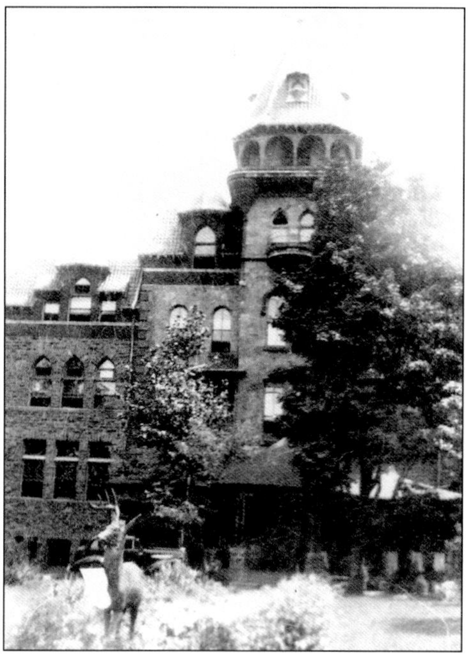

The sprawling campus of the orphanage had many benefits and features. The kids loved to take pictures around the statue of a caribou, located on the front lawn of the home. Some years later, the alumni of the home spotted this very statue at another facility and verified that it was the same one, since it had the initials J. F. H. inscribed on its hind leg. (Courtesy of Herb Lyons.)

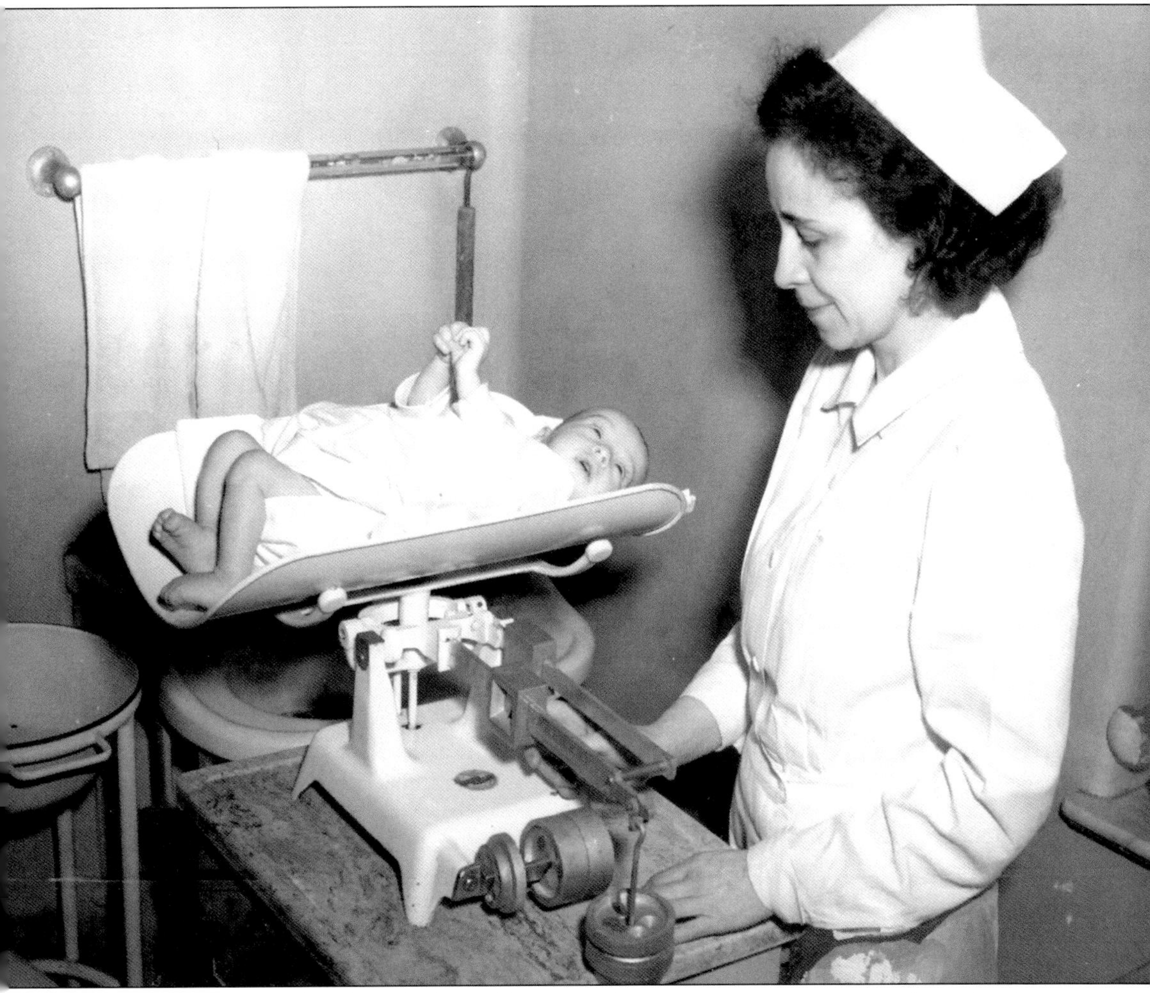

The merger in 1929 of the Jewish Foster Home and Orphan Asylum with the Hebrew Orphans Home of Philadelphia consolidated services for children from infants up to the age of 18. The home was renamed once again. From 1929 until its closing in the early 1950s, it was known as the Foster Home for Hebrew Orphans. Shown here is a nurse attending to an infant with great care. (Courtesy of the Philadelphia Jewish Archives Center.)

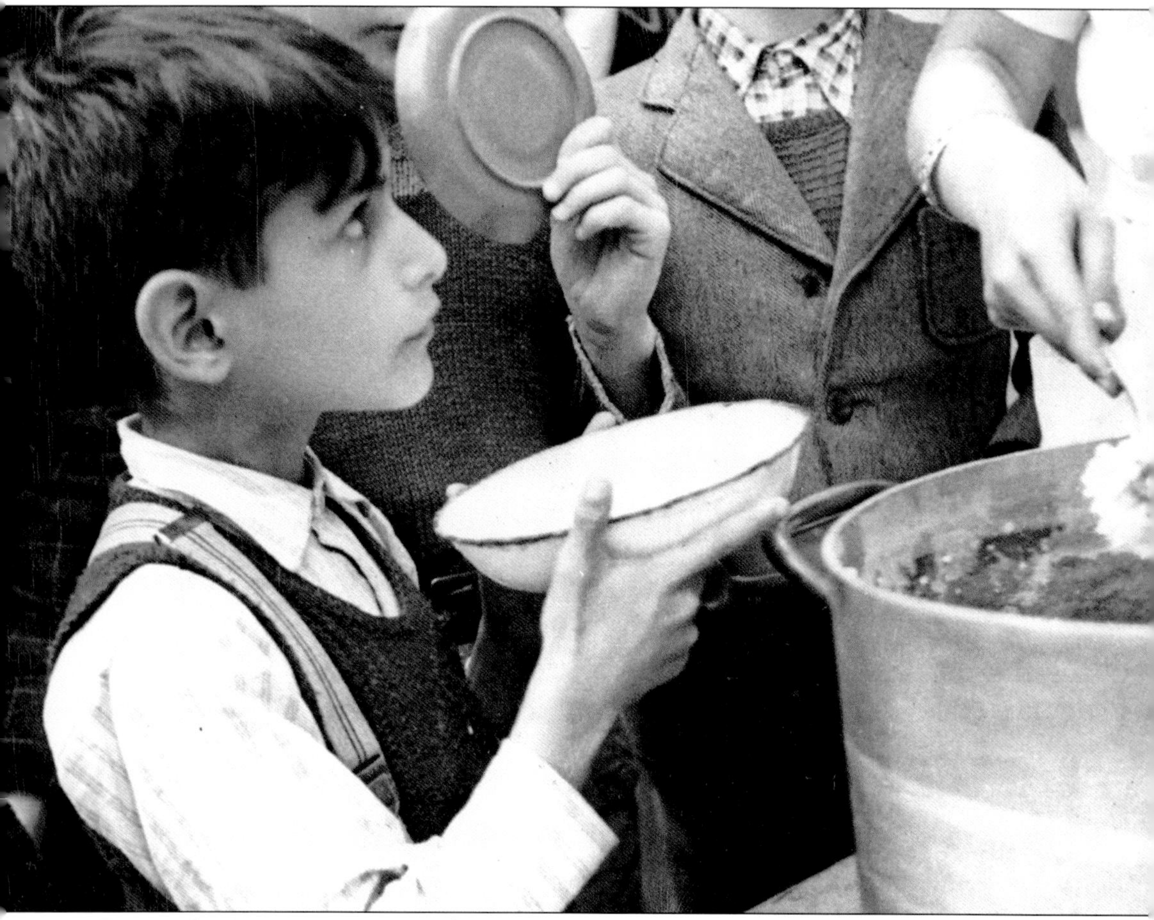

During the Great Depression in the 1930s, as jobs for grown men became scarce, there was a rise in children waiting in soup lines for their only daily nourishment. Some Jewish parents could care for only one child and found the Foster Home for Hebrew Orphans a refuge for other siblings. (Courtesy of the Philadelphia Jewish Archives Center.)

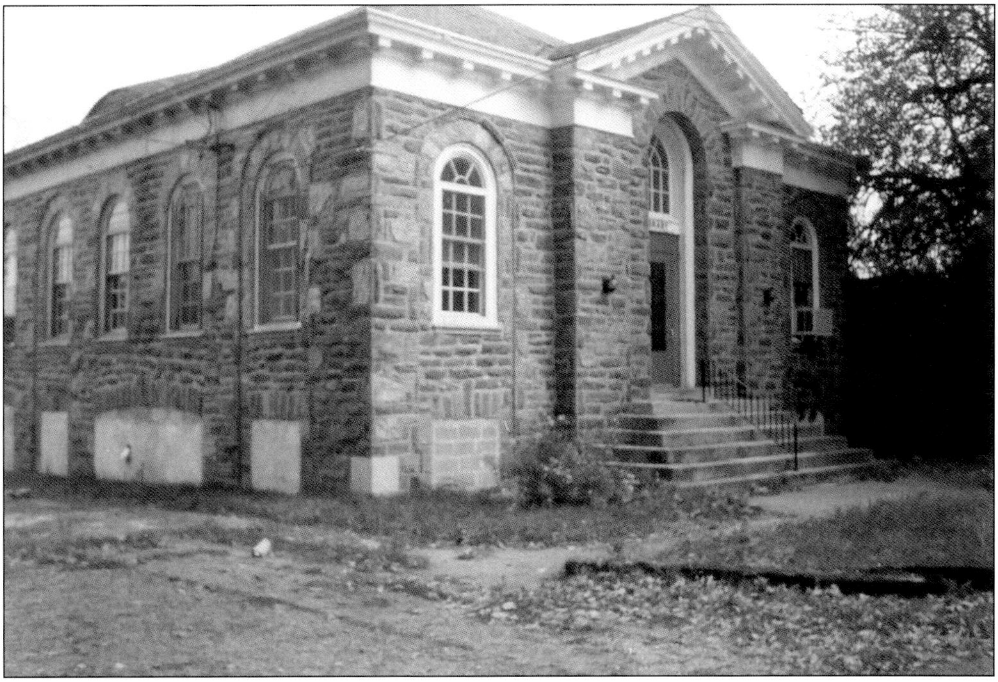

The Teller Synagogue, on the campus of the home, was built in 1900 and became a sanctuary for many to enjoy and share in their Judaism. (Courtesy of Herb Lyons.)

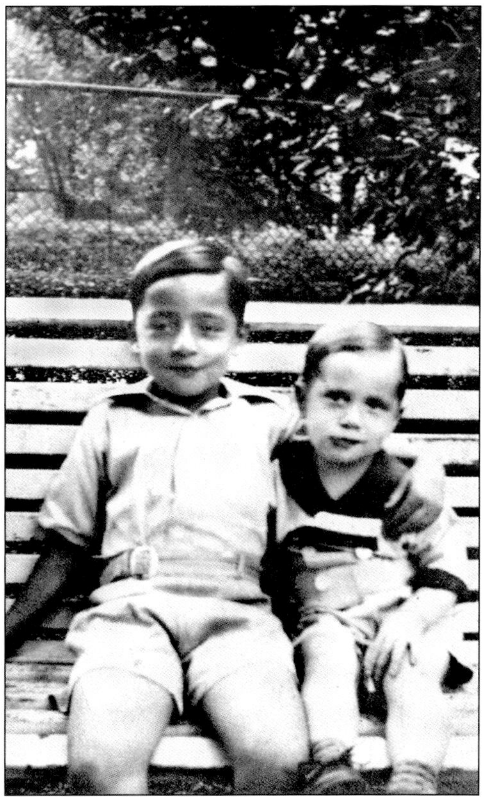

After their mother's death, Albert and Steven Chodowsky were placed in the Foster Home for Hebrew Orphans in the mid-1930s. Many wards of the home were actually from single-parent families who faced hard times and could not care for their children. Many of the home kids also had volunteer sponsors. Albert and Steven benefited from the caring of the Harry Blatstein family, owners of Ben Hur's ice-cream store in Strawberry Mansion. (Courtesy of Albert Chadler.)

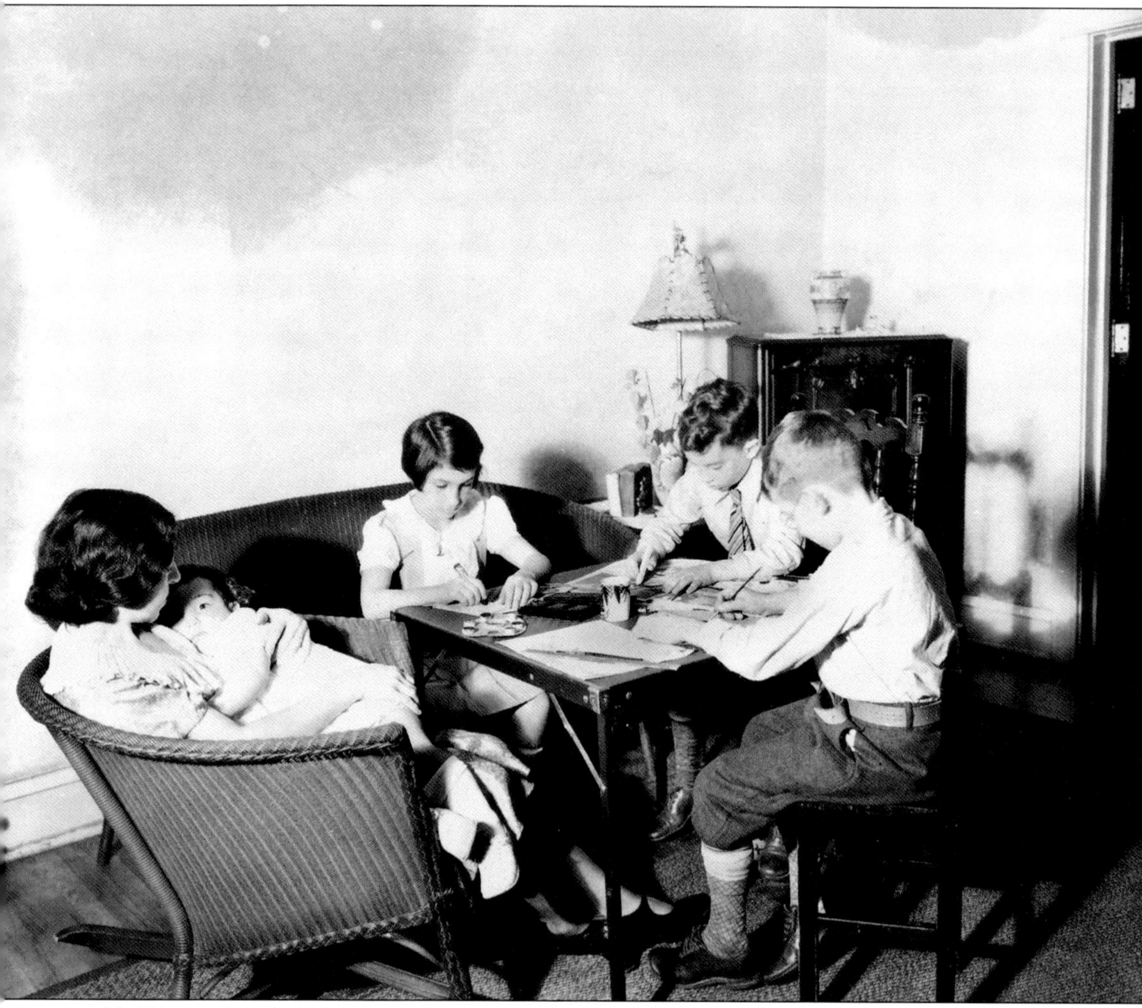

Children gather for some quieter moments. The home held as many as 200 kids in its heyday, so life was far from quiet most of the time. (Courtesy of the Philadelphia Jewish Archives Center.)

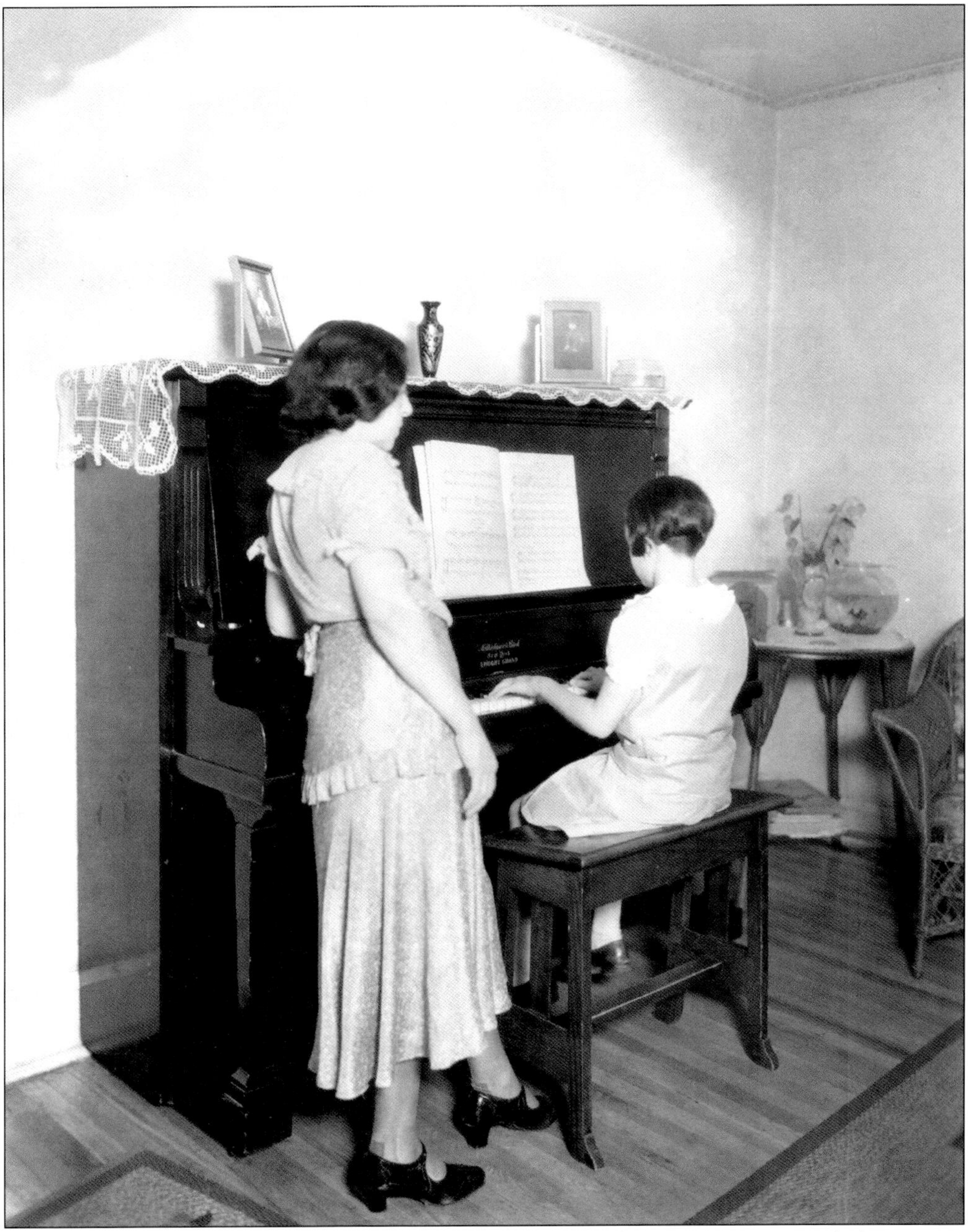

The home kids had many opportunities for cultural enrichment activities, including piano lessons. (Courtesy of the Philadelphia Jewish Archives Center.)

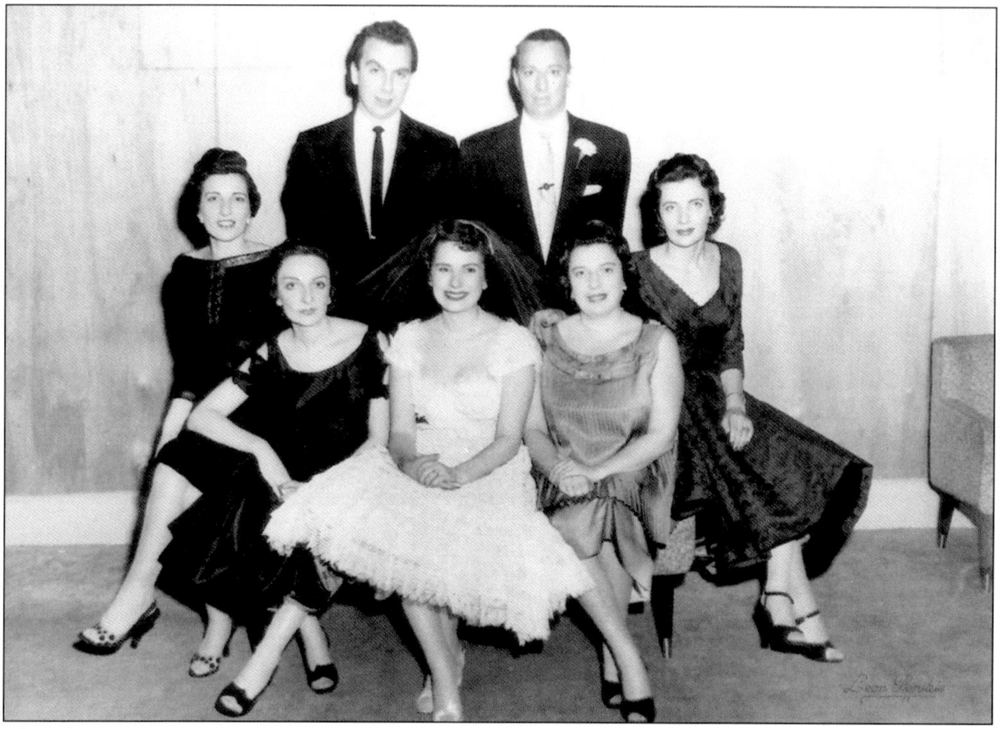

The Bloom sisters (Lucy and Irene), who are pictured on the cover of this book, had other siblings who did not live at the home. Pictured from left to right are (first row) Lucy, Mildred, Margie, Irene, and Hannah; (second row) Stanley and Jack. (Courtesy of Lucy and Irene Bloom.)

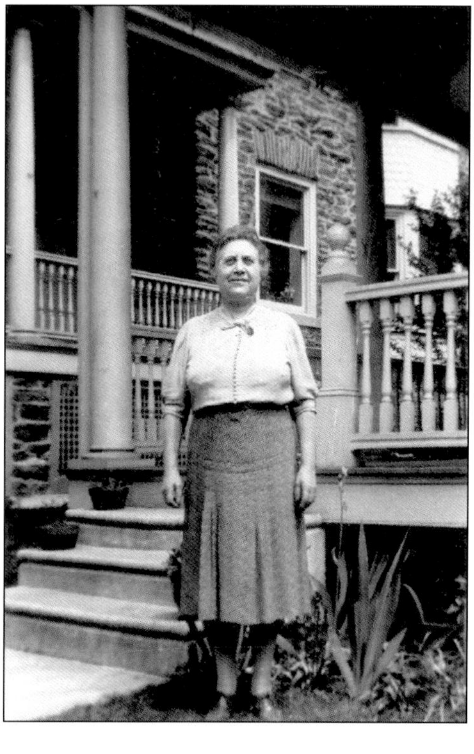

The large size of the home did not prevent the personal touch from children's lives. Take for example, "Aunt" Ethel Newman, housemother, who taught the girls how to run a home at 426 Church Lane. This facility, near the Foster Home for Hebrew Orphans, opened in 1936 and housed up to six young women between 16 and 18 years old from the orphanage, helping them make the transition to adulthood. (Courtesy of Pearl Clavner.)

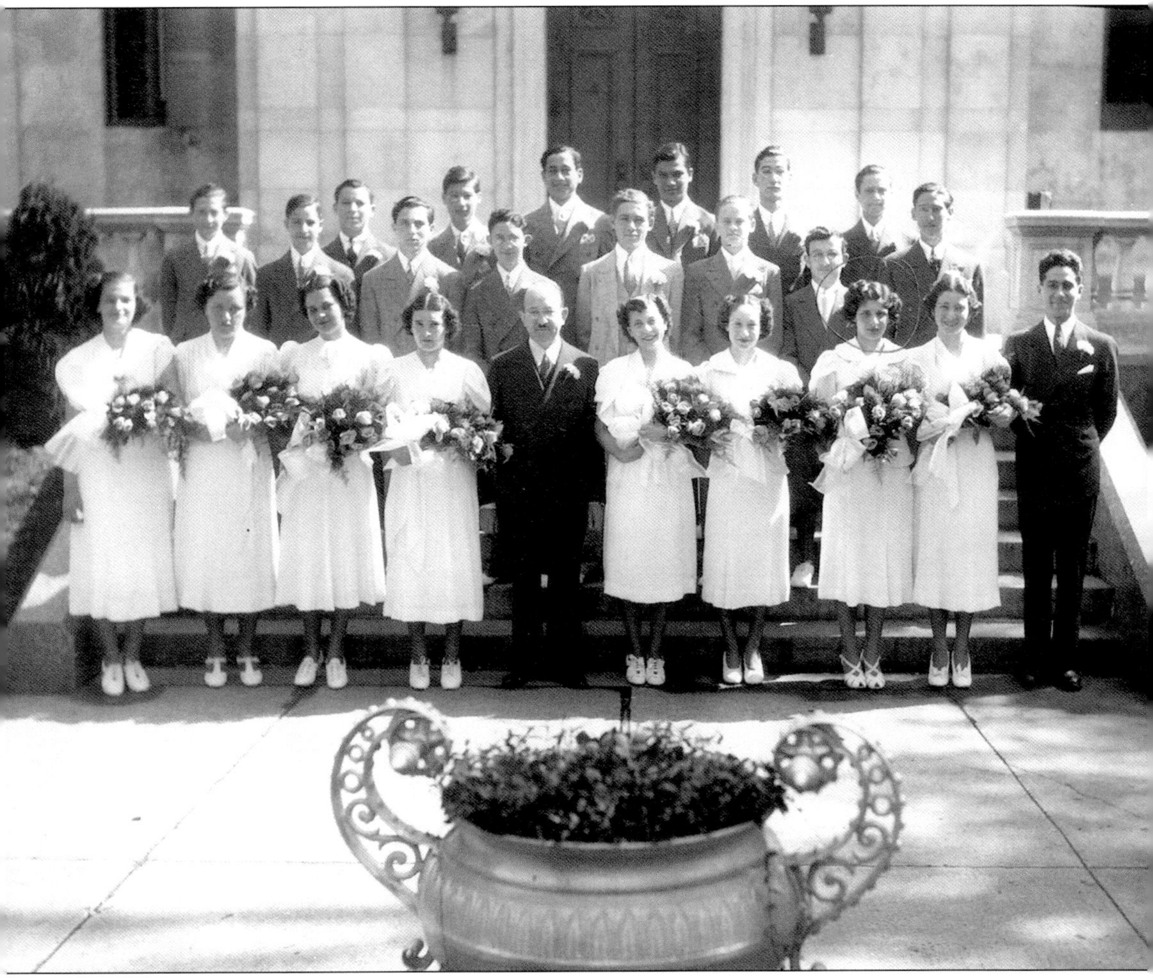

Confirmation of students at the age of 16 years old after extended study of Judaism and biblical texts meant a huge achievement. The home kids joined in the fanfare, too. Herman Gumnit, superintendent of the home, poses proudly with the confirmands. (Courtesy of Dorothy Mitchell.)

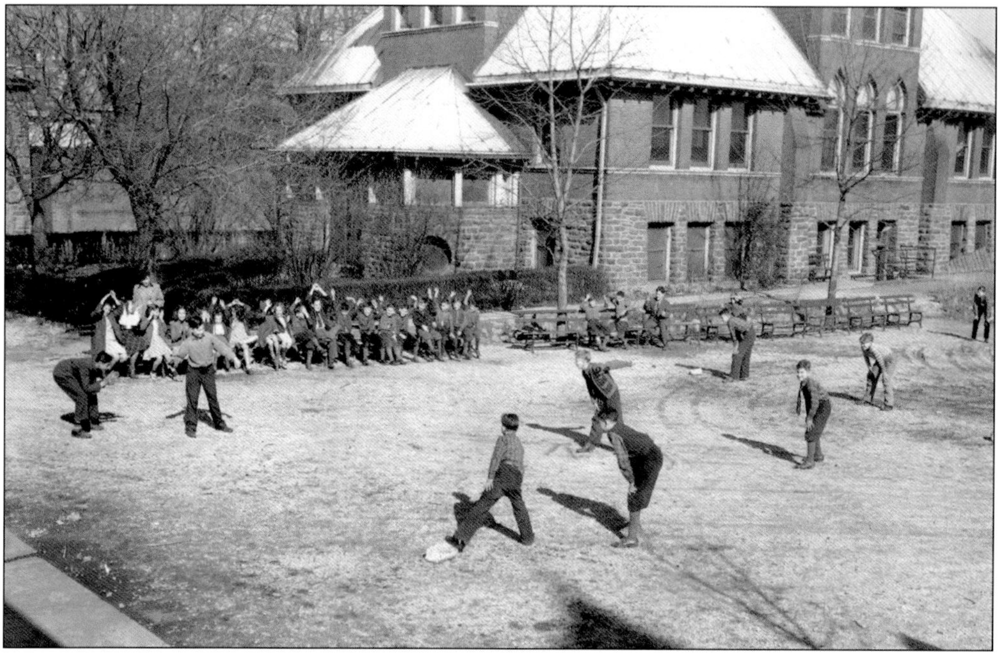

The large grounds of the Foster Home for Hebrew Orphans doubled as a serene setting for many youngsters to enjoy their childhood years. All the amenities were available, including a baseball diamond where the kids could watch and participate in America's greatest pastime sport. (Courtesy of the Philadelphia Jewish Archives Center.)

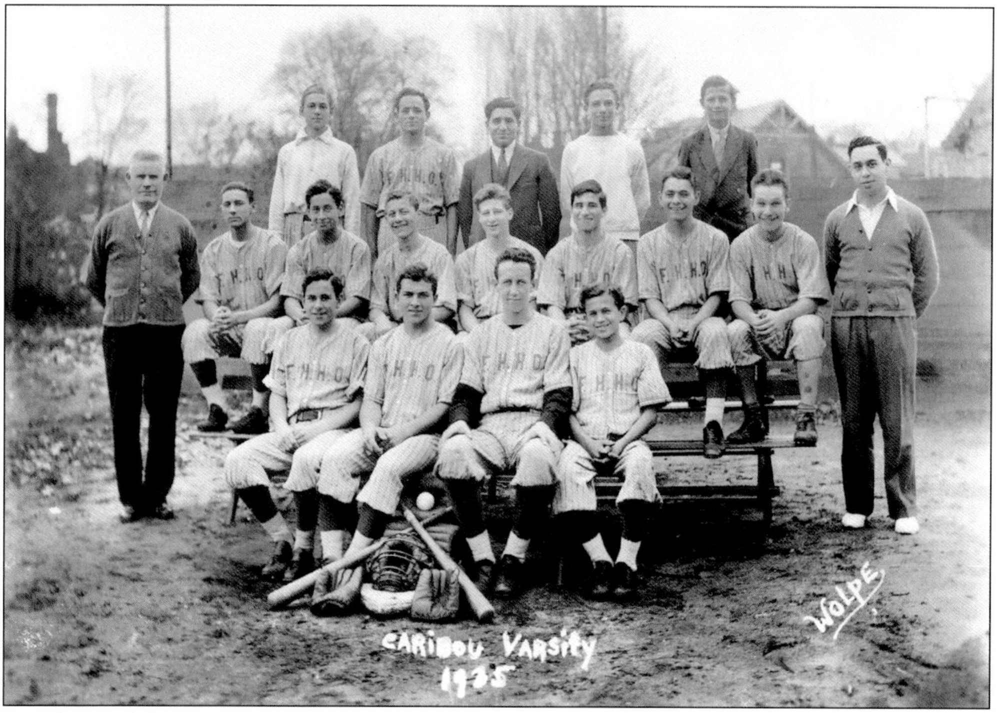

Members of the Caribou Varsity Club "home team" suit up for a game. (Courtesy of the Philadelphia Jewish Archives Center.)

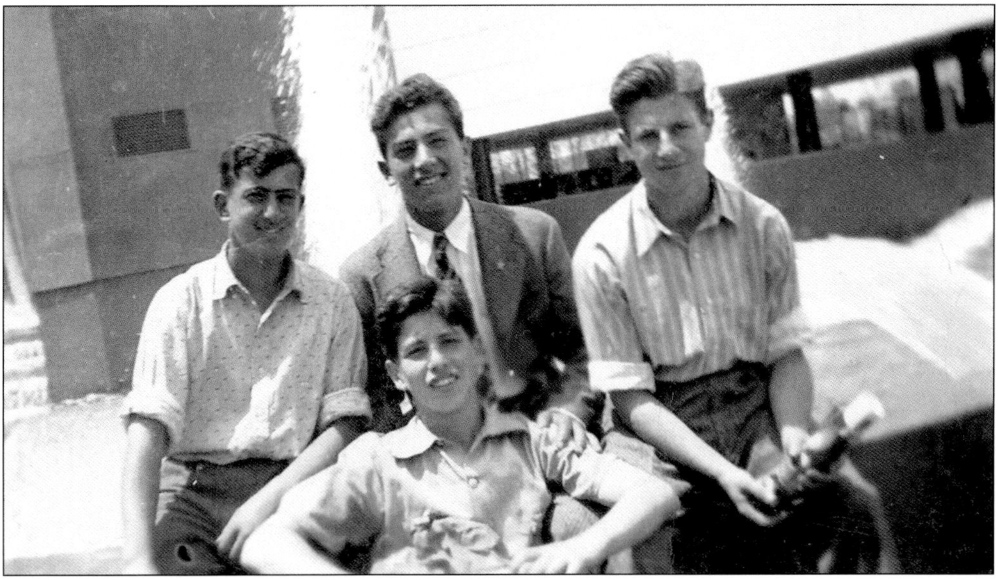

The home kids took trips to many places in the Pennsylvania countryside. Outings sometimes included trolley car visits to Willow Grove amusement park. Shown are Sammy, Leon, Bernie, and Jack. (Courtesy of Pearl Clavner.)

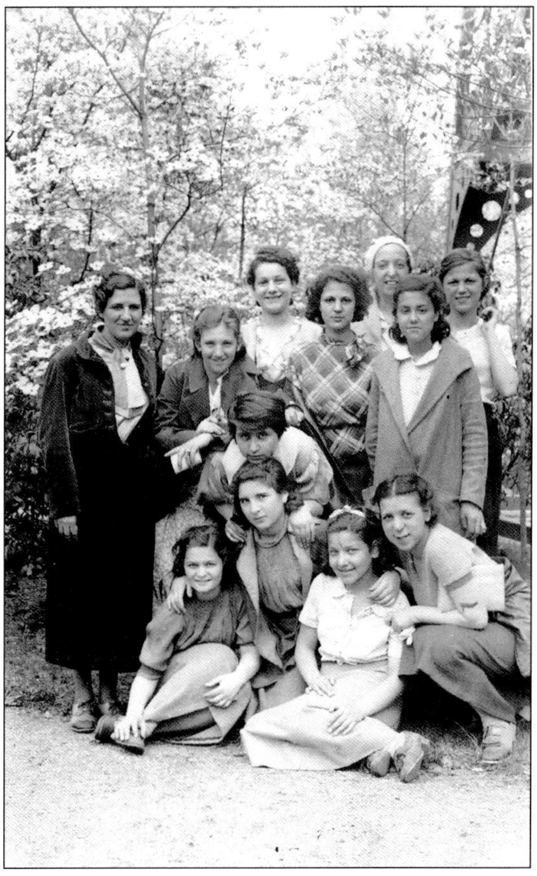

Home kids regularly participated in school trips. A spring outing in 1933 found these girls enjoying a treat in Valley Forge State Park and getting a history lesson all at the same time. (Courtesy of Herb Lyons.)

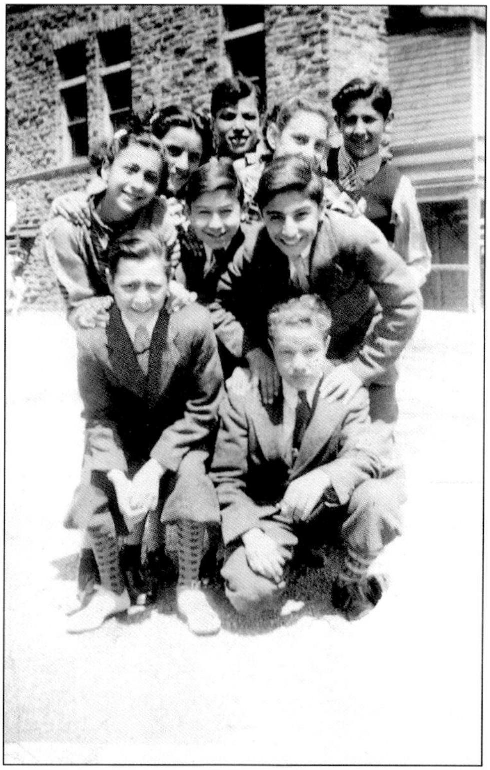

The kids at the home formed a close-knit family of their own. (Courtesy of Herb Lyons.)

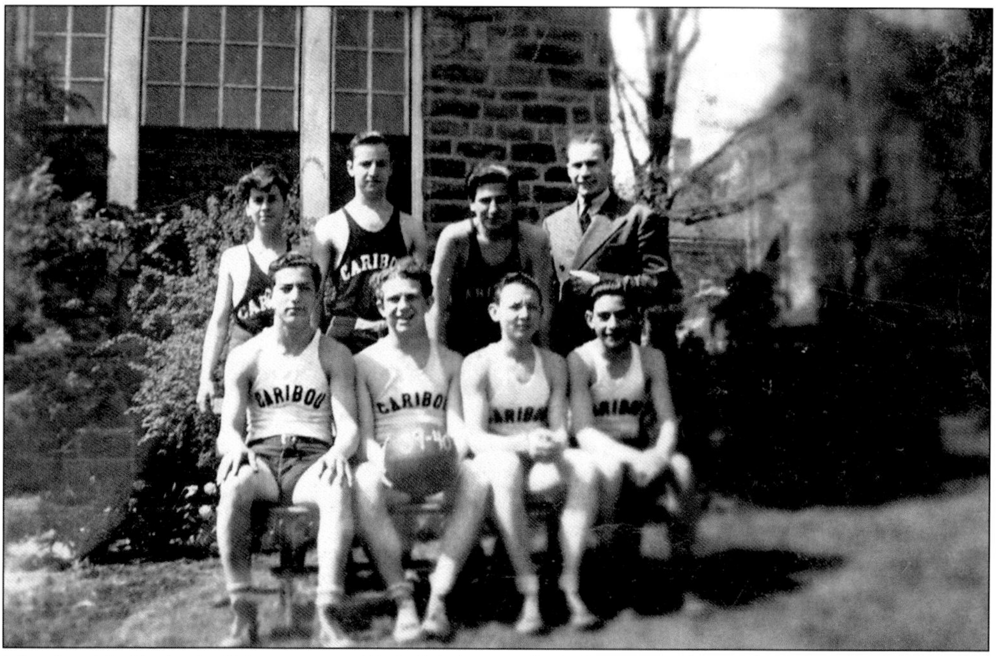

The Jewish Basketball League in Philadelphia included a team from the home on its roster. The 1940 team consists of, from left to right, (first row) Bernie Cohen, Mitsy Driss, Abe Weinshellbaum, and Len Feldman; (second row) Frank Shapiro, Jack Goldberg, Leonard Lee, and Eddie Lance. (Courtesy of Pearl Clavner.)

The mascot of the home, the statue of the caribou, became a focal point for picture taking. The friendships that were made by Pearl Speckert and Silvia Gold lasted a long time beyond this moment in September 1940. (Courtesy of Pearl Clavner.)

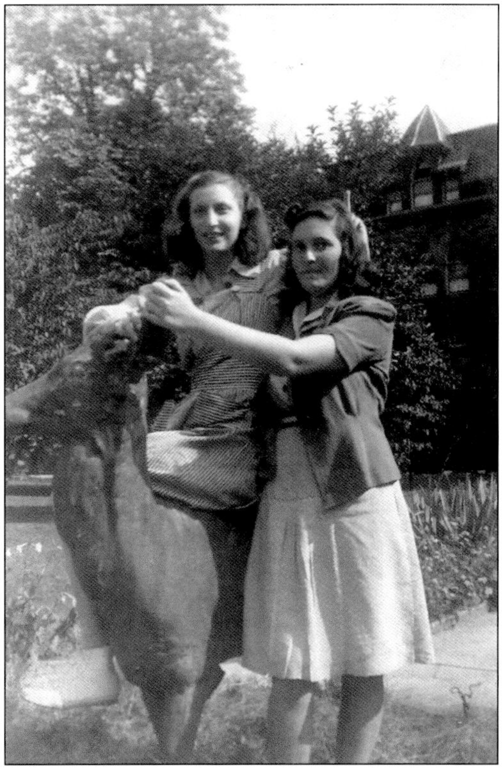

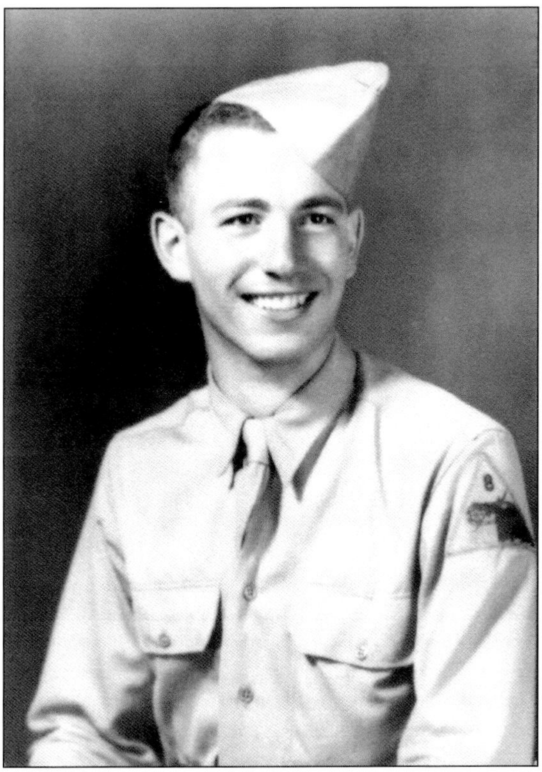

Childhood came to an end when some of the boys, including Dan Harris, became draftees in the military service in the early 1940s at the age of 18. (Courtesy of Pearl Clavner.)

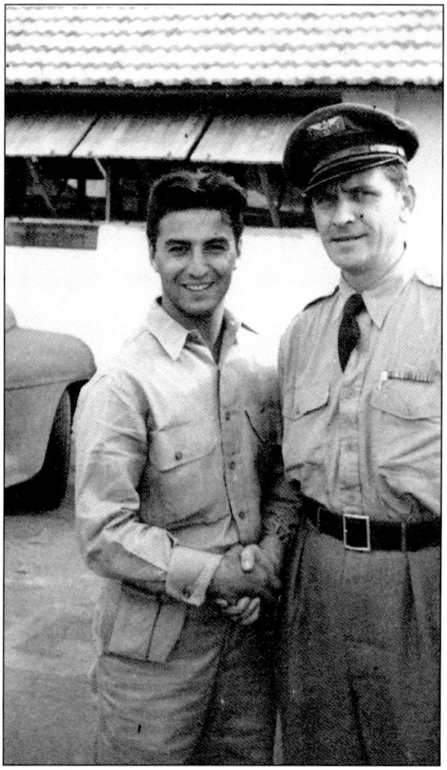

Many of the boys from the home served their country during World War II with great honor. Some said that the regimentation of life in a large institution like the home prepared them well for military life. Pictured are home alumnus Herb Lyons (left) and Fredric Narch. (Courtesy of Herb Lyons.)

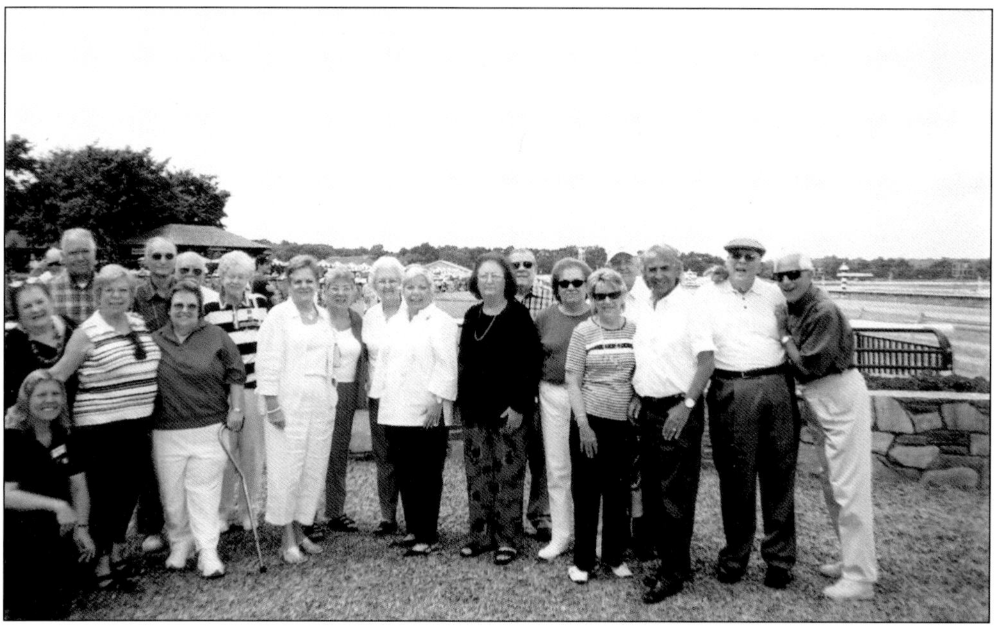

For some, a lifetime is made up of friendships formed years ago. The alumni of the home, some of whom met more than 70 years ago, have a lot to give thanks for, including their health, longevity, and, especially, the joys of growing together as one big family. This group regularly dines together at Casino Delicatessen on Welsh Road in Northeast Philadelphia. (Courtesy of Paul Bass.)

Four

Modern Leaders

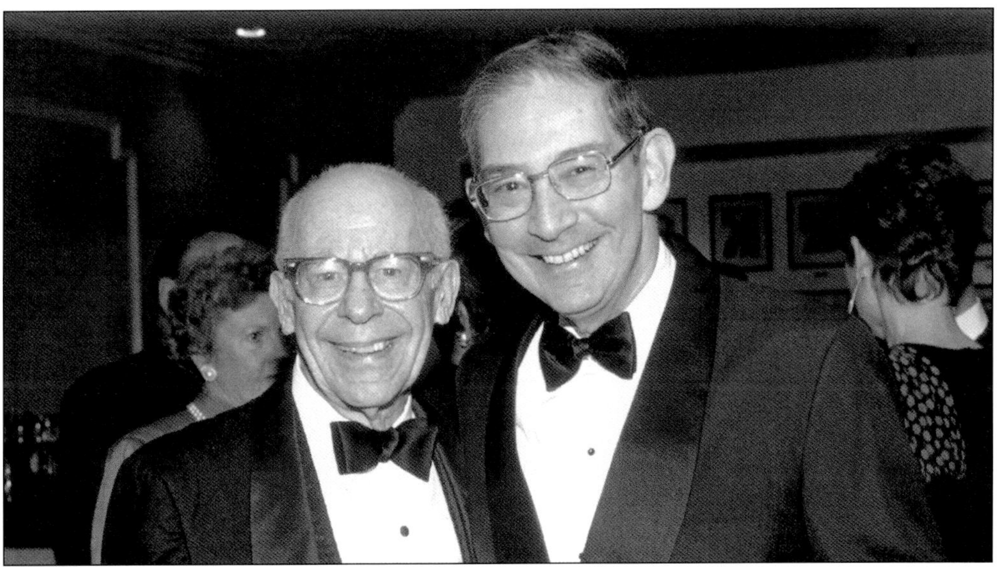

When JFS merged with the AJC in 1983, leaders from both agencies worked together closely to ease the transition. Shown here at a special event from the early 1980s are two of those leaders: Benjamin Sprafkin (left), the last executive director of JFS, and Ivan Gabel, a JFS board member, who in 1983 became copresident with Samuel Frieder of the new merged agency. (Courtesy of Ivan Gabel.)

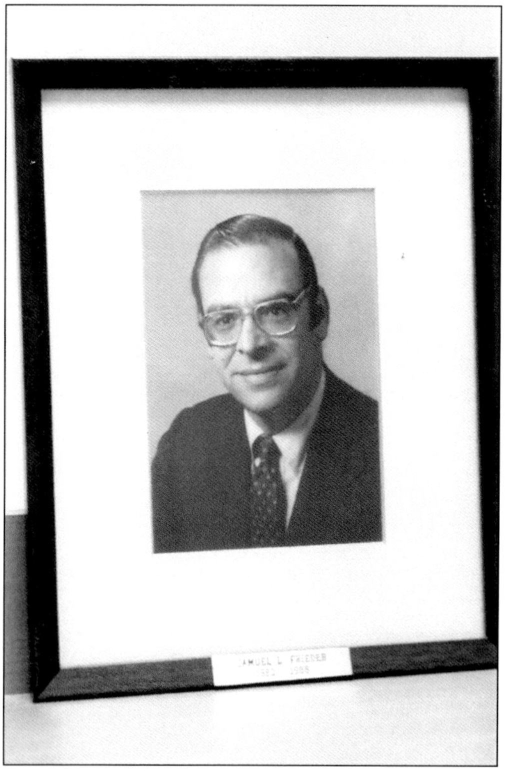

Samuel Frieder, a board member of the AJC, served as copresident with Ivan Gabel of the merged agency from 1983 to 1985. The two men had been friends since childhood. While the JFS had worked with children as an adjunct to dealing with families, the AJC had put the emphasis on kids. The marriage of the two agencies approached the families with unified services, a "win-win" situation, Frieder said. (Courtesy of JFCS.)

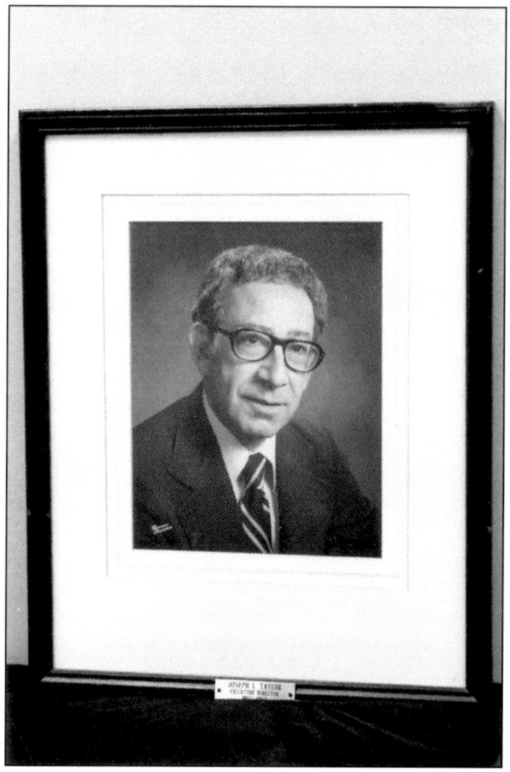

A vital part of the transition team, Joseph Taylor served as the last executive director of the AJC. His leadership of that agency spanned 25 years, from 1957 to 1982. During that time, the AJC moved increasingly away from institutional care toward more community-based services, such as services to families in their own homes and foster care. The last AJC group home closed in 1984, a year after the merger. (Courtesy of JFCS.)

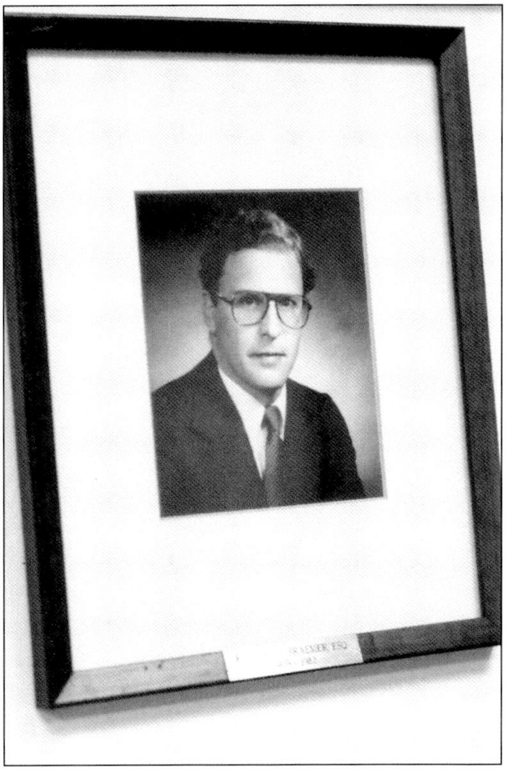

Richard Braemer (right), the last president of the AJC, and Arnold Kessler (below), the last president of the JFS, were a part of the leadership team that played a key role in planning for the merger of what is now Jewish Family and Children's Service of Greater Philadelphia. (Courtesy of JFCS.)

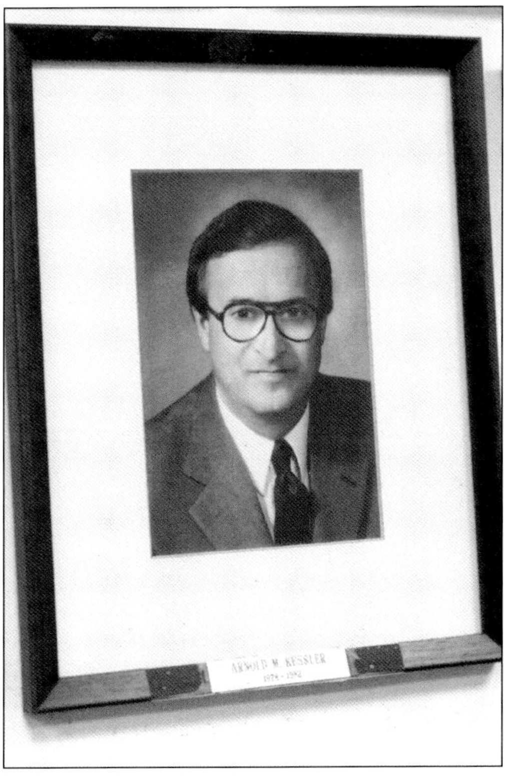

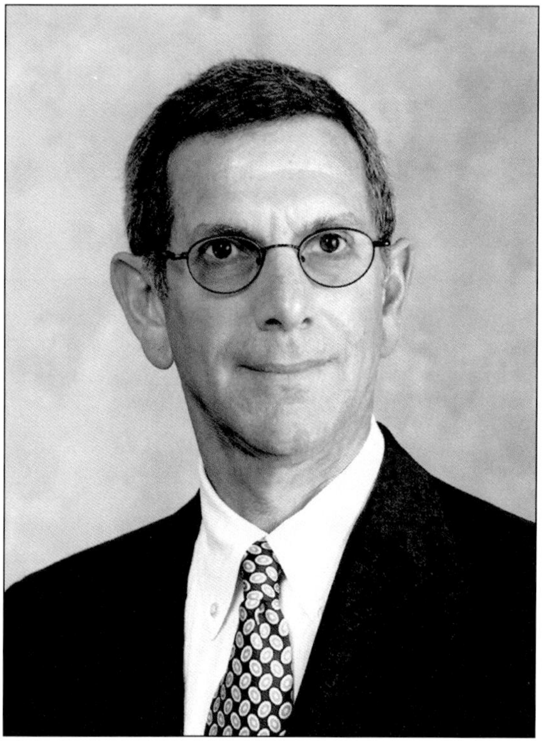

Following the copresidency of Ivan Gabel and Samuel Frieder, there have been six men and women to date to hold the top board leadership position at JFCS, beginning with Henry Miller (1985–1988). He followed a proud family tradition. His father, Lester Miller, was board president of the AJC from 1959 to 1962. (Courtesy of Wolf, Block, Schorr and Solis-Cohen LLP.)

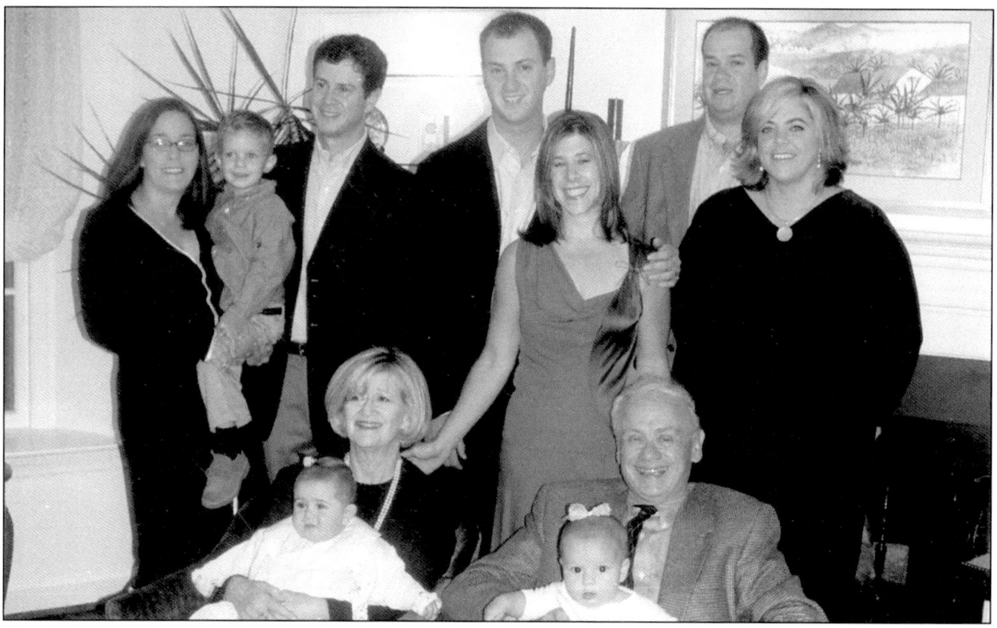

Owen Knopping, past board president (1988–1991), continues to serve JFCS year-round as a board leader, including taking on the recent role chairing the JFCS Tomorrow Fund—the planned giving campaign to secure the agency's future. Pictured here, he enjoys a more personal moment as he gathers with (second row, from left to right) Hillary, Max, Jamie, David, Denise, Eric, and Kristen. Proud parents and grandparents are Margaret, with Ava, and Owen, with Remy. (Courtesy of Owen Knopping.)

Leonard Cooper, past board president (1991–1994), first became involved with JFCS through his law firm, Wolf, Block, Schorr and Solis-Cohen LLP, when he provided legal research for the AJC. After decades of service to JFCS and its predecessors, he took on the role of chairman of the agency's 150th anniversary celebration in 2005. (Courtesy of Wolf, Block, Schorr and Solis-Cohen LLP.)

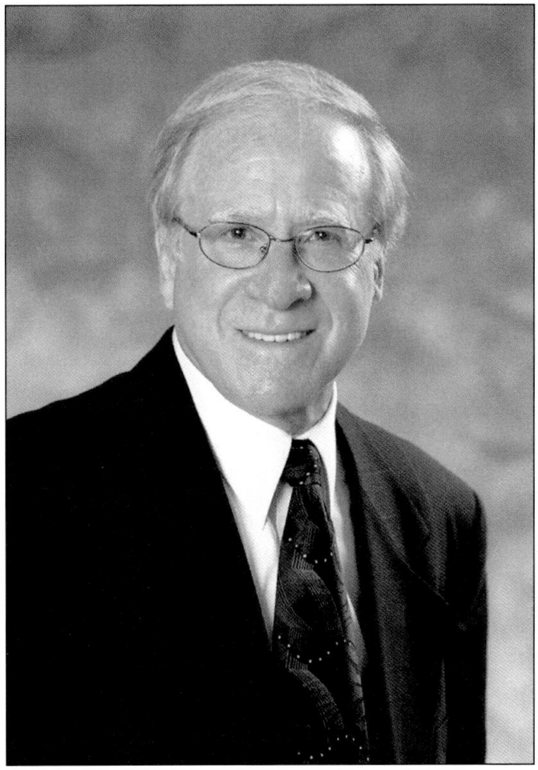

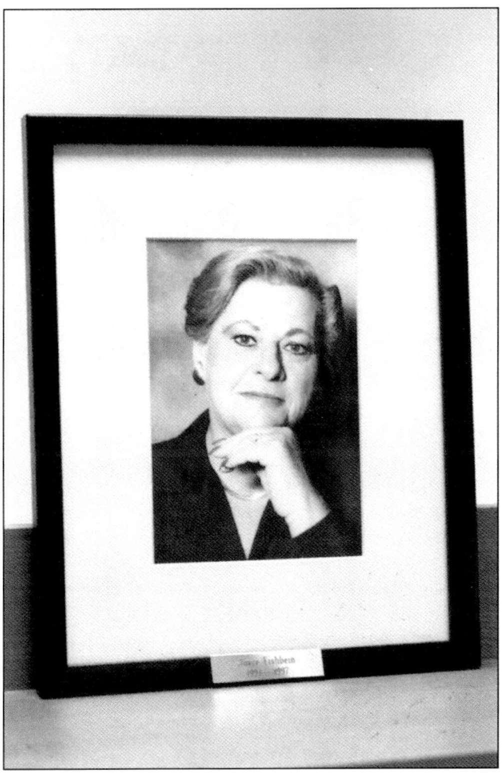

As JFCS board president, Joyce Fishbein (1994–1997) often inspired her colleagues with "Did You Know?" vignettes culled from the daily work of JFCS. Her personal connection to the agency and the clients it serves began years earlier when she assisted with educational and psychological testing of children in the group homes of the AJC. JFCS programs to serve vulnerable populations expanded under her presidency. (Courtesy of JFCS.)

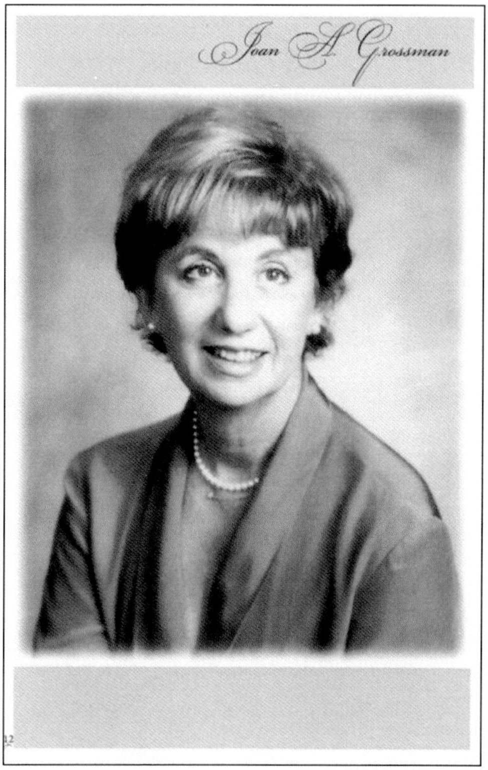

Joan Grossman led efforts to create a chaplaincy and healing center at JFCS and also served as admissions director at the Raymond and Ruth Perelman Jewish Day School during her JFCS board chairmanship (1997–2000). Her dual roles and broad perspective on communal services helped the agency strengthen its community collaborations in providing counseling, education, and support programs for children and families. (The board leadership title changed to chairman in 1997.) (Courtesy of JFCS.)

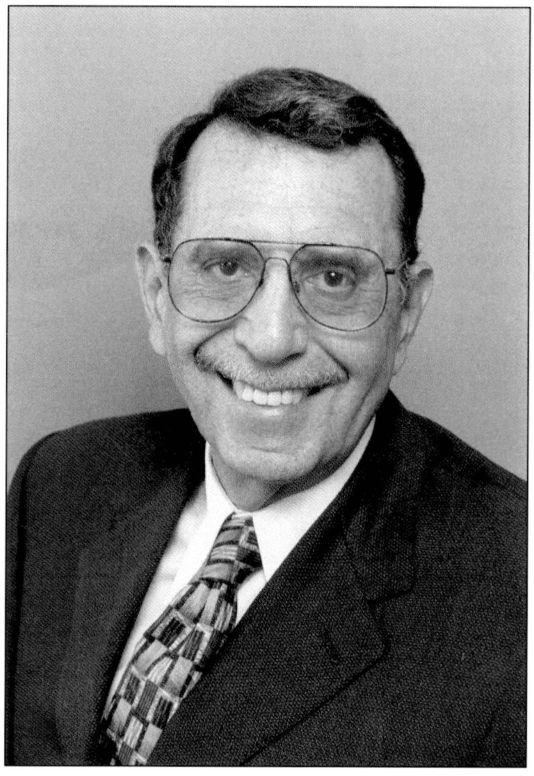

Board chairman Carl Schneider's tenure (2000–2003) saw the agency move from 1610 Spruce Street to modern, new quarters in the Jewish Community Services Building at Twenty-first and Arch Streets. Focusing on the need for JFCS to remain financially strong to best perform its mission of *tikkun olam* (repairing the world), he created a new annual membership drive and helped to expand other resource development efforts. (Courtesy of JFCS.)

Board chairman James Kahn (2003–2006), a former Jewish "big brother" with JFCS, led the agency during its historic 150th anniversary year. Calling JFCS crucial to maintaining and expanding a "higher and wider" Jewish social safety net, he continued the development of agency services and fund-raising programs and oversaw a new strategic plan for the JFCS of the 21st century. (Courtesy of JFCS.)

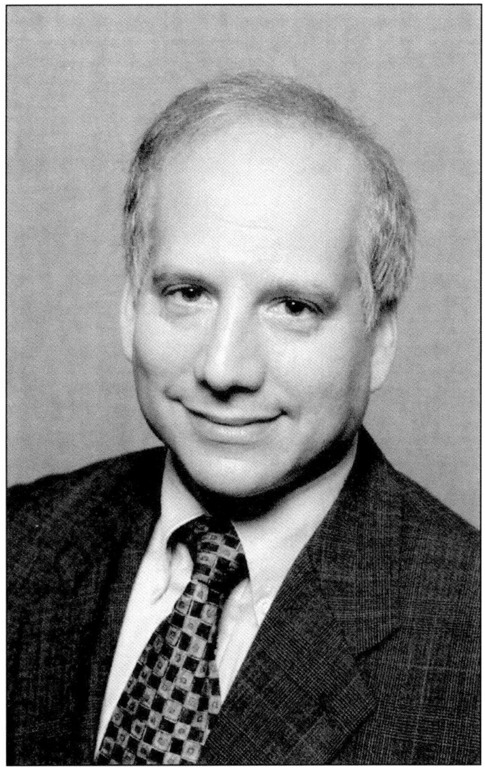

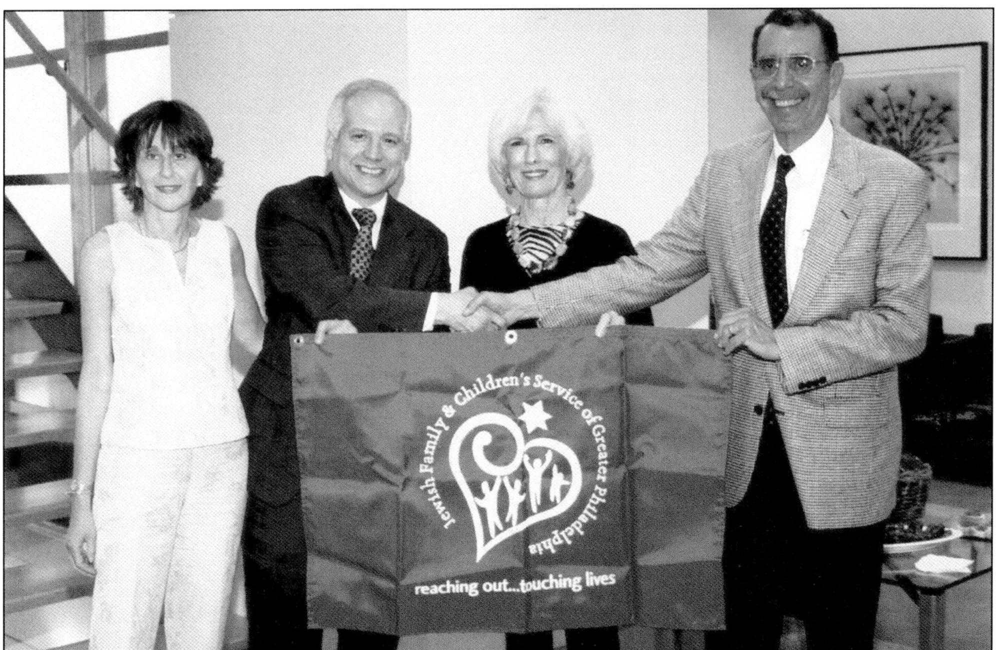

Incoming JFCS board chairman James Kahn (second from left with wife Debra) and outgoing board chairman Carl Schneider (with wife Mary Ellen) share a handshake and a smile at a moment of transition in agency leadership. (Courtesy of JFCS.)

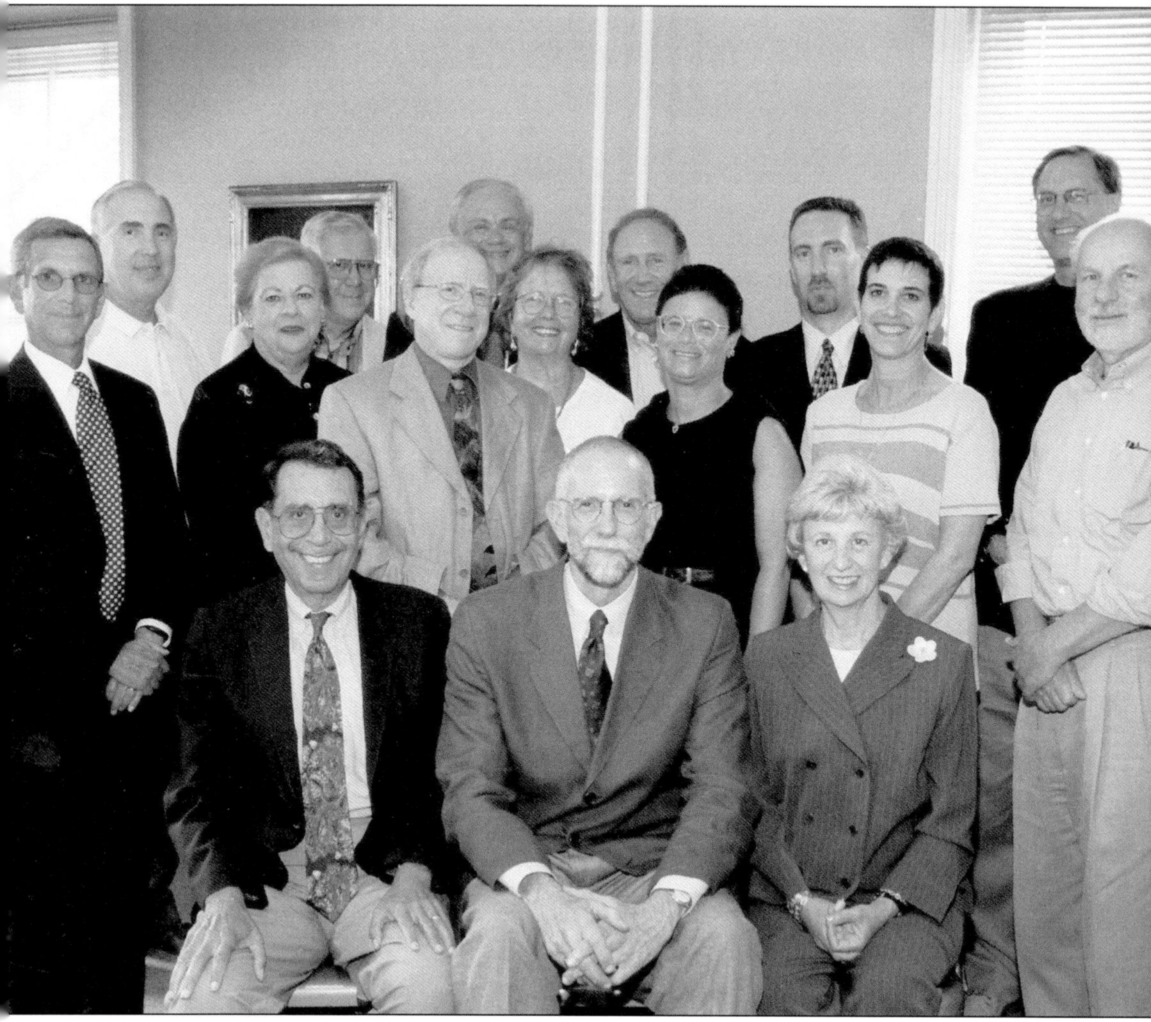

While JFCS is a family service agency, those who work there are also a family. A group of longtime JFCS leaders pose for this group photograph taken at the end of Dr. Harold Goldman's presidency. Their contributions are measured not by individual talent alone but also by their spirited teamwork carrying out the mission of Jewish Family and Children's Service. Pictured from left to right are (first row) Carl Schneider (then chairman of the agency), Harold Goldman, and Joan Grossman; (second row) Henry Miller, Joyce Fishbein, Leonard Cooper, Miriam Finkel, Patricia Cramer, Lois Manowitz, and Edward Brown; (third row) Robert Horen, Howard Magen, Owen Knopping, Raymond Alexander, Mark Schneider, and Paul Stark. (Courtesy of Harold Goldman.)

Dr. Harold Goldman began at JFCS as its associate executive director in 1983 and succeeded JFCS's first executive director, Donna Pressma (1983–1984). He served as executive director and president of the agency until 2000 when he became president of the Jewish Federation of Greater Philadelphia. Looking back on his JFCS years, he said, "I can honestly say I fell in love with the mission of this agency, which is to provide a social safety net for those less fortunate that ourselves." (Courtesy of JFCS.)

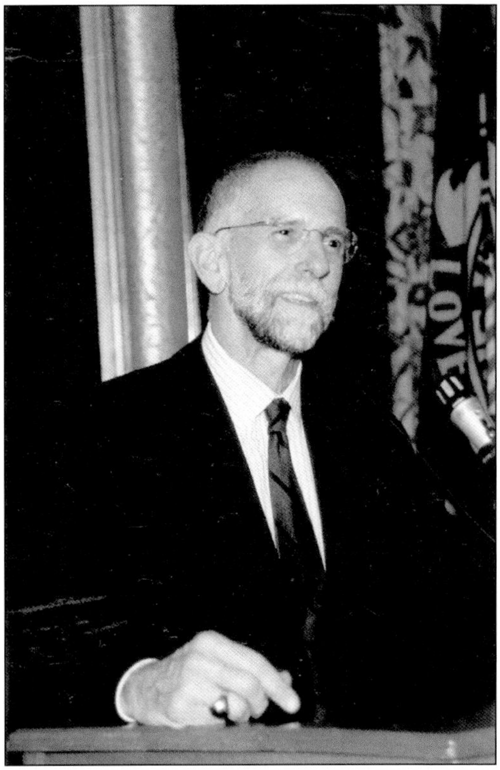

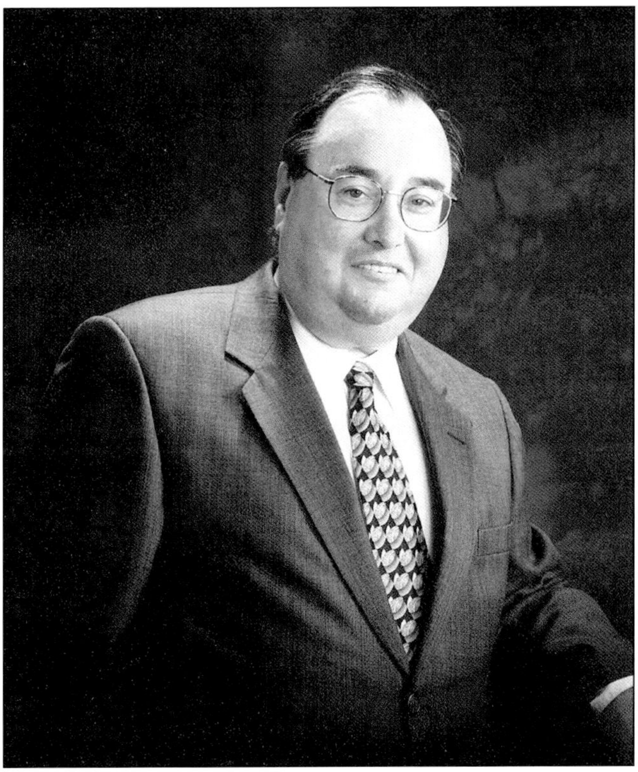

Little more than a month after assuming the position of JFCS president and CEO, Drew Staffenberg (2001–2005) mobilized the agency to reach out to the community with trauma response counseling and support in the wake of 9/11. JFCS reached out immediately because, as he said, "the hallmark of any good social service agency is to be proactive, up front and ahead of the curve." (Courtesy of JFCS.)

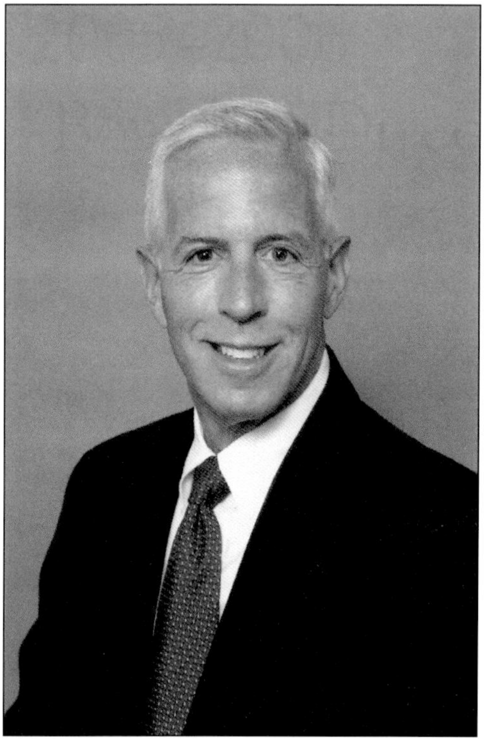

In 2005, JFCS's current president and CEO, Jack Dembow, took the helm of a well-established 150-year-old agency that has served hundreds of thousands of people over the years. Still, he says, challenging times presen*t an opportunity to adapt anew to "meet the needs of a changing community and marketplace and enable the agency to further expand its wonderful, mission-driven work." (Courtesy of JFCS.)

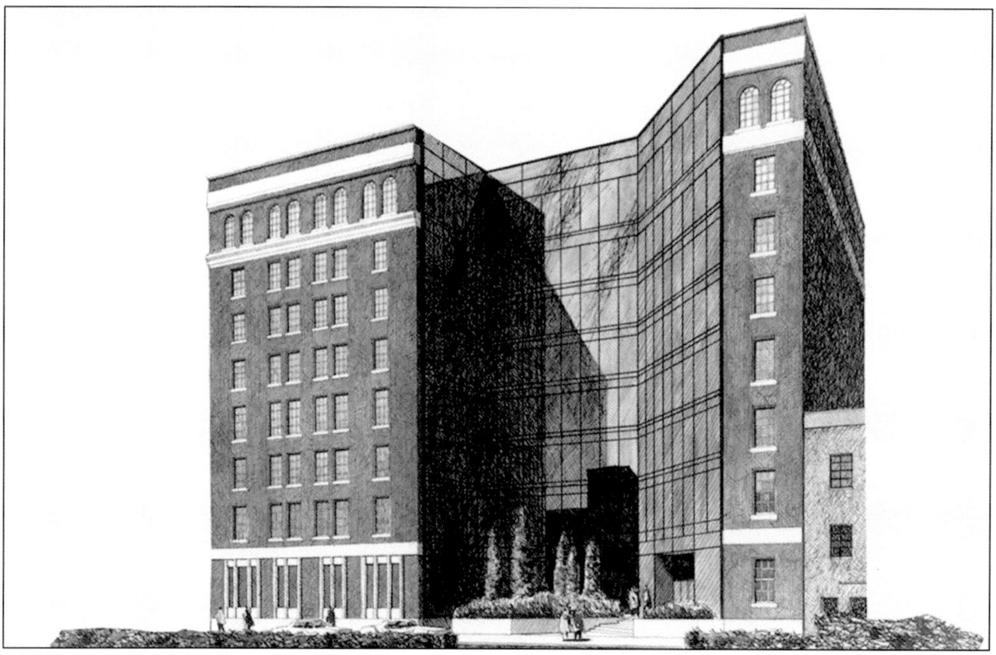

The modern era at JFCS is reflected in the modern look of its current headquarters, located in the Jewish Community Services Building at 2100 Arch Street. The central office of the Jewish Federation of Greater Philadelphia and a number of other communal organizations are housed there also, fostering close communal collaborations. (Courtesy of the Jewish Federation of Greater Philadelphia.)

2005–2006 Board of Directors

Raymond Alexander
Donald Bean
Martin Blumberg
Phyllis Bookspan
Samuel Brand
Iris Brownstein
Scott Brucker
Henry Cohen
Ronald Cohen
Stephen Cohen
Michael Coleman
David Colman
Leonard Cooper
Sheri Cozen Resnik
Patricia Cramer
Judith Creed
Kelly Dalsemer
Stephen Dubin
Alison Erlbaum Sussman
Donna Feinberg
Miriam Finkel
Joyce Fishbein
Ricki Fisher
Joel Freedman
Ivan Gabel
David Glickman
Suzanne Goldstein
David Grunfeld
Robert Horen
James Kahn
Owen Knopping
Amy Kurland
Adam Laver
Murray Levin
Barbara Lincow
Alan Lindy
Francine Lipstein
Irwin Lipton
Howard Magen
Bruce Marks
Henry Miller
Ruth Nathanson
Rosalind Neff
Norman Olson
Eve Orlow
Mark Patlove
Curtis Pontz
David Rosenberg
Peter Rosenberg
Douglas Schleicher
Mark Schneider
Carl Schneider
Ira Schwartz
Jeffrey Schwartz
Michael Schwartz
Toni Seidl
Carrie Shapiro
Cindy Smukler Dorani
Jessica Solomon
Marjorie Stein
Diane Steinbrink
Ted Wasserman
Peter Weintraub
Matthew White
Michael Willner
Flora Barth Wolf
Vivian Young

2005–2006 Officers

Chairman of the Board
James R. Kahn

President and CEO
Jack H. Dembow

Executive Vice President
and COO
Lois Manowitz

First Vice Chairman
Douglas F. Schleicher

Vice Chairmen
Miriam Finkel
Mark Schneider
Vivian Young

Secretary
Toni Seidl

Assistant Secretaries
Patricia Cramer
Barbara Lincow
Rosalind S. Neff
Peter Rosenberg

Treasurer
Howard M. Magen

Assistant Treasurers
Raymond S. Alexander
Robert Horen
Bruce Marks
Ted N. Wasserman

General Counsel
Matthew A. White

Honorary Officers
Donald Bean
Martin J. Blumberg

JFCS board officers and board members for the historic anniversary year (2005–2006) are listed above. (Courtesy of JFCS.)

2005–2006
Board of Trustees

Jack Adler
Charna Axelrod
Stuart Beck
Daniel Behrend
Charlotte Bernstein
Dene Bernstein
Paul Brenman
Edward Brown
Allan Cohen
Ruth Cohn
Lana Dishler
Ruth DuBois
Richard Freundlich
Samuel Frieder
Jeffrey Garson
Irving Gerber
Joseph Gerber
Carol Gerstley
Jerilyn Getson
Janet Ginns
Michael Goldberg
Julia Greenbaum
David Gutin
May Bert Gutman
Theodore Halpern
Joan Jaffee
Rachelle Kaiserman
Matthew Kamens
Lillian Karsch
Ruth Krawitz
Rabbi William Kuhn
Seymour Kurland
Marlene Lachman
Harold Lampert
Aaron Landes
Herman Lefco
Joseph Levine
Judith Lynn
Julie Marcus Paul
Norma Meshkov
Jay Ochroch
Sheldon Pavel
Grace Portner
Adena Potok
Lois Rosenau
M. William Schwartz
Robert Segal
Betsy Sheerr
Joseph Smukler
Joanne Stoloff
Harold Sukonik
Edith Toll
Robert Wachter
Dorothy Wasserman
Isa Welsch
Joan Wohl
Nancy Wolfson

Fifty-eight men and women served as JFCS trustees during the agency's 150th anniversary year. (Courtesy of JFCS.)

Five

REMARKABLE MOMENTS

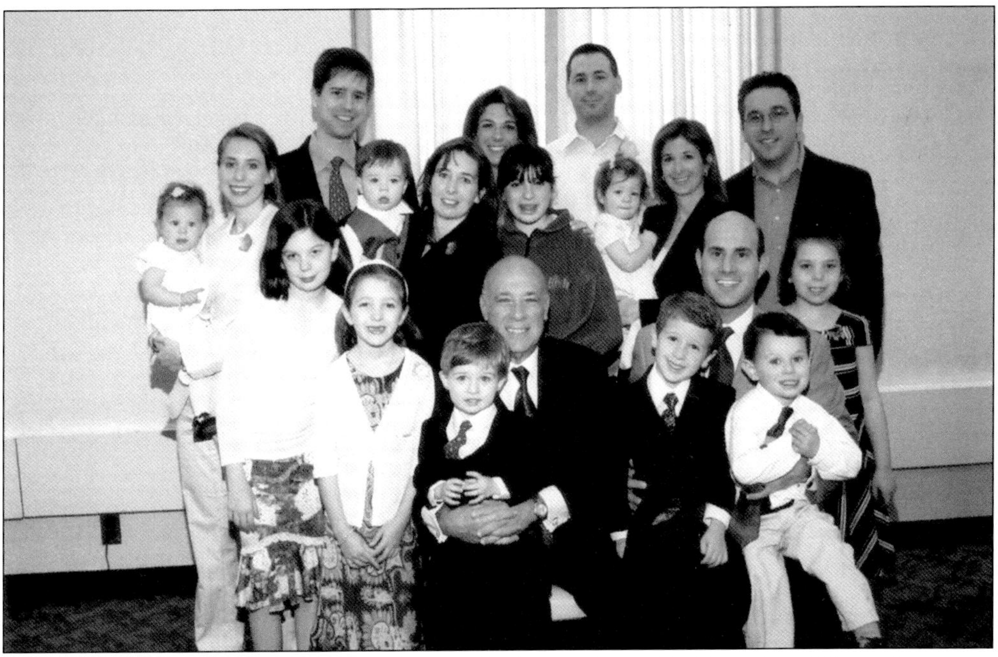

Surrounded by his daughters, sons-in-law, and a bevy of grandchildren, Dr. Gilbert Grossman enjoys a memorable moment at the formal dedication of the Joan Grossman Center for Chaplaincy and Healing. The center is named in memory of his wife, a former JFCS board chairman, whose vision and advocacy helped inspire its creation. It provides Jewish spiritual care to those living with illness, to caregivers, and to the bereaved, volunteer para-chaplaincy training, community education and support programs, and more. The dedication ceremony took place in 2004 at Beth Sholom Congregation in Elkins Park. (Courtesy of JFCS.)

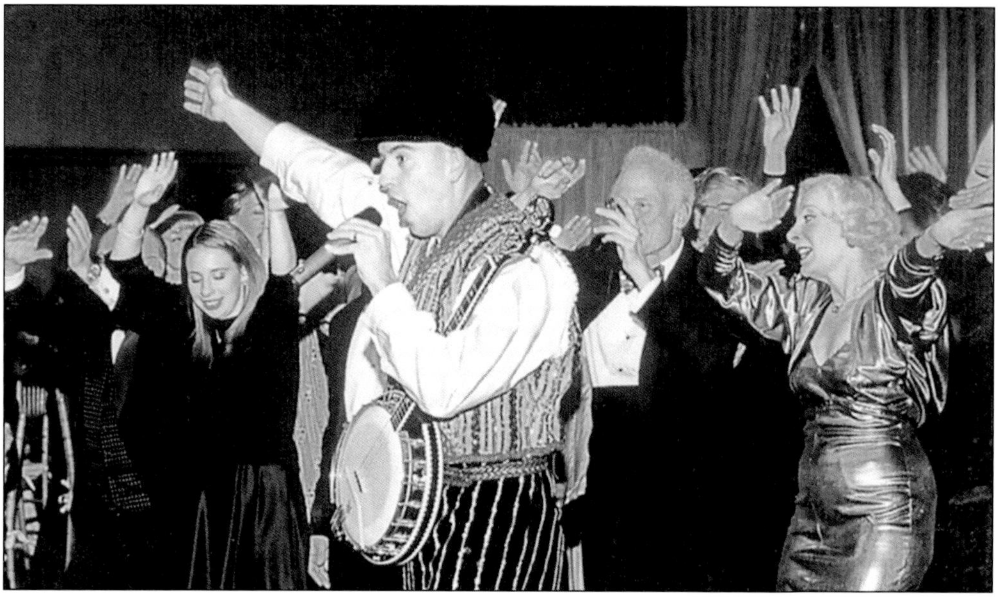

JFCS fund-raising events are a tradition dating back to the 19th century. JFCS's 19th-century predecessor, the United Hebrew Charities, for example, held an annual Purim Ball to help support its services. In a more recent JFCS gala fund-raiser, members of the famed Philadelphia Mummers added a special flair to the festivities. The theme of that gala, "Another Philadelphia Treasure," highlighted JFCS's role in reaching out, touching lives throughout the Greater Philadelphia community. (Courtesy of JFCS.)

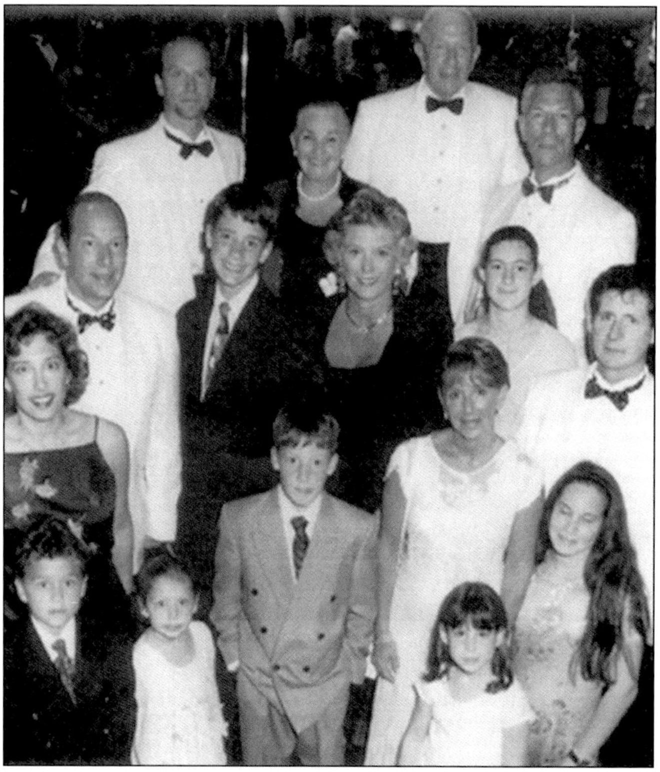

"From Generation to Generation" has been a theme to celebrate with many families over JFCS's long history. Four generations of the Leonard and Dorothy Wasserman family were honored for this tradition of caring at the 2001 JFCS gala. Dorothy and Leonard are pictured in the top row (middle and second from right). Whether volunteering on behalf of kids at an AJC group home, being a Jewish "big brother," delivering challahs to Jewish hospital patients, chairing JFCS's Faithways interfaith outreach program advisory committee, serving as board members, or in a multitude of other ways, family members continue to lend a hand and a heart where needed. (Courtesy of Dorothy and Leonard Wasserman)

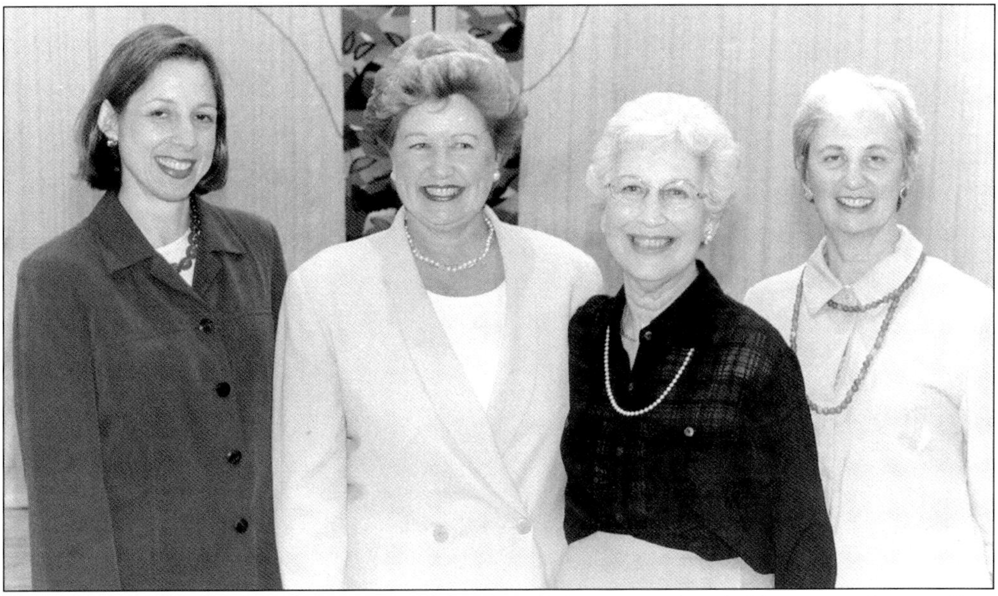

This 1990s event, held at the National Museum of American Jewish History in Center City, celebrated more than a century of JFCS adoption services. Pictured at the event from left to right are Margo Bloom, then museum executive director; keynote speaker Pennsylvania first lady Michele Ridge; honoree Shirley Sagin, past director of the adoption program under JFCS and its predecessor, the AJC; and JFCS board chairman Joan Grossman. Ridge received JFCS's Friend of the Family Award for her support of adoption. (Courtesy of JFCS.)

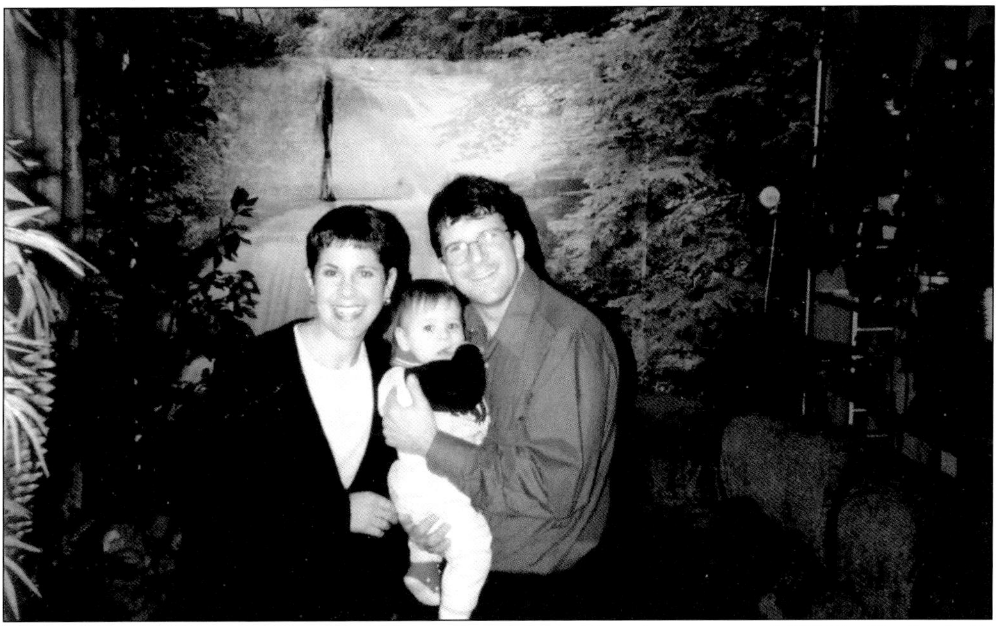

A child's love knows no borders. The Paths to Parenthood program of JFCS's Elizabeth B. Binswanger Adoption Service helps to place children from Eastern Europe, Guatemala, and China with adoptive families locally and nationally. Leza Raffel and her husband Mark Rake adopted their son Ilya with the help of JFCS. They are pictured here in Moscow in 1999 on the day they first met Ilya. (Courtesy of Leza Raffel and Mark Rake.)

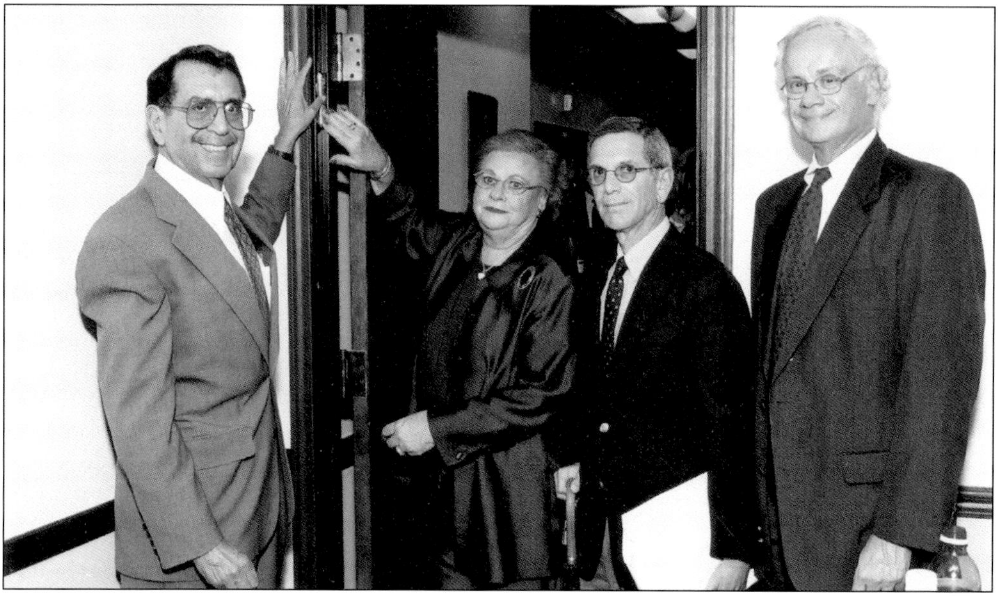

Carl Schneider (left), then JFCS board chairman, joins in the formal mezuzah hanging at the entrance to the new JFCS office at the Jewish Community Services Building, located at Twenty-first and Arch Streets. The posting of a mezuzah on the doorpost of a Jewish home is an age-old tradition dating back to biblical times. With Schneider at the 2001 ceremony from left to right are former JFCS board presidents Joyce Fishbein, Henry Miller, and Owen Knopping. (Courtesy of JFCS.)

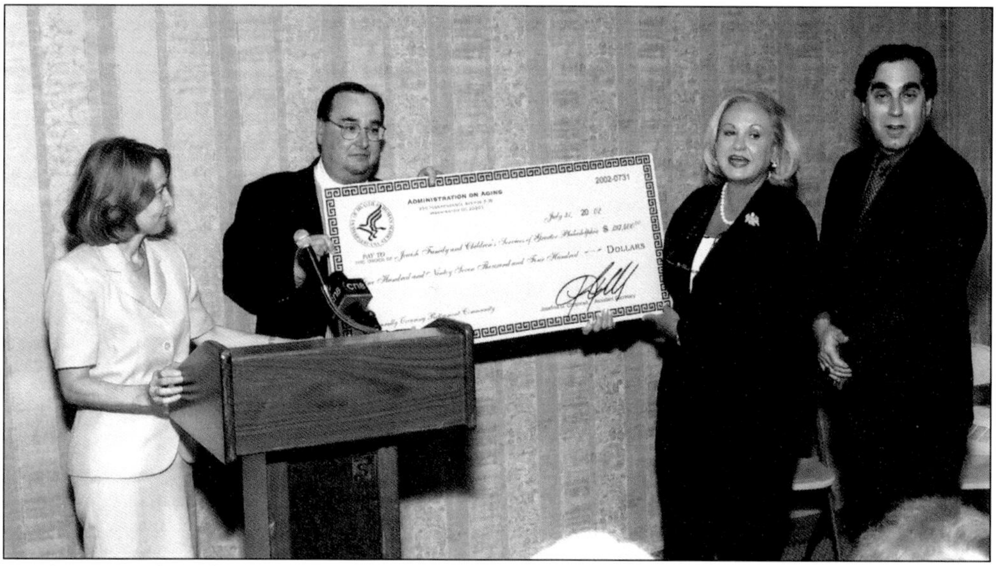

Josefina G. Carbonell, assistant secretary for aging in the U.S. Department of Health and Human Services, presents a check for $197,400 to JFCS's then president and CEO Drew Staffenberg. Pictured are Diana Aviv (at far left) of the United Jewish Communities' Washington Action Office and Gary Guiran (at far right), U.S. Department of Health and Human Services regional representative. JFCS was one of the first five recipients nationwide to receive a federal grant in 2001 to fund a new model program for "naturally occurring retirement communities." (Courtesy of JFCS.)

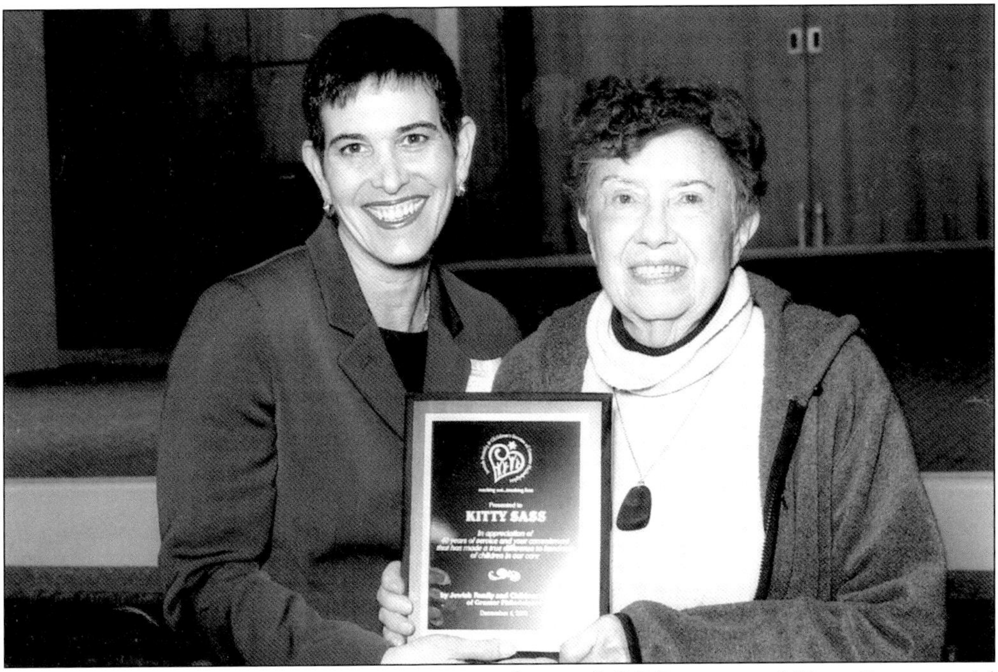

Lois Manowitz (left), JFCS executive vice president and COO, presented Kitty Sass, a social worker in the Child Welfare Department, with an award for 40 years of service during the agency's 2002 All Staff Day. Sass helped locate families for children needing foster care and to evaluate candidates who were interested in becoming foster parents. Throughout all those years of service, she rarely missed a day of work. (Courtesy of JFCS.)

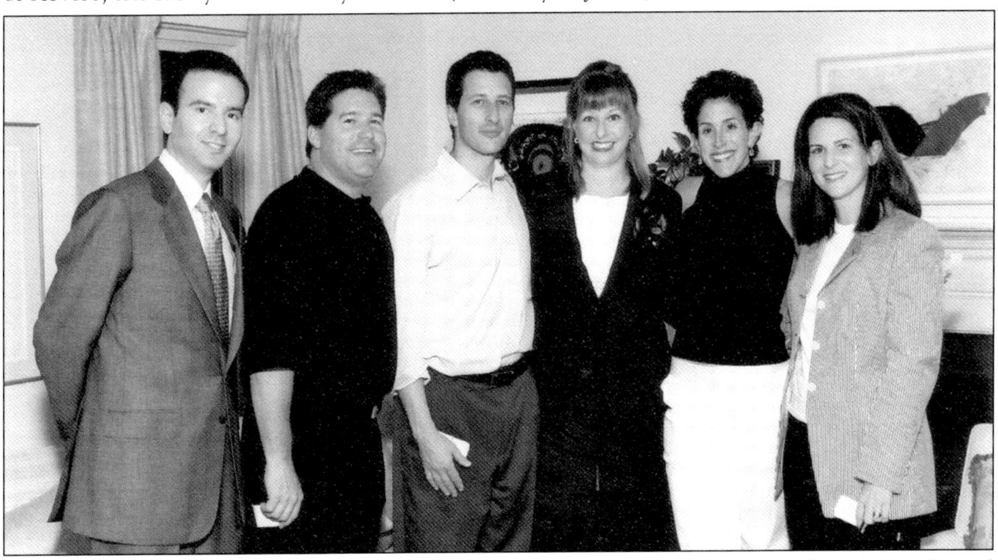

Developing new leadership is crucial to sustaining an organization over time. Jewish Family and Children's Service formed a young leadership organization, the JFCS Advocates, to connect a younger generation of adult leaders to the organization and to help support JFCS's work. Pictured at the JFCS Advocates's inaugural event in 2003 from left to right are Adam Laver, Larry Brownstein, Peter Rosenberg, Iris Davis Brownstein, Sheri Cozen Resnik, and Jessica Solomon. (Courtesy of JFCS.)

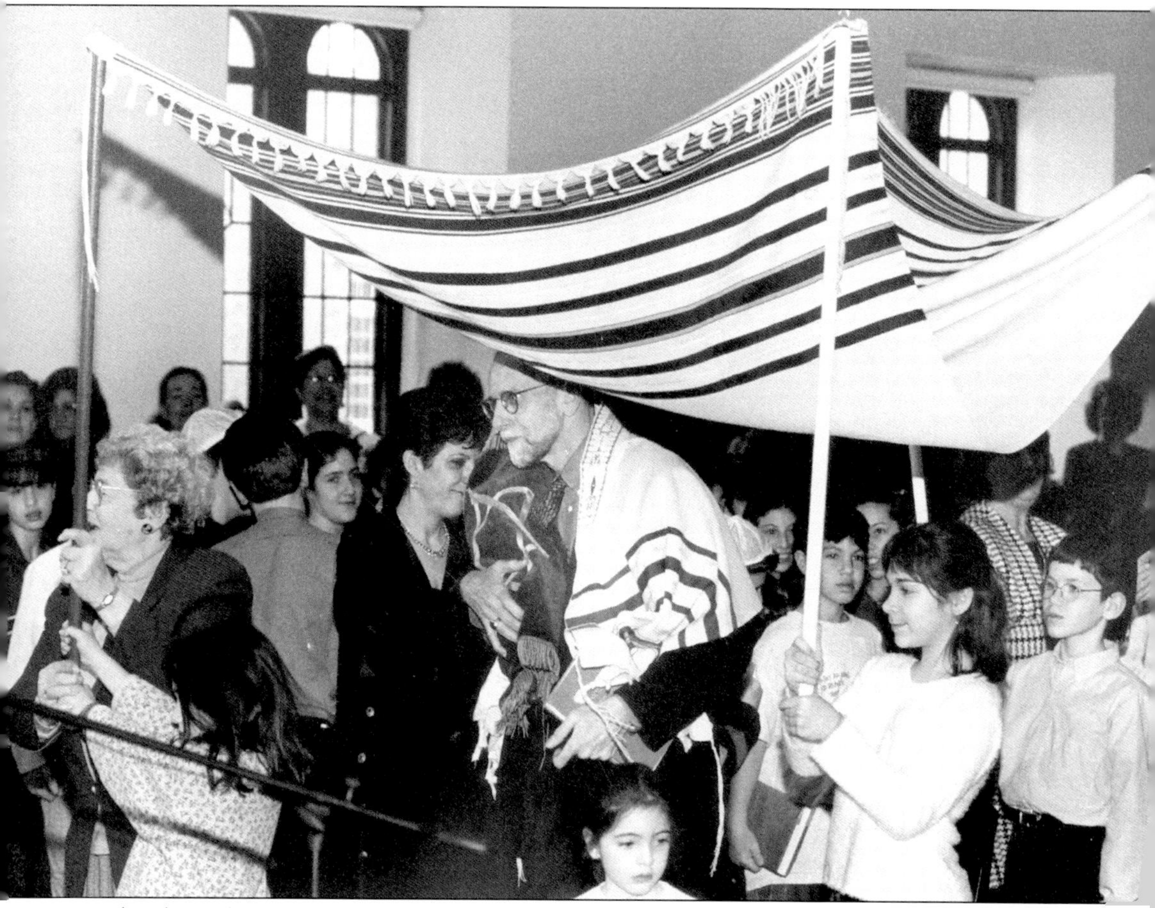

The chuppah, a religious symbol in Judaism, is used at weddings. The Torah, used by the Foster Home for Hebrew Orphans at 700 East Church Lane, remained in storage after the home closed in 1951 until JFCS leaders thought of making a *shidduch* (match) between the former Jewish institution and the Stern branch of the Raymond and Ruth Perelman Jewish Day School in Lower Merion. JFCS's then president Harold Goldman carries the Torah in a procession during the ceremony in the school's sanctuary. (Courtesy of JFCS.)

Six

Caring for Those in Crisis and in Need

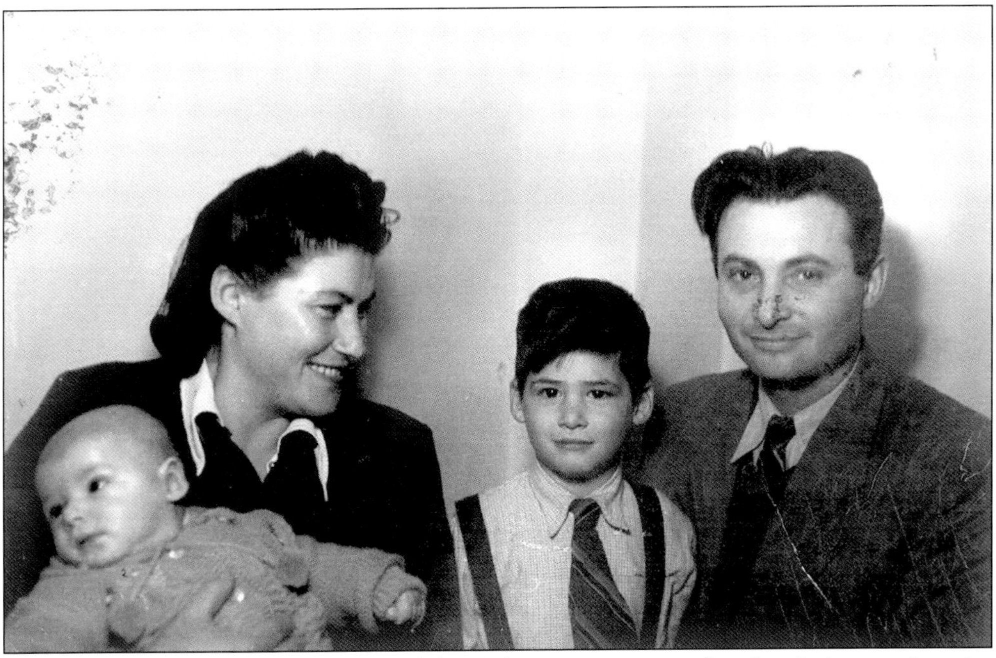

Toba and Leo Zeisler, both survivors of the Holocaust, immigrated to Israel, then to America after World War II. Toba was bedridden, and a family member arranged for a homemaker's assistance through JFS. Working from 7:00 a.m. to 5:00 p.m. each day, Mrs. Gratman, the caregiver, made meals, got the kids off to school, and cleaned the house. While today's JFCS no longer has homemakers on staff, the agency continues to arrange for home care, chore services, and other critical in-home assistance for clients who need it. (Courtesy of Ron Zeisler.)

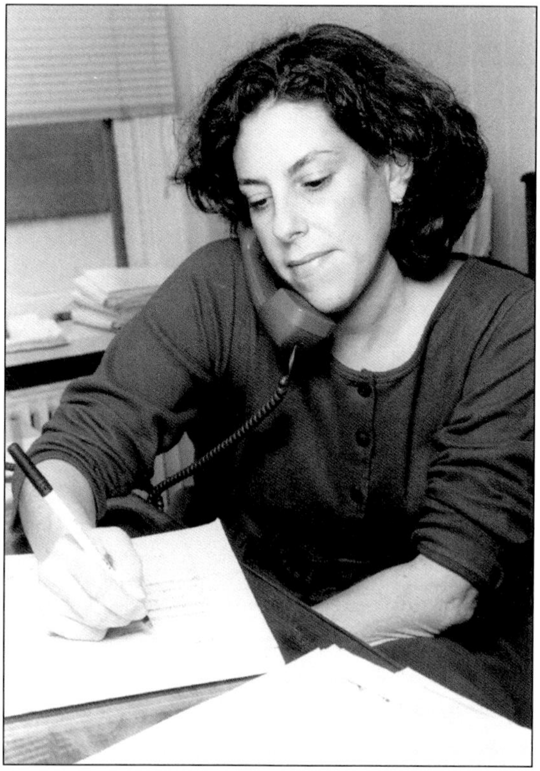

JFCS's Critical Needs program is staffed by social workers, like manager Joanne Lippert, who help people in financial crises. The social workers know that an illness or disability, a sudden rise in the cost of heating, or a job loss, can push individuals and families over the financial edge. While statistics showing that one quarter of the Philadelphia Jewish community is poor or near-poor might surprise some, those on the front lines of JFCS's critical needs response see that reality daily. (Courtesy of JFCS.)

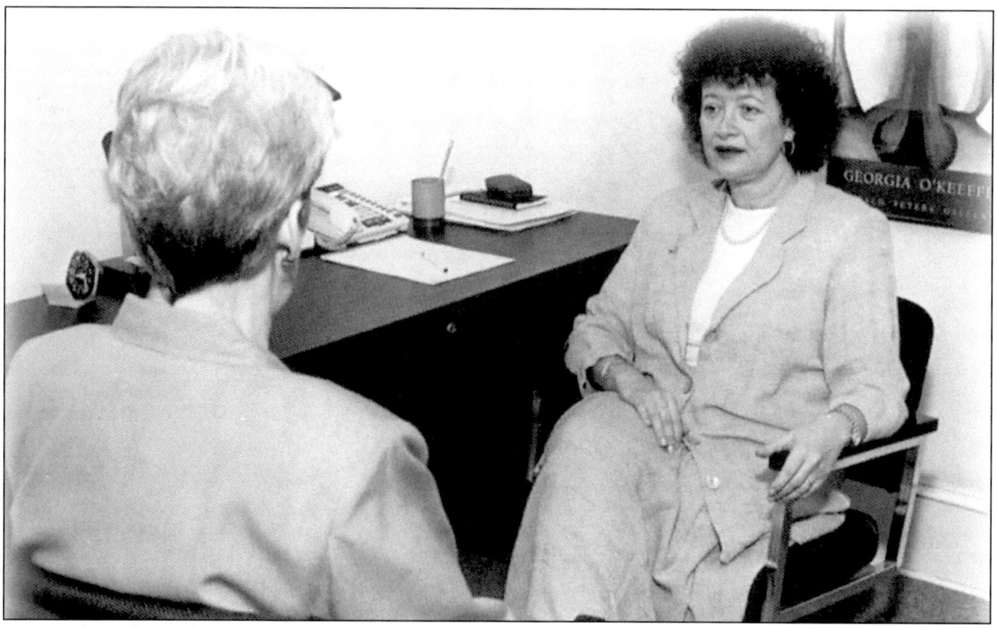

Counseling has always been at the heart of JFCS's work. Whether it is crisis issues, such as bereavement or divorce, or the more ordinary stresses that can be a part of everyday life, problems can become overwhelming for individuals and families. "Turning hurt into hope," JFCS's compassionate, experienced counselors promote emotional healing and help empower their clients to live their lives to the fullest potential. (Courtesy of JFCS.)

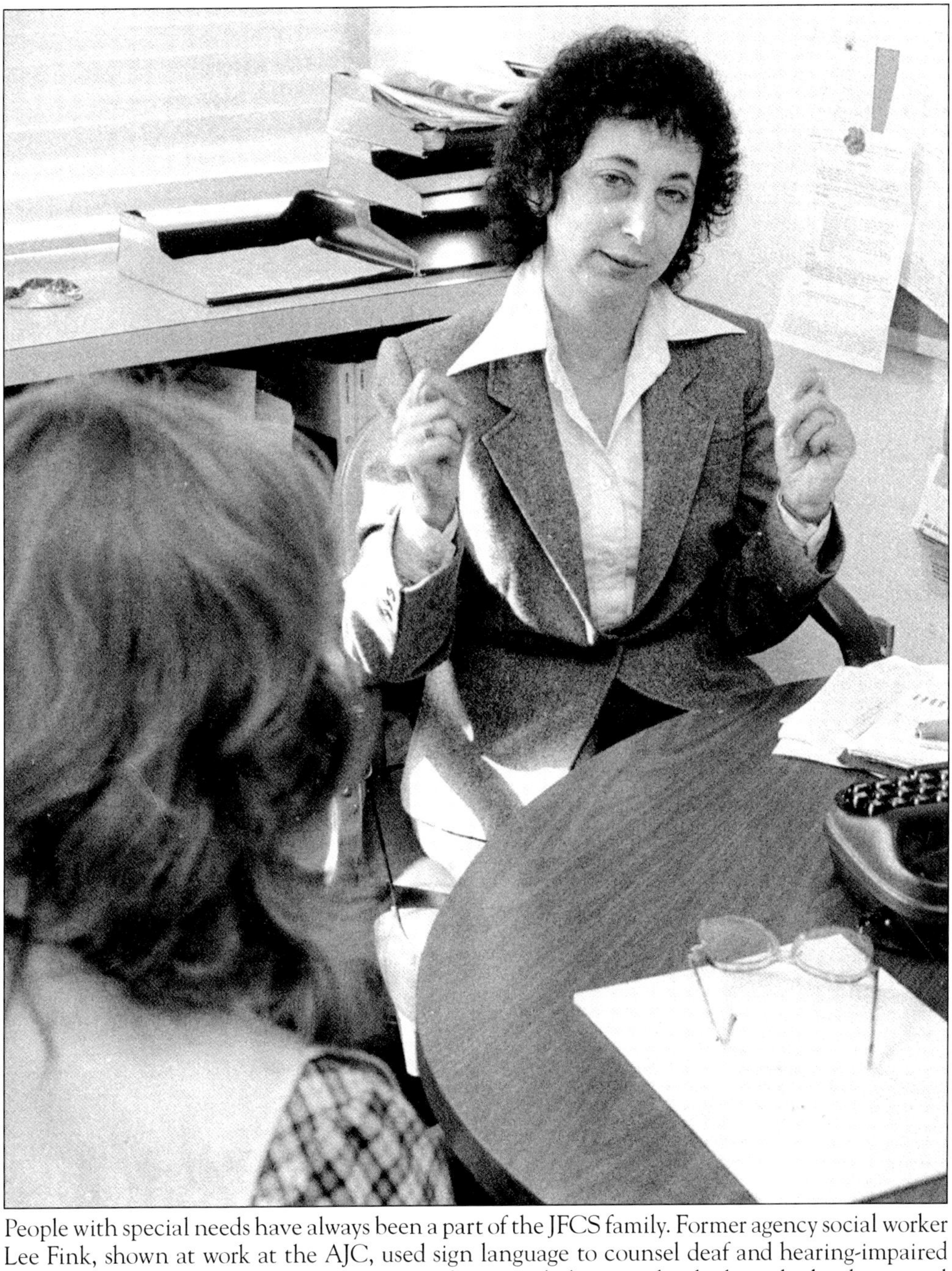

People with special needs have always been a part of the JFCS family. Former agency social worker Lee Fink, shown at work at the AJC, used sign language to counsel deaf and hearing-impaired clients. JFCS special needs services today focus on helping individuals with developmental disabilities and their families. (Courtesy of the Philadelphia Evening Bulletin, Photojournalism Collection, Temple University Libraries, Urban Archives, Philadelphia, Pennsylvania.)

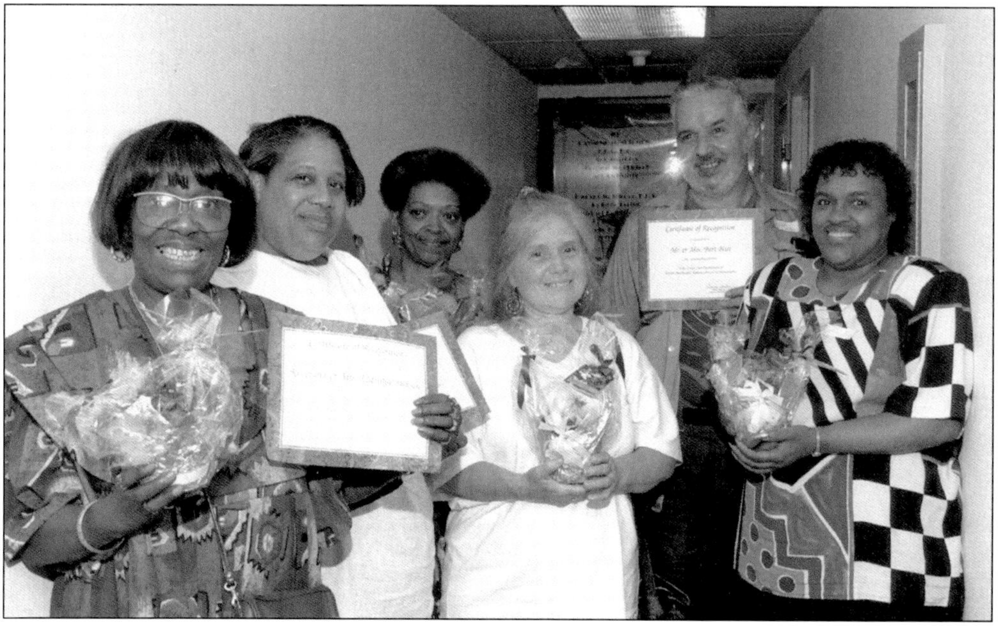

Helping members of the community at large is another role of JFCS. Working with the Philadelphia Department of Human Services and other county agencies, JFCS serves children in need of child foster care and other child welfare programs. These foster parents were among those honored at a JFCS foster parent recognition event in the 1990s. Foster parents provide temporary homes for children whose parents cannot care for them—often children who are abused or neglected, emotionally troubled, or who have special medical needs. (Courtesy of JFCS.)

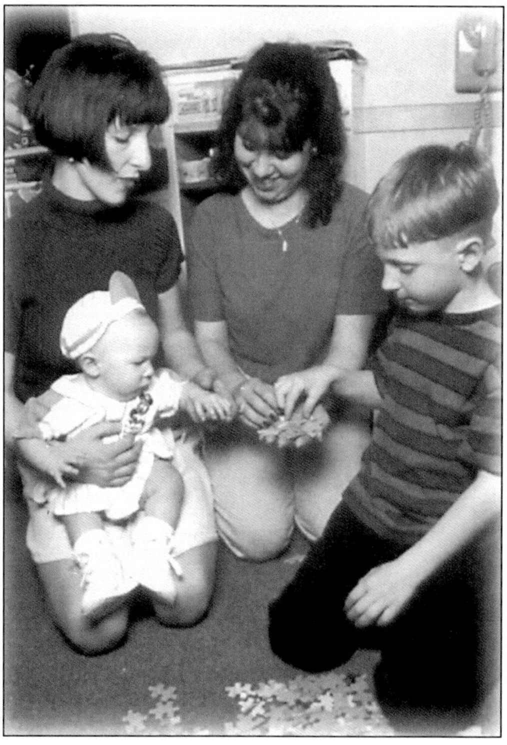

Raising children is a timeless challenge, and some families need intensive help. Through its SCOH (Services to Children in their Own Homes) program, JFCS provides intensive in-home services to children and families at risk to avoid out-of-home placement of the children when possible. (This photograph is not of actual clients.) (Courtesy of JFCS.)

Seven

Honoring Our Mothers and Fathers

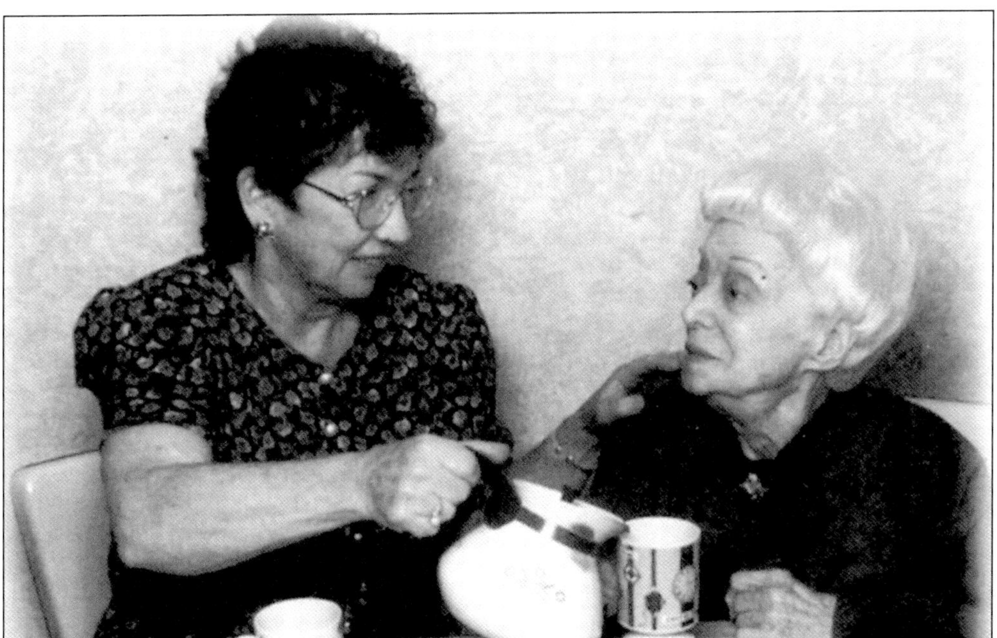

Home visits are a key part of JFCS's social work services for older persons. They often provide a lifeline to clients who are increasingly frail and isolated. A social worker's informal communication and firsthand observations of an elderly client's living situation can yield important information about difficulties the client is experiencing. (Courtesy of JFCS.)

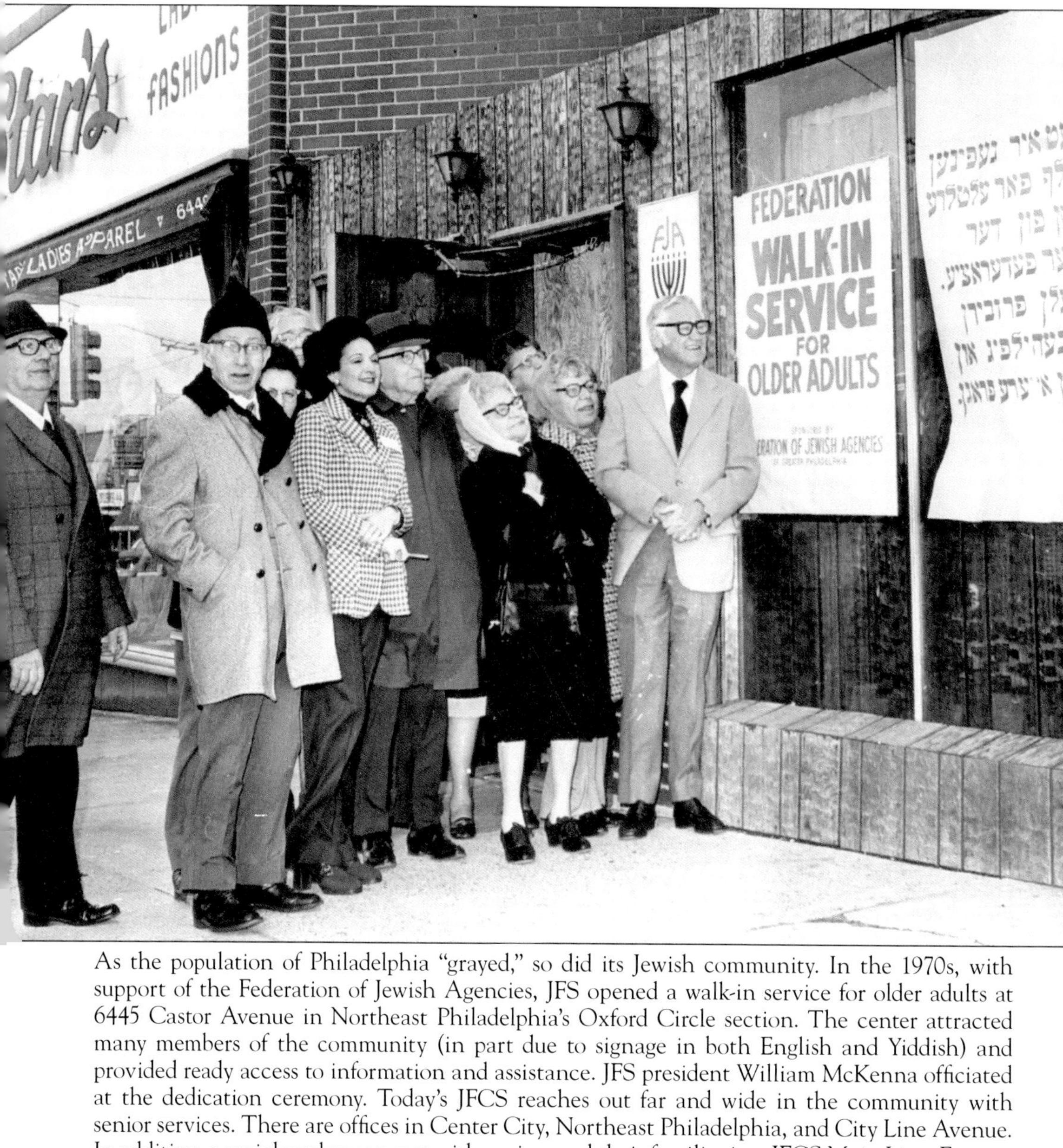

As the population of Philadelphia "grayed," so did its Jewish community. In the 1970s, with support of the Federation of Jewish Agencies, JFS opened a walk-in service for older adults at 6445 Castor Avenue in Northeast Philadelphia's Oxford Circle section. The center attracted many members of the community (in part due to signage in both English and Yiddish) and provided ready access to information and assistance. JFS president William McKenna officiated at the dedication ceremony. Today's JFCS reaches out far and wide in the community with senior services. There are offices in Center City, Northeast Philadelphia, and City Line Avenue. In addition, a social worker can met with seniors and their families in a JFCS Main Line, Eastern Montgomery County, Bux-Mont, or Chester County offices or in the older person's home. (Courtesy of the Philadelphia Jewish Archives Center.)

Bringing joy at holiday time, volunteer clowns pay a visit to elderly residents of an area boarding home. Such celebrations really bring cheer to everyone's day, especially when the clowns are having a little fun on the job. Social work, chaplaincy, and volunteer services for elderly Jews in local boarding homes are part of a unique JFCS outreach project initiated through the agency's Services for Older Persons Department. (Courtesy of JFCS.)

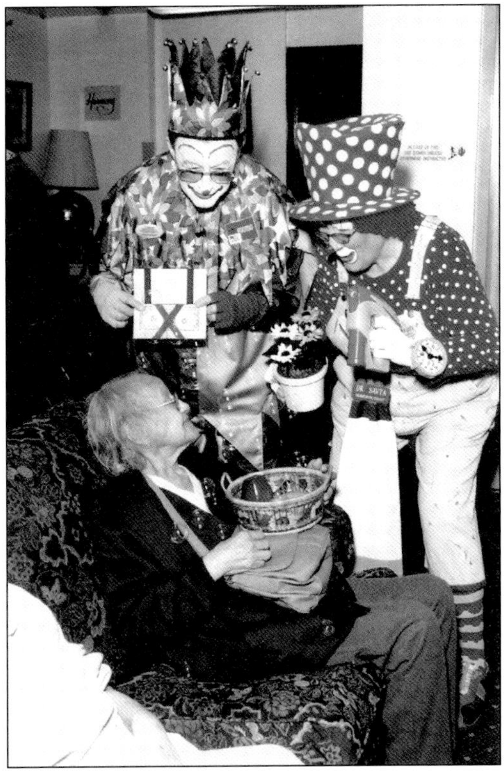

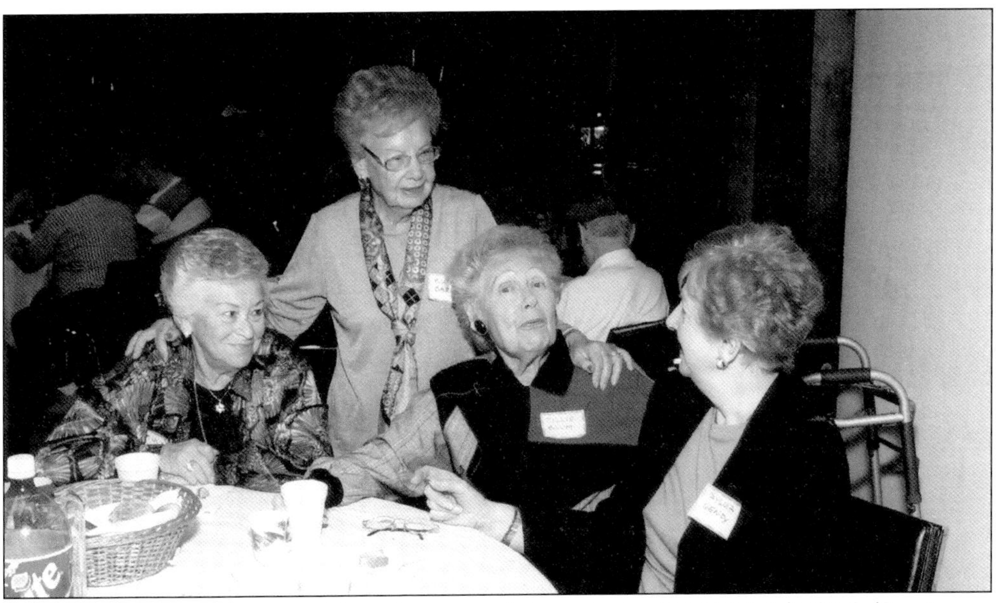

Participants enjoy a "lunch-and-learn" sponsored through the JFCS STAR/NORC (Services to Area Residents/Naturally Occurring Retirement Communities) program. The program reaches out to residents in a number of Center City high rises, in neighborhoods in the Lower Northeast and Overbrook sections of Philadelphia, and in the eastern Montgomery County area—helping seniors access the help they may need to remain independent and fostering social connections, wellness, and community. (Courtesy of JFCS.)

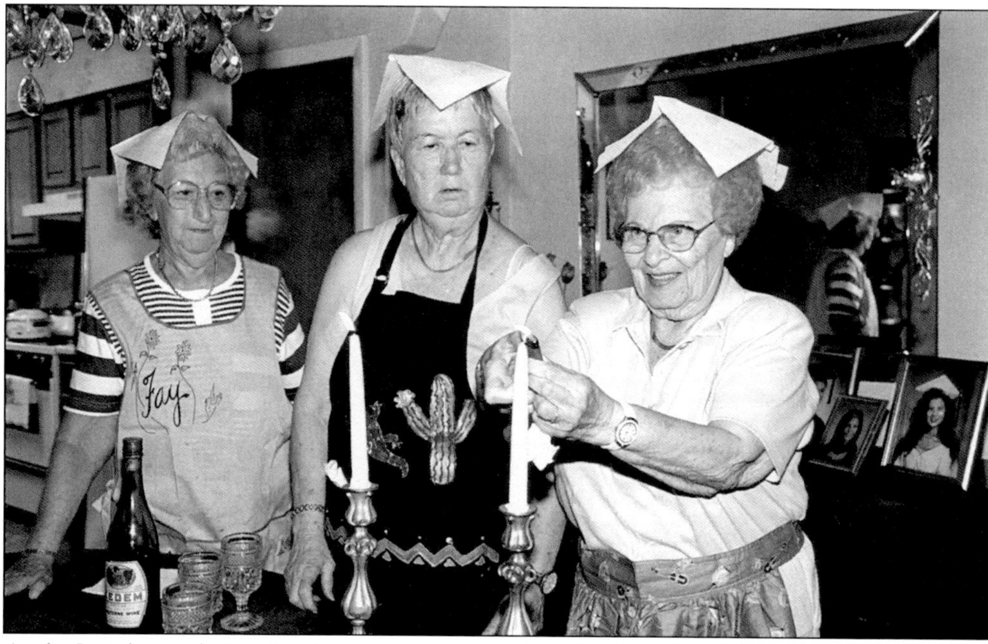

As the Jewish population shrinks in some areas, such as South Philadelphia, JFCS is a continuing presence for those Jews who remain, most of whom are elderly. Social workers can make home visits to clients and connect them to services they need to remain independent. Exemplifying the spirit of South Philadelphia's Jewish community (from left to right) are Fay Kauffman, Alice Freeman, and Bernice Hoffman lighting Sabbath candles to usher in the Jewish day of rest. (Courtesy of Harvey Finkle.)

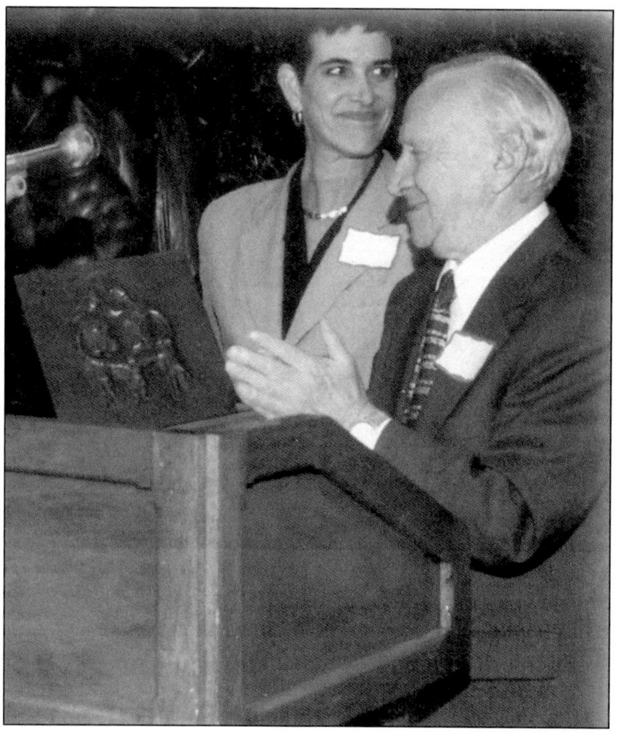

JFCS honored Philadelphia's Association of Jewish Holocaust Survivors and presented its president, Abram Shnaper (right), with the agency's Friend of the Family Award in this recognition event held at city hall. Shnaper serves on the JFCS advisory committee for the Jewish Holocaust Survivor's Project, which assists survivors in need of such services as counseling, home care, and emergency assistance. Presenting the award is Lois Manowitz, JFCS executive vice president and COO. (Courtesy of JFCS.)

Eight

Education for Life

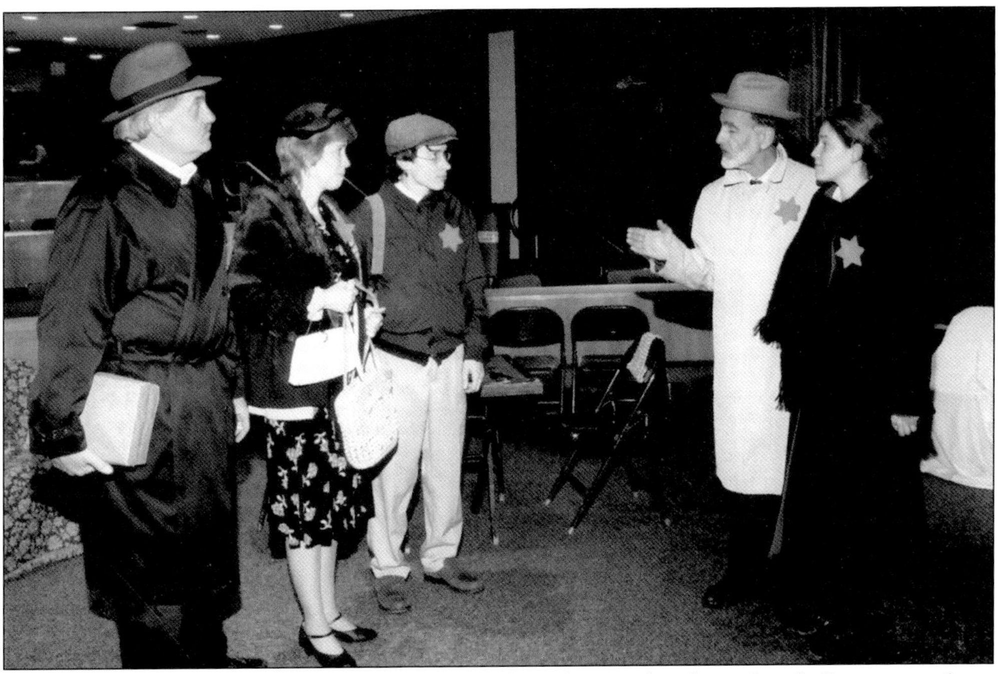

JFCS's Anne Frank Theater Project has played to thousands of people of all ages, teaching history and life's lessons. Audiences see an abridged version of the play *The Diary of Anne Frank* and engage in a post-play discussion led by a JFCS facilitator on the various themes raised by the play. Holocaust history comes alive through this production, with the tale of one teenage girl and the drama of how people's actions and their indifference make a difference—in the secret annex and in the world. (Courtesy of JFCS.)

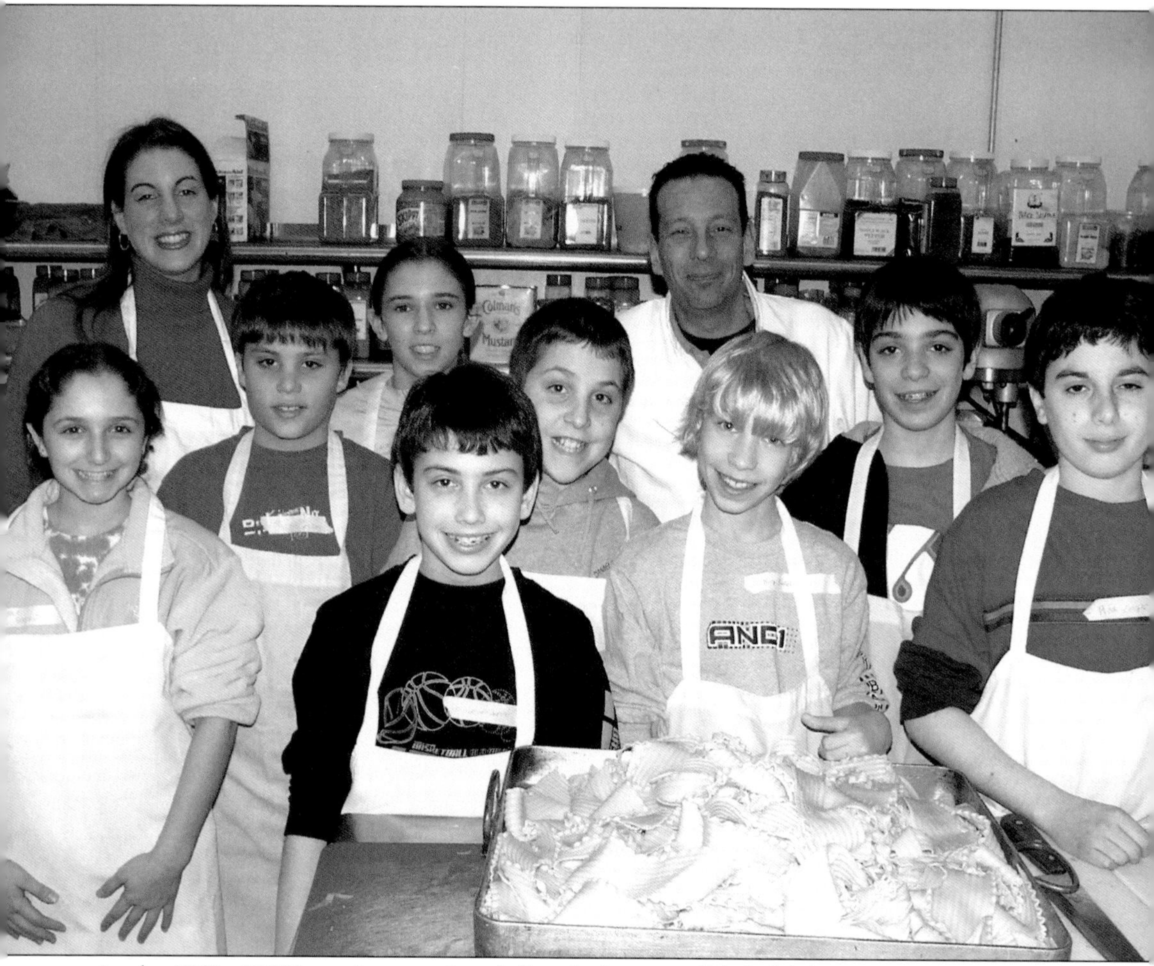

In the 1950s, JFCS's predecessor, Jewish Family Service of Philadelphia, inaugurated family life education programs, bringing expert knowledge and advice on family matters to synagogues, community centers, home and school organizations, youth groups, and other community organizations. Today JFCS's Lieberman Jewish Family Life Education and Group Services program continues its creative, proactive approach to family life issues through discussion groups and workshops, theater education, and conferences. One of its newer ventures, the Youth Mitzvah Corps, a pre–bar/bat mitzvah service-learning project, combines *mitzvot* (good deeds) with the teaching of Jewish values. Shown here, Youth Mitzvah Corps kids prepare a Mother's Day feast for mothers and children at a Project H.O.M.E. residence for formerly homeless families. Peachtree and Ward Catering of Willow Grove and its kosher division, Peachtree Kosher, teamed with JFCS and Project H.O.M.E. to initiate this cooking project. With the kids are Adrienne Madnick (top left), JFCS facilitator for the project, and Marc Zaslow (top right), executive chief of Peachtree Kosher. (Courtesy of the Communication Solutions Group.)

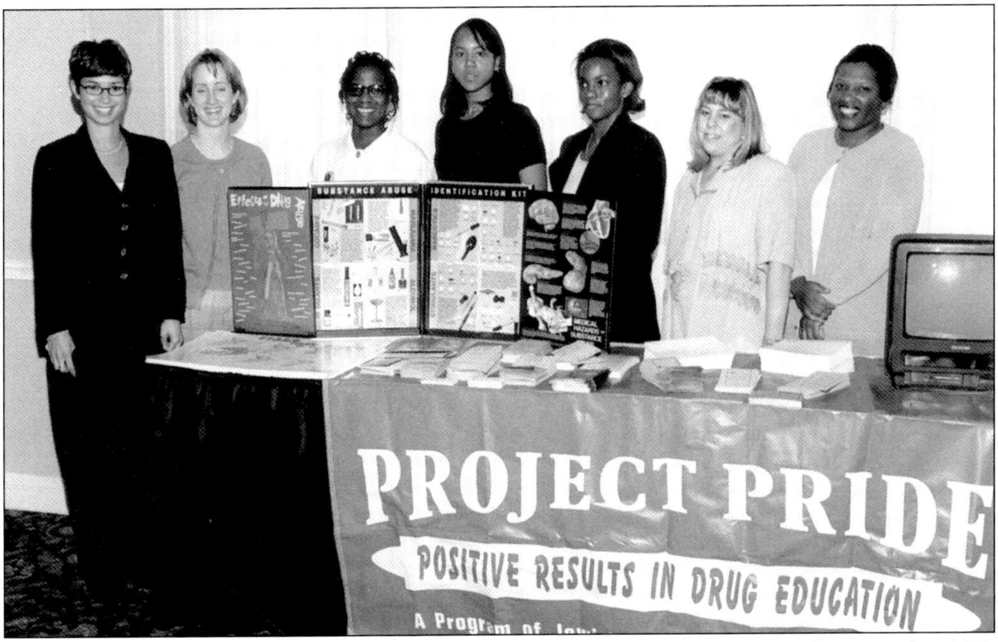

Project PRIDE (Positive Results in Drug Education), originated by JFCS's predecessor, the AJC, operates in Philadelphia and suburban public and private schools. The program works with adolescents in a peer group setting, helping them to build self-esteem and make good decisions so they can avoid substance abuse and other high-risk behaviors. Pictured above, members of the Project PRIDE staff showcase the program at a community outreach event. (Courtesy of JFCS.)

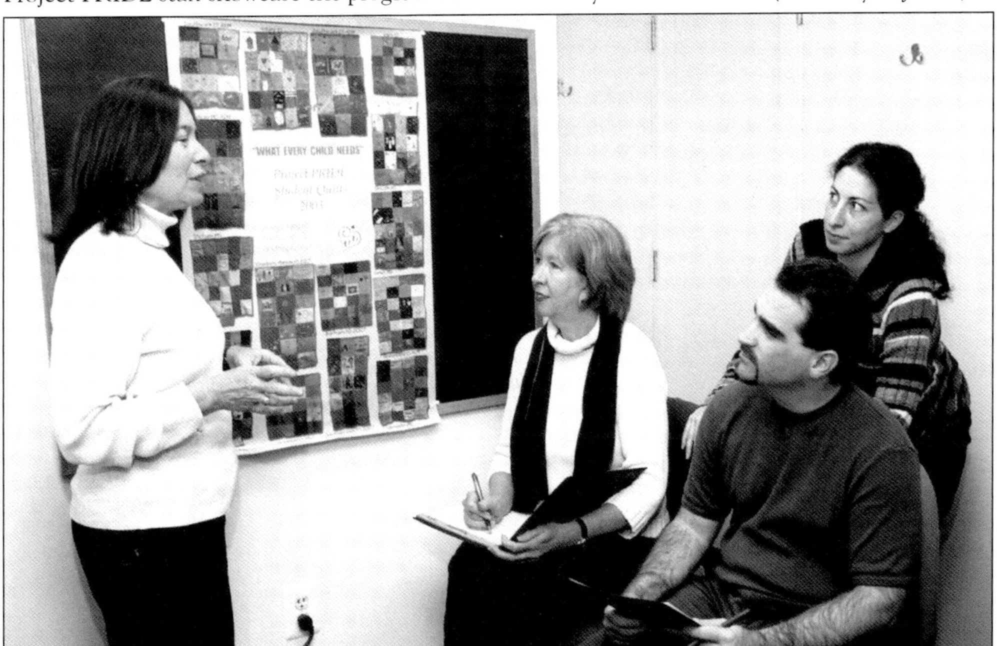

Adrienne Tomlinson (left), assistant director of Project PRIDE, and Project PRIDE staff view a framed poster depicting quilts created by children in an artwork project. Kids made squares on the theme of "What Every Child Needs." (Courtesy of JFCS.)

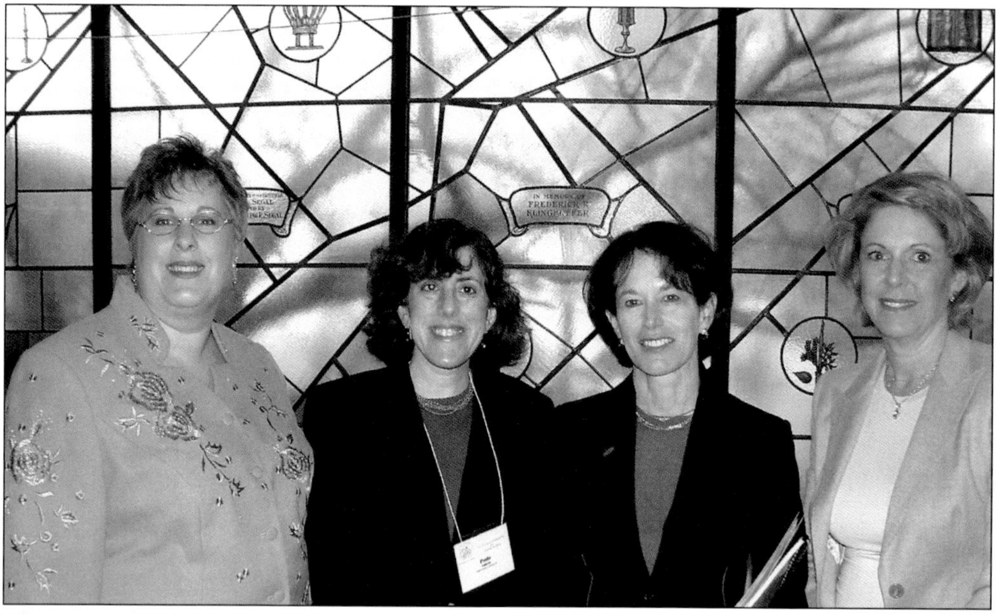

The 2005 Edna S. Tuttleman Symposium on Jewish Women, presented by JFCS in cooperation with other community agencies, focused on Jewish women and caregiving. Pictured above from left to right are symposium cochairpersons Susan Goldfinger Bilker and Paula Goldstein of JFCS; keynote speaker Dr. Terri Apter, psychologist and author; and Dr. Jan Tuttleman, director of the Tuttleman Family Foundation, which funded the symposium to honor Edna S. Tuttleman for her leadership and vision. (Courtesy of JFCS.)

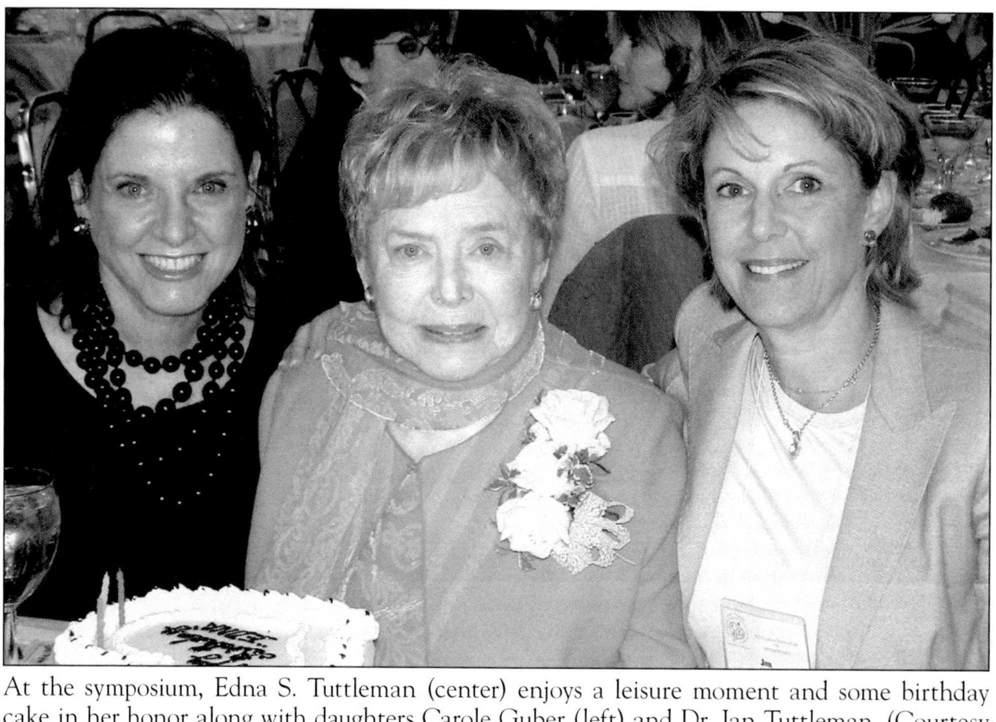

At the symposium, Edna S. Tuttleman (center) enjoys a leisure moment and some birthday cake in her honor along with daughters Carole Guber (left) and Dr. Jan Tuttleman. (Courtesy of JFCS.)

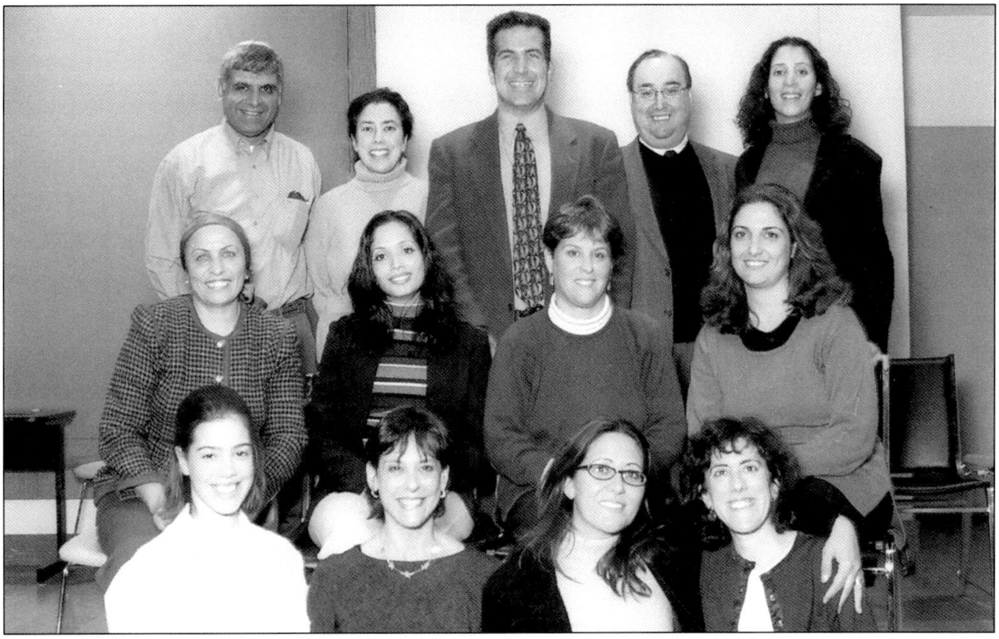

Israeli social workers visited JFCS through the Jewish Federation's Partnership 2000 program that links the Philadelphia Jewish community with that of the Netivot Sedot Negev region of Israel. They pose with members of JFCS staff, including then president and CEO Drew Staffenberg (top row, second from right), for this picture. Also pictured are an actress from the Anne Frank Theater Project (first row left), Sara Wenger and Paula Goldstein of JFCS (first row, second from left and far right), and Robert Levin (top row, center), of the Jewish Federation. (Courtesy of JFCS.)

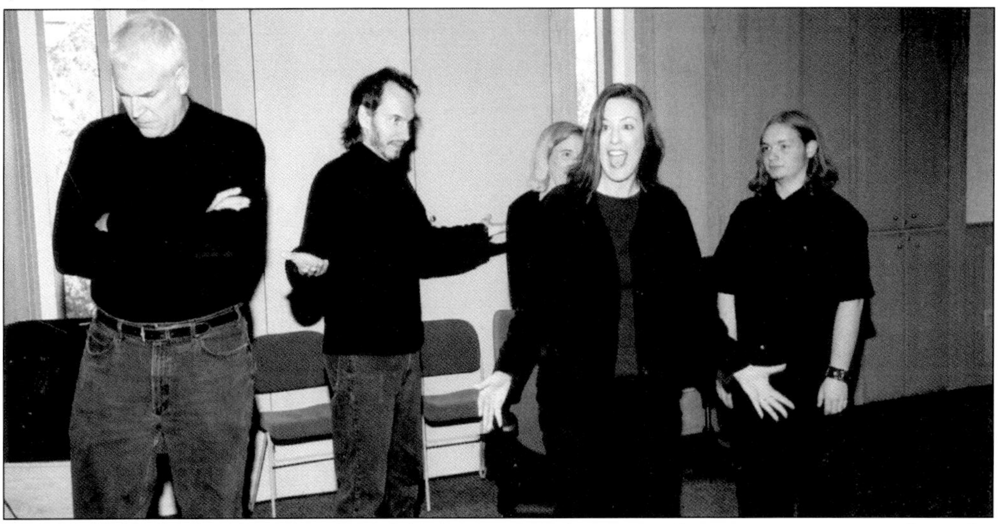

Intermarriage in the American Jewish community hit over 50 percent, as reported in the national Jewish population studies of the early 1990s. JFCS developed a new program entitled Faithways Interfaith Family Support Network to provide an "open door" to interfaith families and welcome their inclusion in the Jewish community. Above, a performance by Theatre Ariel highlights interfaith issues during the Faithways conference "Interfaith Families at Home and in the Community." (Courtesy of JFCS.)

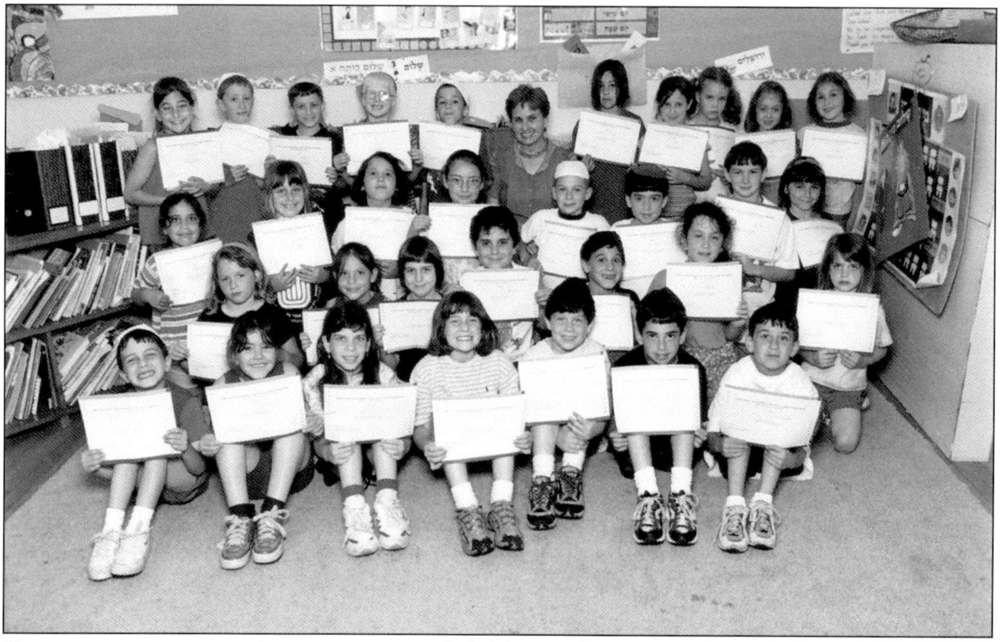

Community service is a key component of children's education. Sandy Fryer, JFCS director of Volunteer Services, meets with children at the Raymond and Ruth Perelman Jewish Day School who participated in a mitzvah project on behalf of JFCS clients. (Courtesy of JFCS.)

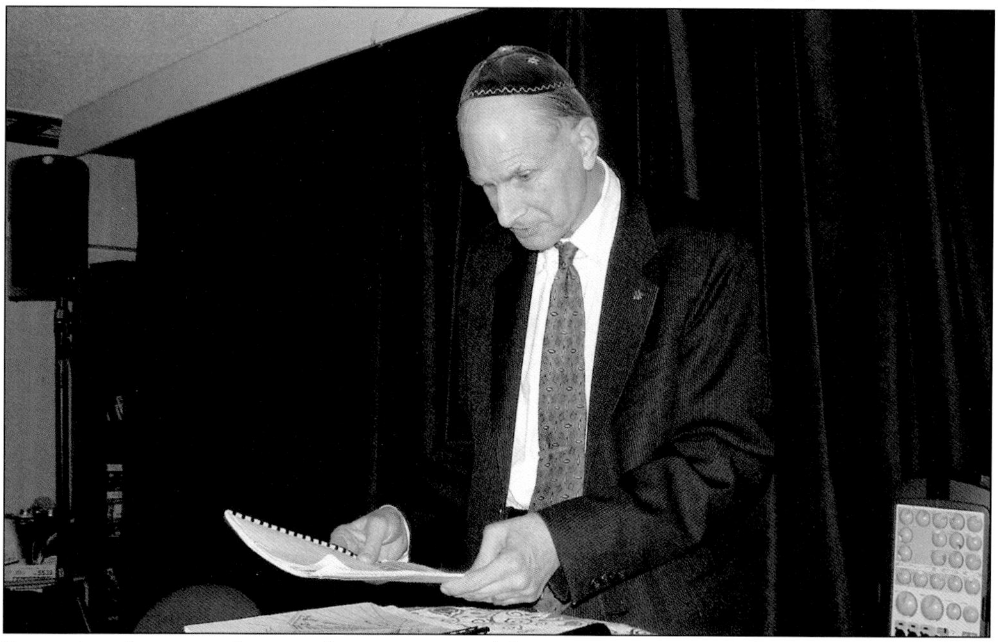

Becoming a bar mitzvah is an achievement to celebrate at any age. JFCS chaplain Rabbi Susanne Greenberg helped Stephen, 68, a resident of Devon Manor, a senior community, to study Hebrew and Judaism to prepare for his 2005 ceremony. Chaplains from JFCS's Joan Grossman Center for Chaplaincy and Healing reach out with pastoral visits, Shabbat and holiday services, and in other ways to connect Jewish residents in senior communities, hospitals, and nursing homes with Jewish tradition and spiritual support. (Courtesy of JFCS.)

Nine

Welcoming New Americans

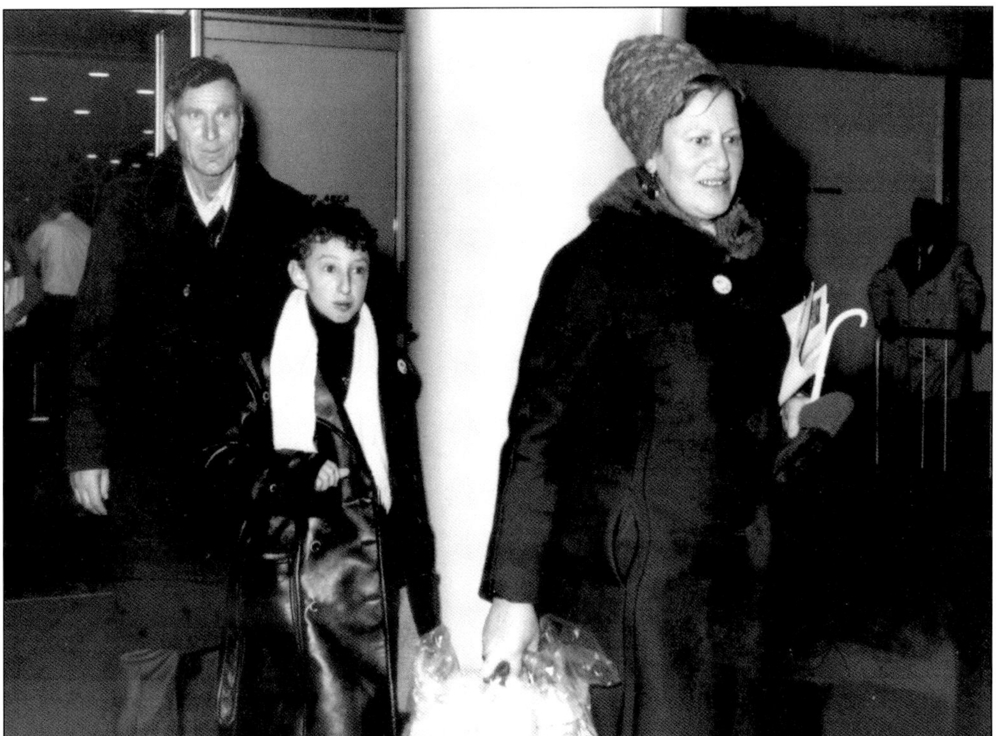

An immigrant family from the Soviet Union realized a dream as they arrived in America. The mass immigration of Soviet Jewish immigrants in the latter part of the 20th century brought new resettlement challenges. (Courtesy of the Philadelphia Jewish Archives Center.)

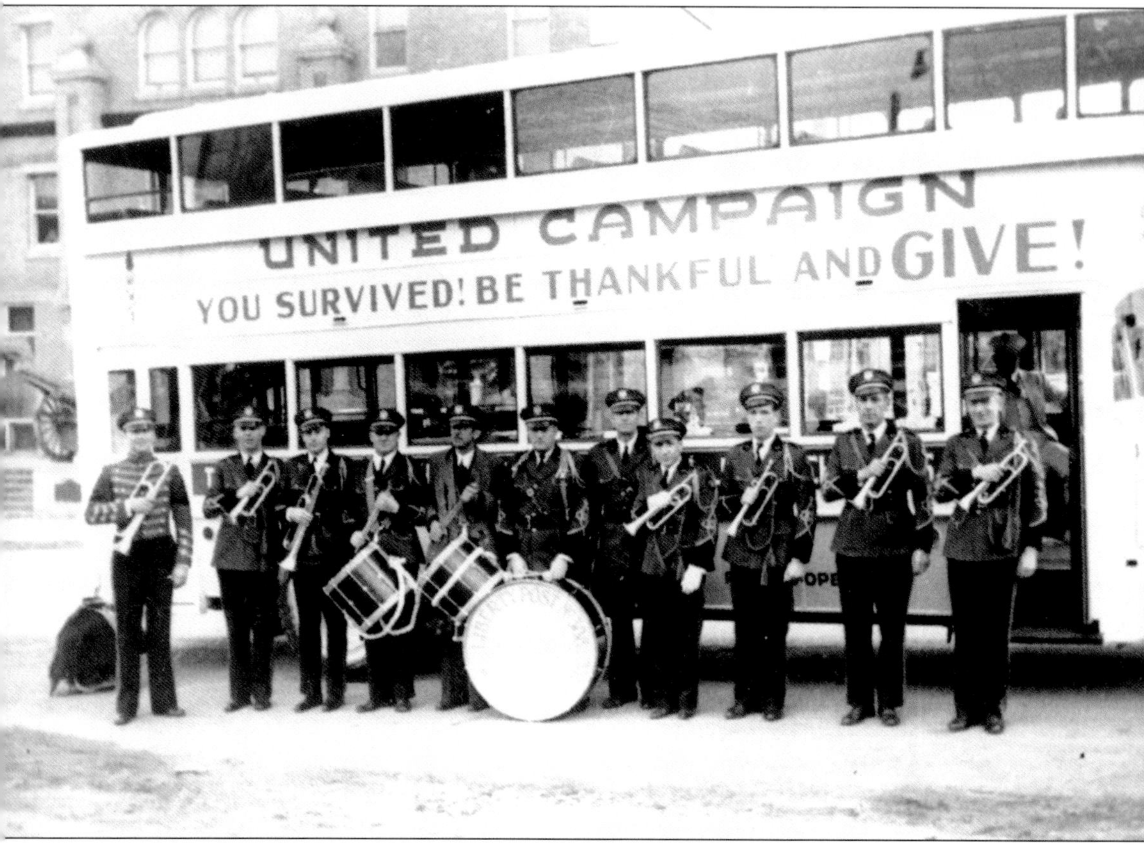

During and after the Nazi era, Philadelphia's Jewish community was active in raising funds and advocating on behalf of their fellow Jews in Europe. The Jewish Welfare Society of Philadelphia, a JFCS predecessor agency, worked to integrate Holocaust refugees into the community. The Hebrew Immigrant Aid Society and the Council of Jewish Women were partners in this effort. While the Jewish Welfare Society had become primarily a counseling agency rather than a relief agency at that time, it provided relief assistance to refugees until they became American citizens and were eligible for public assistance. The society (later renamed Jewish Family Service of Philadelphia) continued to resettle Holocaust refugees in the aftermath of World War II. (Courtesy of the Philadelphia Jewish Archives Center.)

Following the mass immigration of 1880–1920, the next big wave of Jewish immigrants were refugees fleeing Nazi persecution. One of them was Henrik Isenberg, then 12. He came alone to America in 1936 when the American Jewish Congress offered to place German Jewish children in foster homes in the United States. Ida Bellet, a social worker with the AJC, would later help to reunite the family in America in 1938. (Courtesy of Marianne Wallach.)

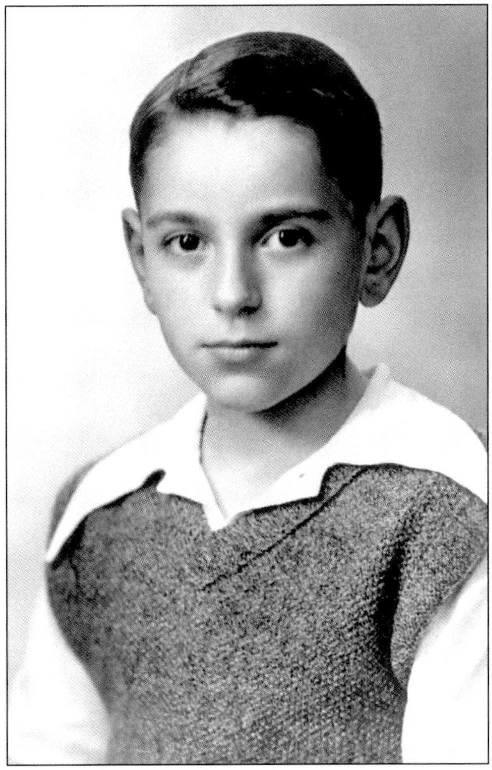

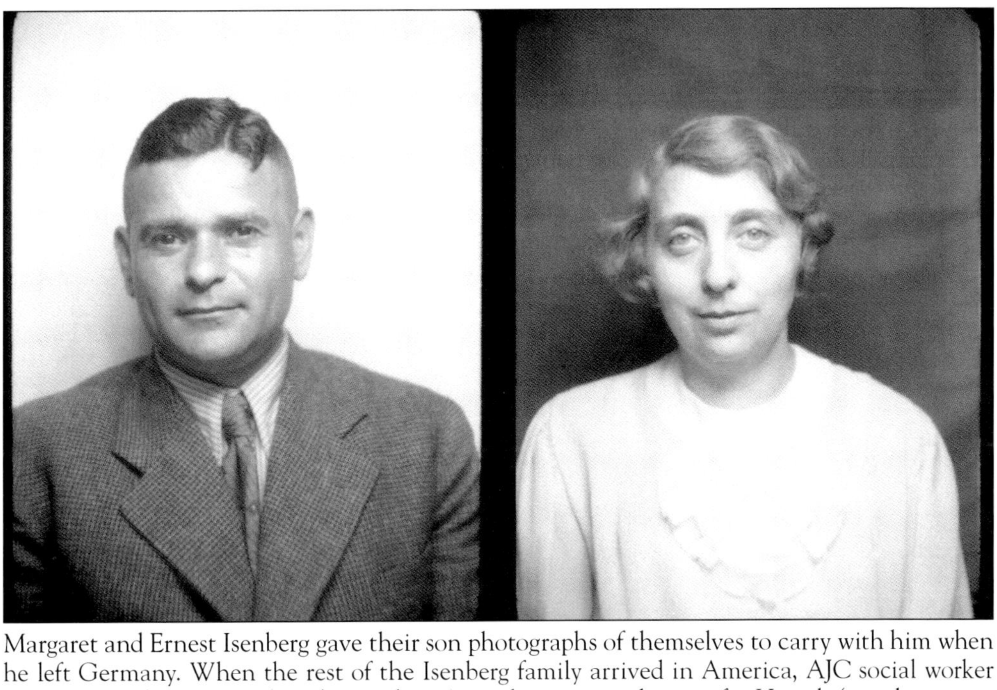

Margaret and Ernest Isenberg gave their son photographs of themselves to carry with him when he left Germany. When the rest of the Isenberg family arrived in America, AJC social worker Ida Bellet had to ensure that the Isenbergs' new home was adequate for Henrik (now known as Henry), who was then in foster care. Bellet stayed in touch with the Isenbergs over the years and helped Henry procure a stipend for college. (Courtesy of Marianne Wallach.)

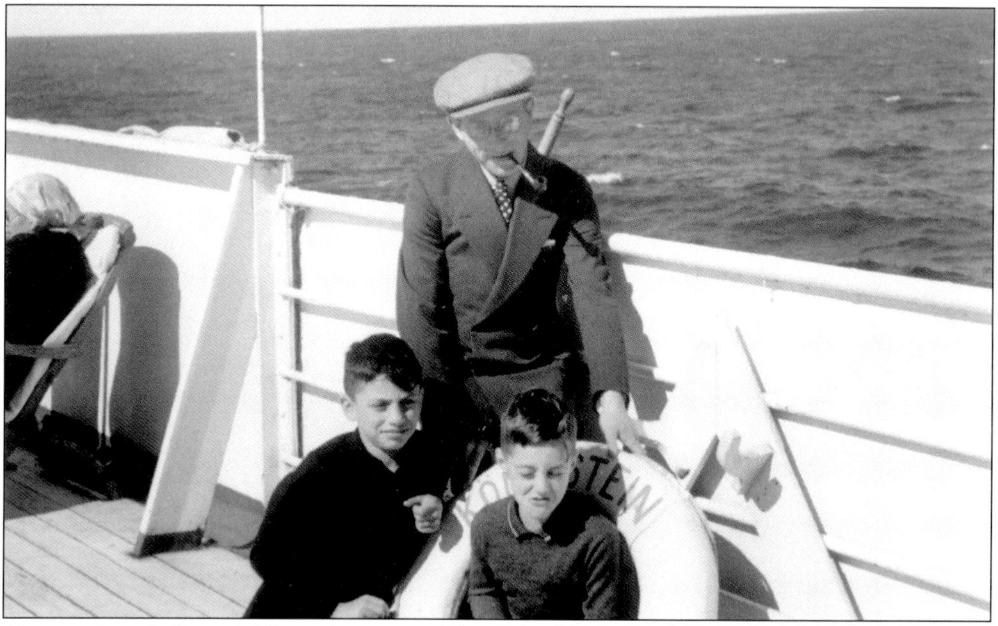

German Jews Lilli and Albert Aaron and their children Daniel (left), 12, and Frank, 8, were among those fleeing Nazi Germany. The boys are shown on board a ship in 1938 with an unidentified passenger during that life-changing journey to the United States. Lilli and Albert Aaron died within the family's first year in America, and both children were placed in foster care through the AJC. (Courtesy of Gerrie Aaron.)

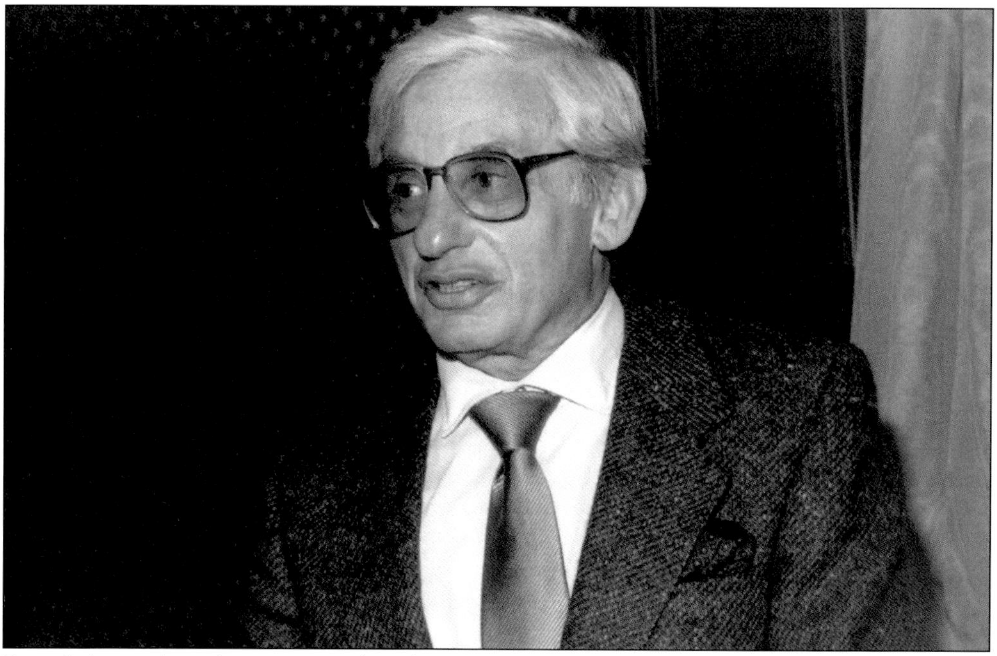

Daniel Aaron later became a cofounder, along with Ralph Roberts and Julian Brodsky, of Comcast Corporation, now America's largest cable television company. Later in life, he renewed his connection with the agency and became a board member of Jewish Family and Children's Service. (Courtesy of Gerrie Aaron.)

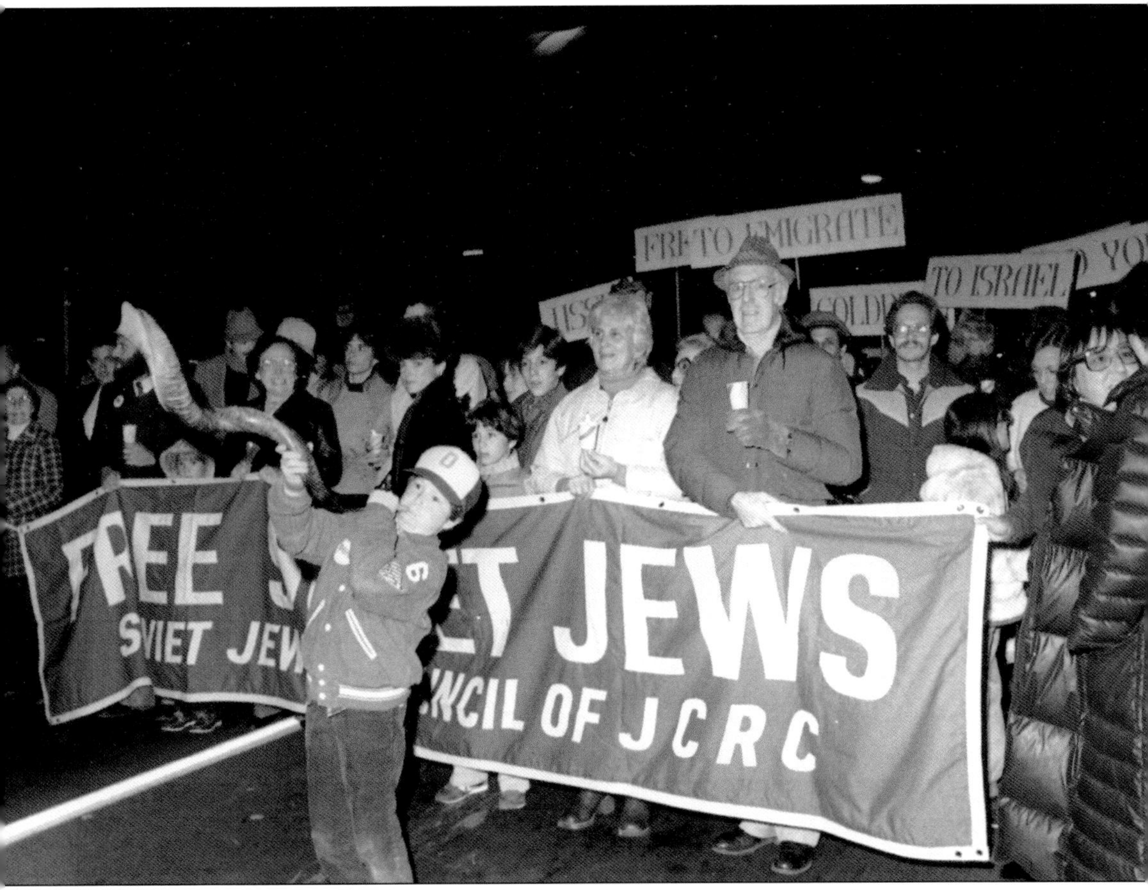

The Philadelphia Jewish community was a leader in the 1970s movement to allow Jews to emigrate from the Soviet Union, where they faced discrimination and religious persecution. Pictured here is a demonstration in Philadelphia sponsored by the local Jewish Community Relations Council. JFS and its successor, JFCS, played a key role in resettling and acculturating as many as 1,500 new Americans a year during the late 1970s and early 1980s and again in the late 1980s. The agency helped new Americans access government resources for refugees and counseled them on adjusting to American life. (Courtesy of the Philadelphia Jewish Archives Center.)

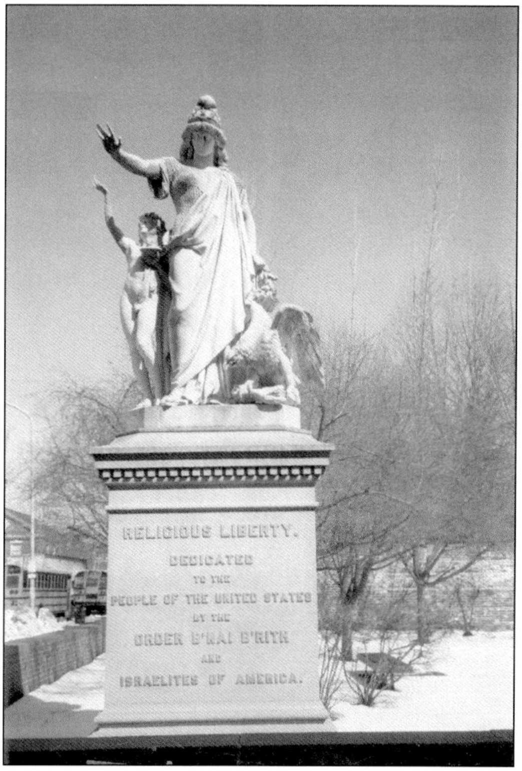

The cause of religious freedom is a well founded and documented part of American history. The statue, *Religious Liberty*, given to Philadelphia and created by Moses Ezekiel in 1876 in appreciation and honor of America's Centennial was located in Fairmount Park on the West side of the Schuylkill River on Belmont Avenue near the former Centennial fair grounds. It was moved to Fifth and Market Streets near Congregation Mikveh Israel in the 1990s. (Courtesy of the Allen Meyers collection.)

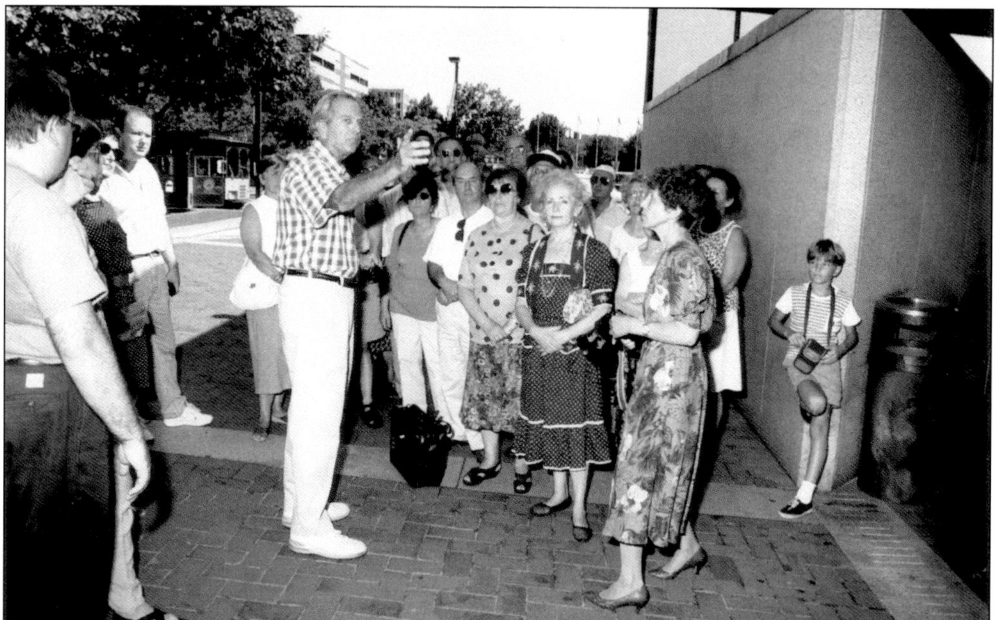

One popular JFCS outreach program was the bus tour, usually led by a JFCS board member, to acquaint new Americans with civic and religious landmarks of Philadelphia. Shown here, JFCS board member Harold Sukonik gathers the group near the *Religious Liberty* statue for the start of the tour.

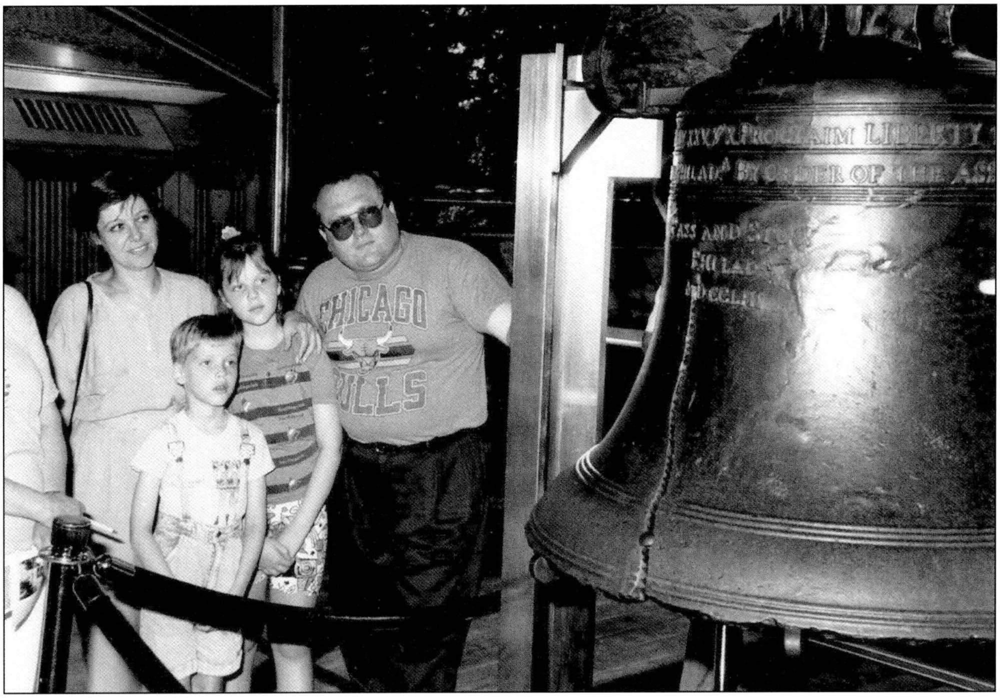

Soviet immigrants viewed a symbol of American freedom during a stop at the Liberty Bell and were welcomed at Temple Beth Zion-Beth Israel by Rabbi Ira Stone for a personal tour of the synagogue and an explanation of its sacred objects. (Courtesy of JFCS.)

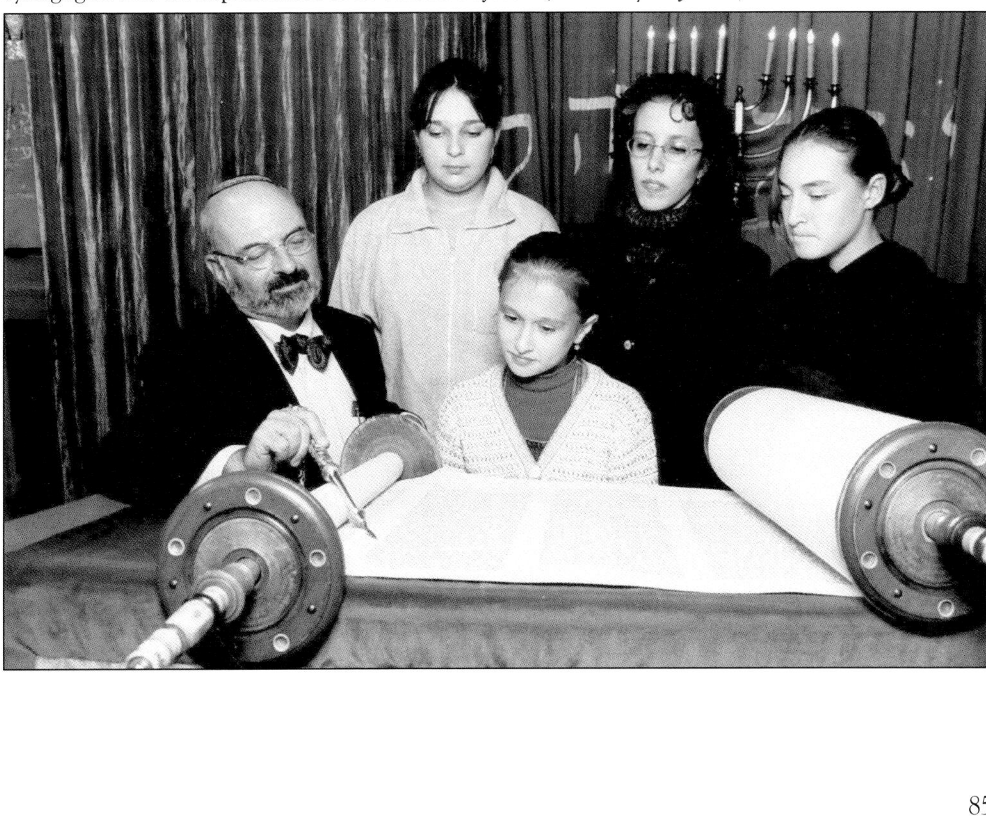

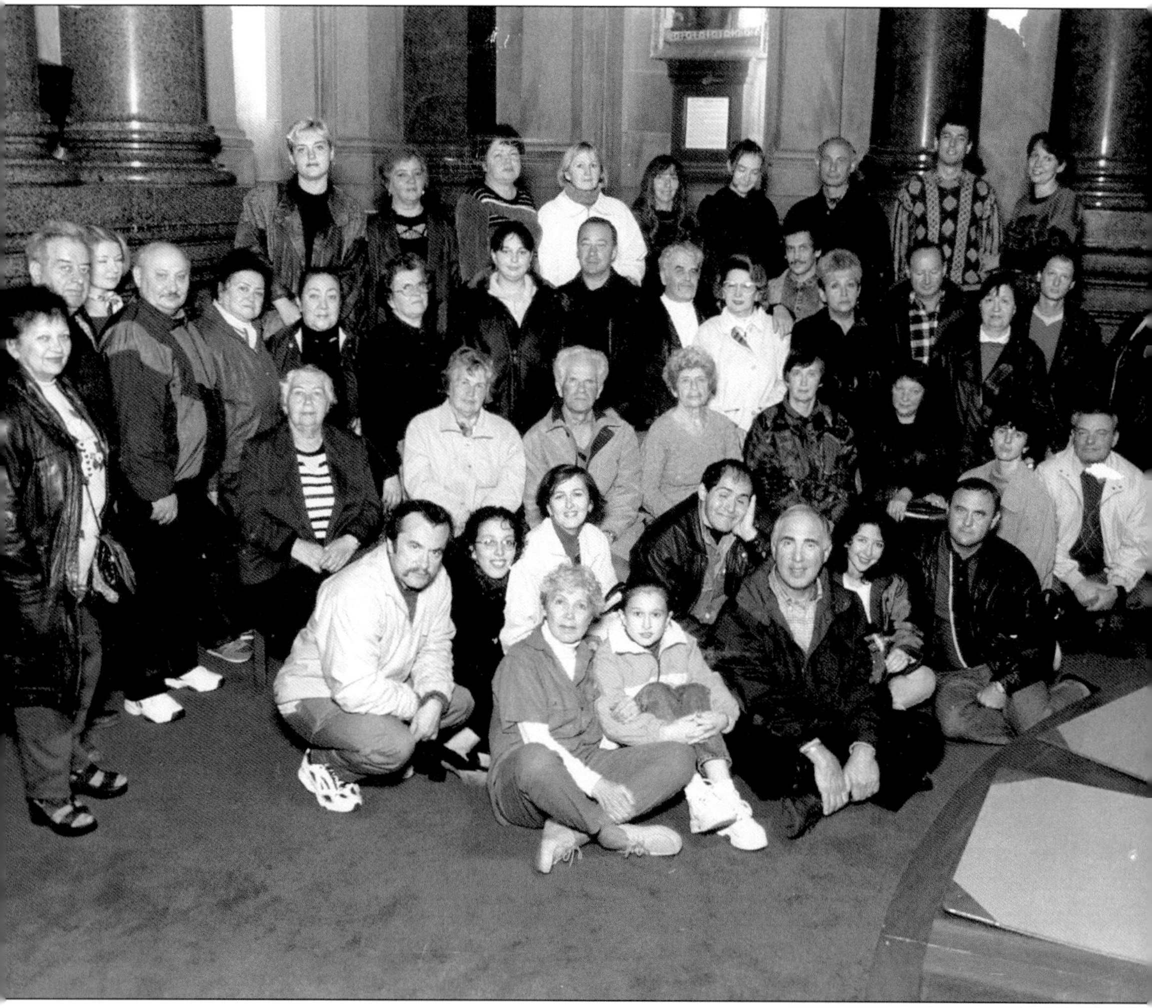

New Americans gathered in Philadelphia's city hall to meet with a member of city council and enjoy a first-hand look at America's democratic institutions. With them (front row, third from left) are JFCS board leader Robert Horen, who led the tour, and (front row, far left) Irma Simuni, JFCS resettlement and volunteer coordinator.

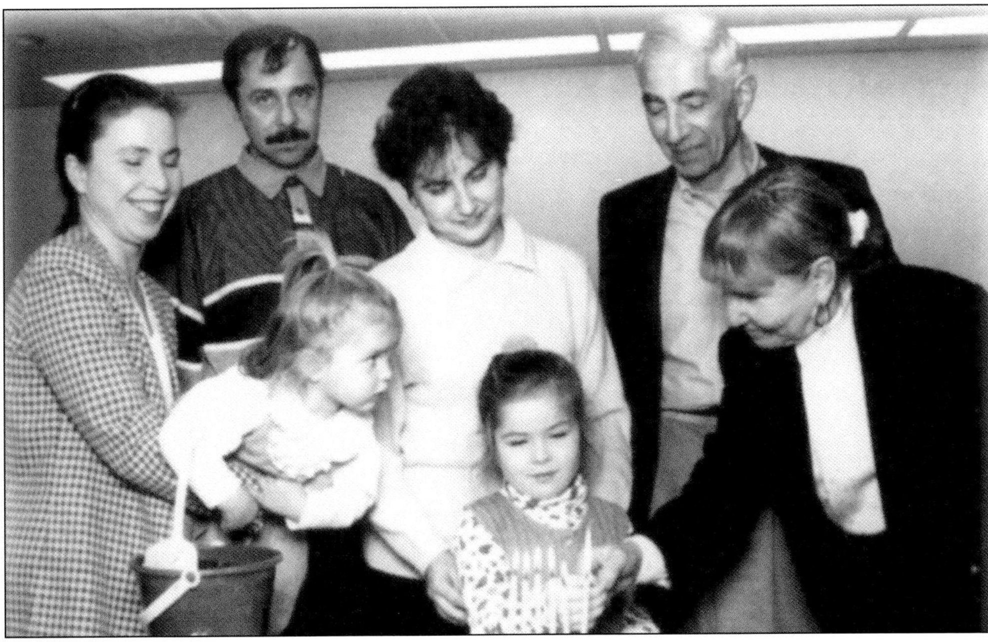

New Americans enjoy a JFCS Chanukah party, part of the acculturation to Jewish life in America. Many new Americans had the opportunity to celebrate Jewish holidays with local families through volunteer matches coordinated by JFCS's Resettlement and Volunteer Departments. (Courtesy of JFCS.)

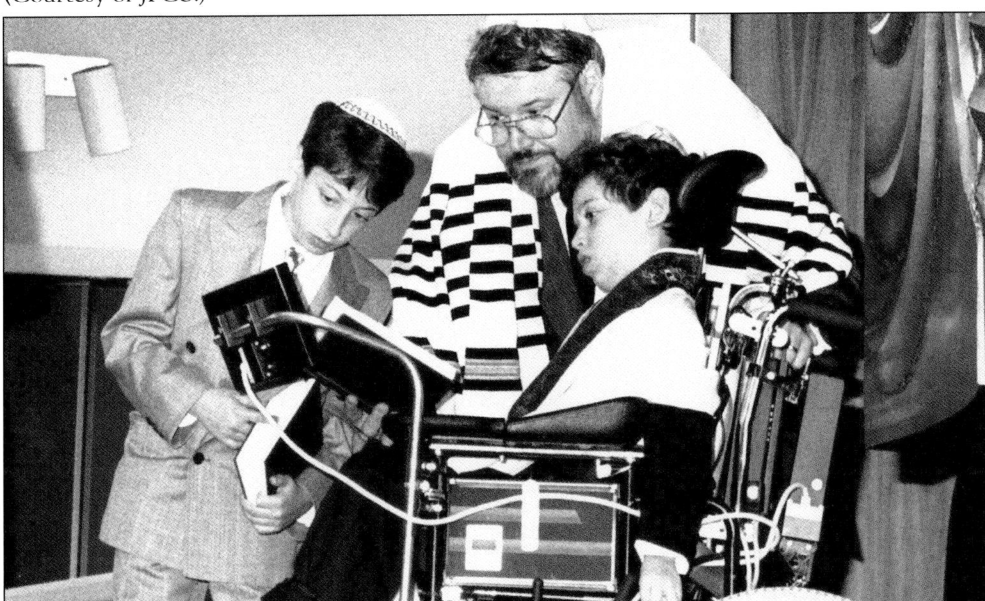

Soviet Jewish immigrants benefited from the Jewish Federation's network of caring. Eugene Chernyakhovsky and his family, for instance, were brought to the United States through HIAS (Hebrew Immigrant Aid Society) and were then resettled by JFCS. Later the Auerbach Central Agency for Jewish Education helped Eugene realize his dream to become a bar mitzvah. With him that day are his brother, Mitchell, and Dr. John Eulenberg of Michigan State University, who consulted on Eugene's computer voice system. (Courtesy of JFCS.)

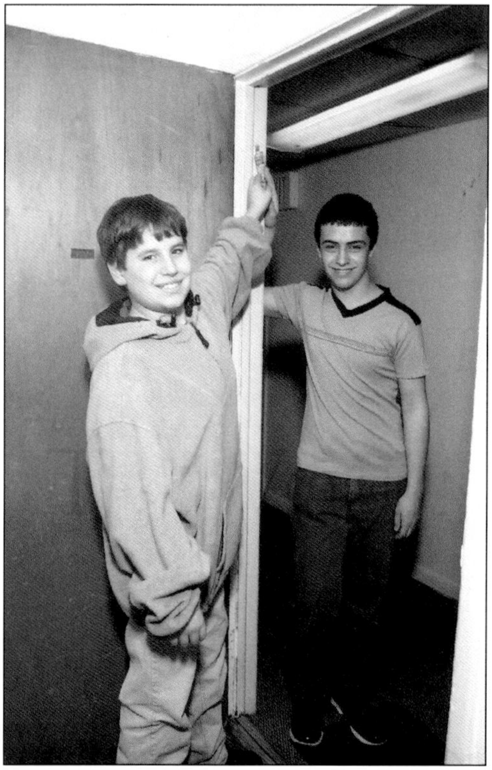

Marc Krawitz of Congregation Beth El–Ner Tamid of Broomall received help from classmates in his Hebrew school class to make many mezuzahs—religious doorpost symbols made of clay and fired in ceramic kilns. Here he meets with recent immigrant Dimitriy Melnikova to affix a mezuzah on the doorpost of Dimitriy's home. JFCS coordinated the match. (Courtesy of JFCS.)

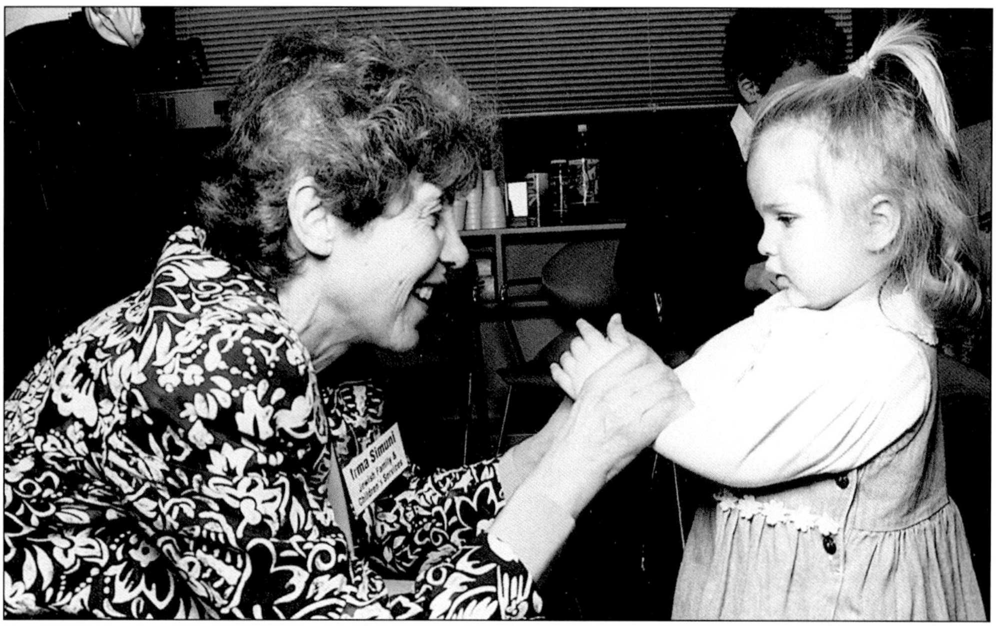

Irma Simuni was once a Soviet refusnik—a Russian Jew denied a visa to leave her homeland. Simuni came to Philadelphia in the 1990s and received help from JFCS in resettling. Her experience and her knowledge of the English language inspired her to become a JFCS volunteer and, later, to work for JFCS in the Resettlement and Volunteer Departments. In the image above, she enjoys a playful moment with a young immigrant client. (Courtesy of JFCS.)

Ten

The Volunteer Spirit

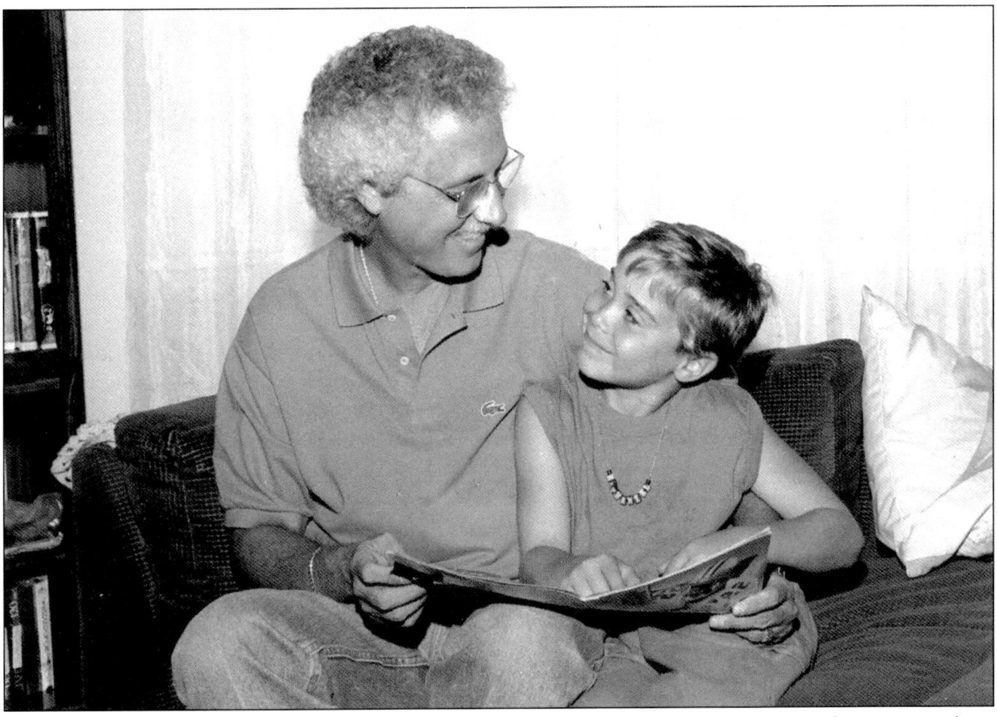

Today JFCS volunteers—individuals, families, synagogues, and groups—contribute more than 20,000 hours of service a year. While that service can be quantified, its value is incalculable. Shown here are Jewish "big brother" Ted Urofsky and his "little brother" getting comfortable for some reading time. (Courtesy of JFCS.)

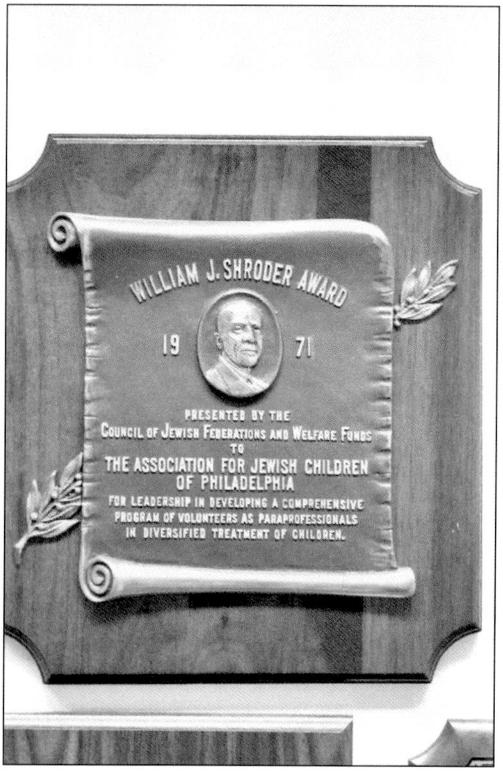

In 1971, the AJC, a JFCS predecessor agency, received the national William J. Shroder Award, sponsored by the Council of Jewish Federations, in honor of its outstanding volunteer programs. Then, as now, volunteers were considered to be extensions of the JFCS team. Often volunteers worked as personal shoppers, tutors, and mentors to assist AJC's child and adolescent clients, many of whom were in foster care or group residences. (Courtesy of JFCS.)

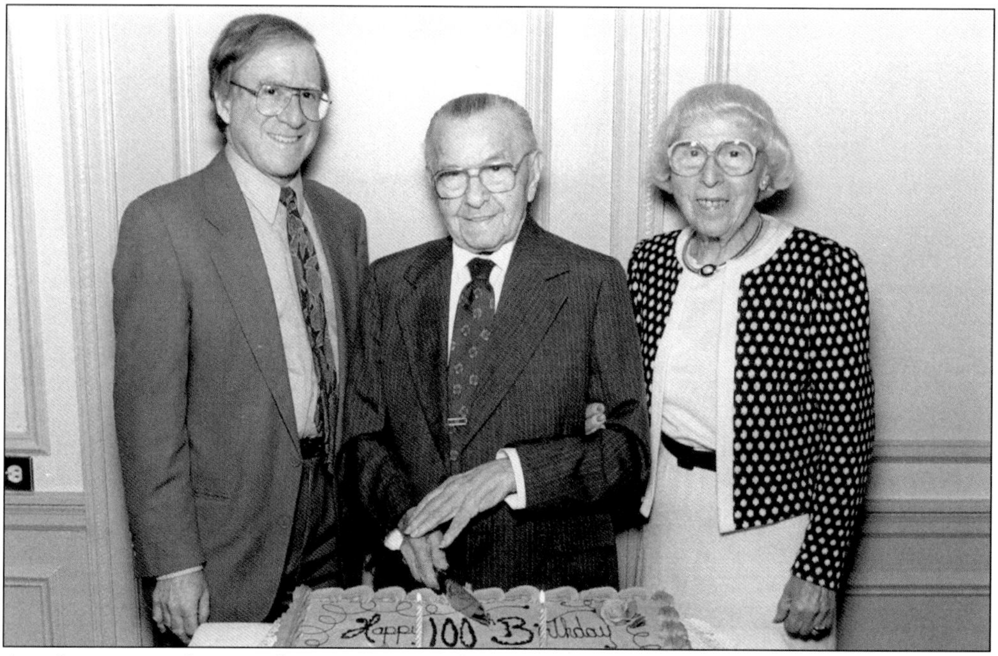

A volunteer can be just about any age. Take for example Albert M. Cohen, who became a centurion in 1999. Albert's friend Elizabeth Colen and former JFCS board president Leonard Cooper were on hand to celebrate Albert's birthday and his 50 years of volunteer service to JFCS. (Courtesy of JFCS.)

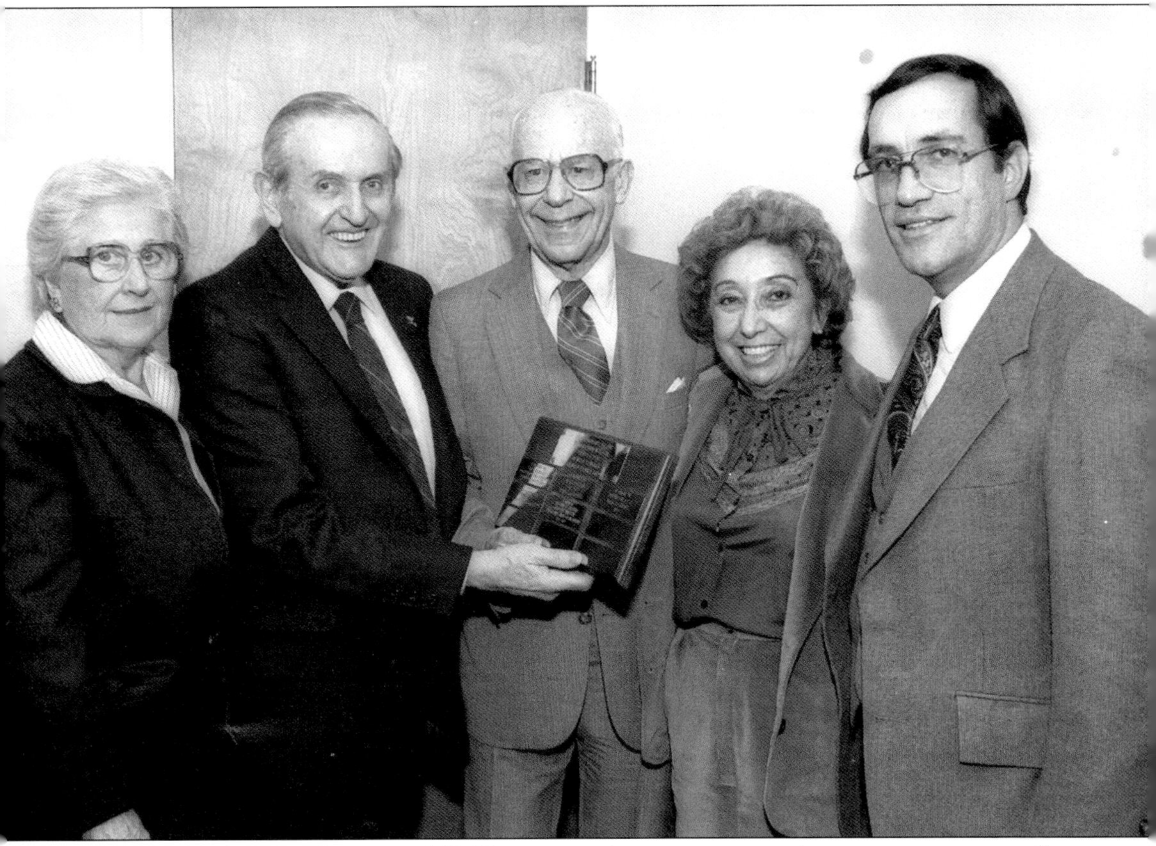

JFS, an immediate predecessor of JFCS, sponsored an extensive volunteer program as well. Volunteers visited, delivered meals, and shopped for the elderly, befriended new American émigrés, provided Thanksgiving and Passover baskets, helped out in JFS offices, and much more. Bertha Rabinowitch (far left) remembers "these beautiful, beautiful experiences" and "the people I wouldn't have met otherwise." She helped the elderly do their income taxes, located apartments and rooms for people who needed them, and shared Jewish holiday celebrations and informal get-togethers with new Americans, many of whom became friends. In 1982, Bertha and Lou Handler were cochairman of the agency's Volunteer Steering Committee and presented an award to Benjamin Sprafkin, JFS executive director. Joining them (second from right) is Ruth G. Cohen, JFS services for older persons director, and (far right) Robert Wachter, chairman for the JFCS committee for senior services. (Courtesy of Bertha Rabinowitch.)

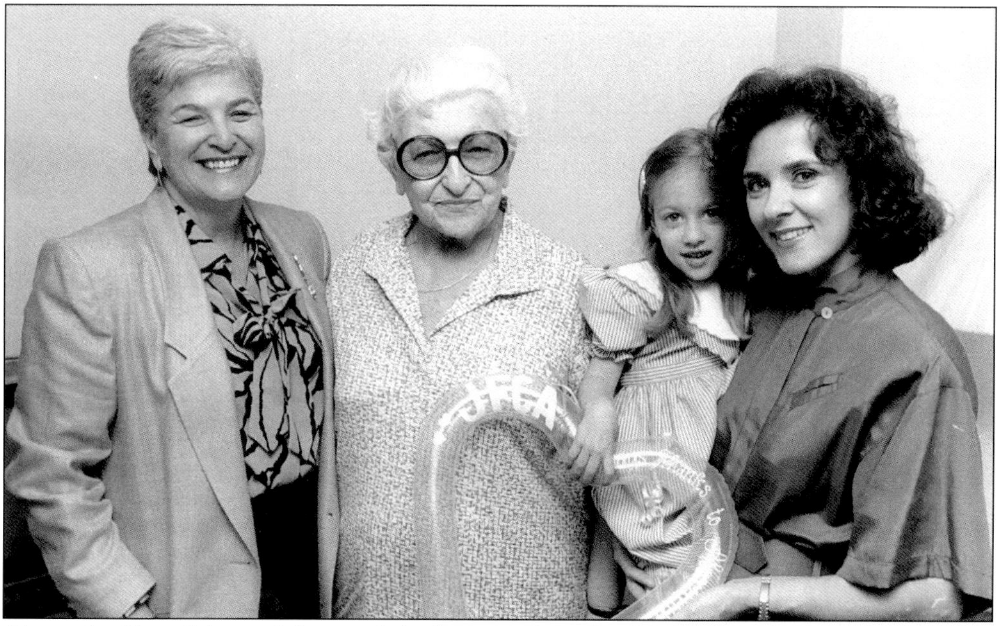

Alexandra Kanoff (second from right), then age four, was honored as the agency's youngest volunteer in 1987. Alexandra and her mother Susan Kanoff (far right) were "friendly visitors" to Jane Fox (second from left) and assisted her with grocery shopping. Such community matchmaking is one of the great satisfactions of JFCS's Volunteer Department. Joining in the ceremony was JFCS's then volunteer director Helene Tulsky. (Courtesy of JFCS.)

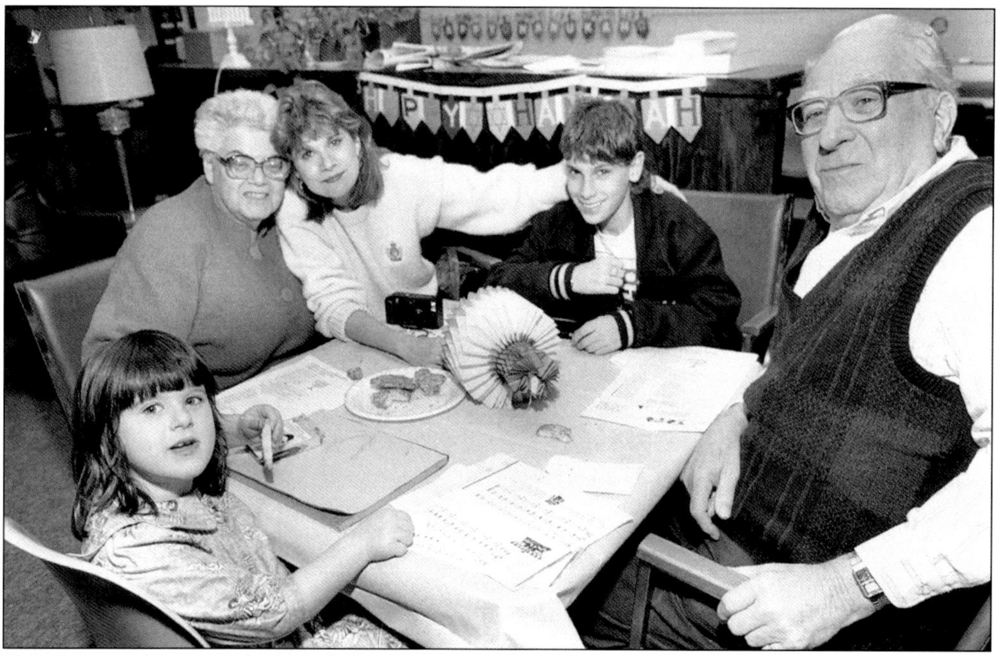

Celebrating the joys of Chanukah is a ritual for all ages. Giving presents and eating latkes (potato pancakes) with apple sauce are enjoyed by all participants at this JFCS Project JOY Chanukah party. JFCS's Project JOY matches volunteers aged 50 and older with children in need of the special extra attention that volunteer grandparents can give. (Courtesy of JFCS.)

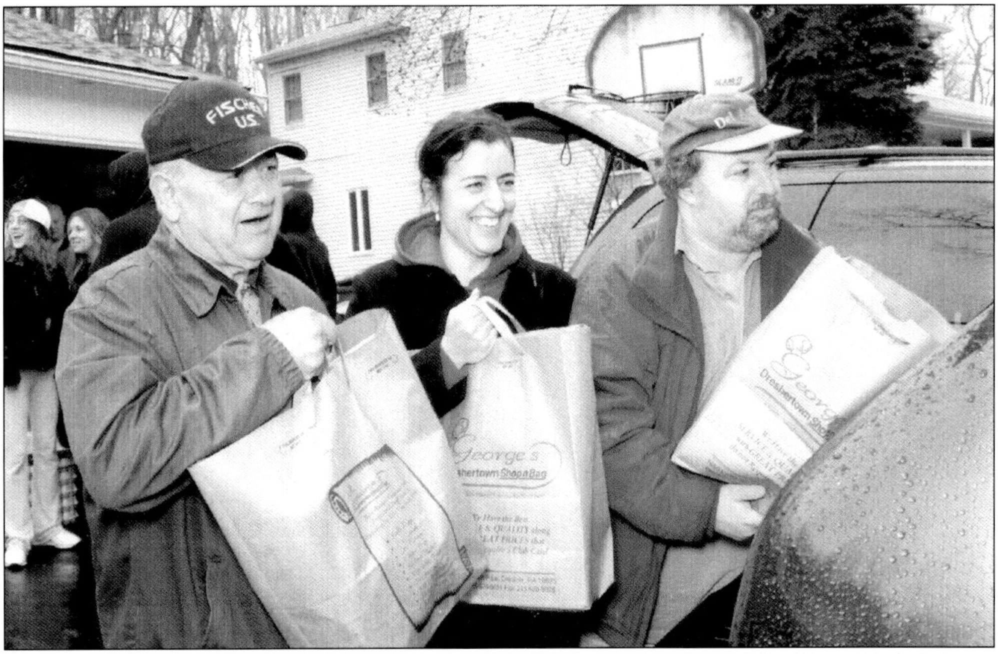

In Jewish tradition, *tzedakah* means justice, not charity. In that spirit, the B'nai B'rith Liberty Region, through its Project H.O.P.E. (Help Our People Everywhere), teams up with JFCS for an annual Passover project. Hundreds of B'nai B'rith members procure, pack, and deliver Passover food on behalf of hundreds of JFCS clients in need. Often children and teens come too for the mitzvah experience. (Courtesy of JFCS.)

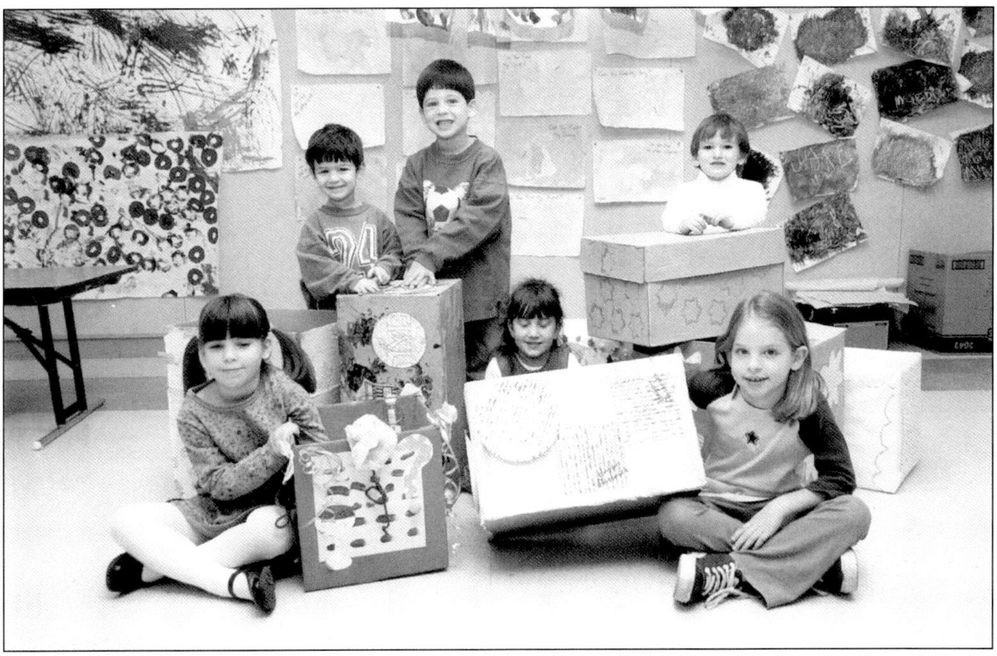

Even the little ones can join in the action. The preschool children at Congregation Beth Or in Spring House participate in an art project in 2000 that included decorating boxes to serve as Passover baskets. (Courtesy of JFCS.)

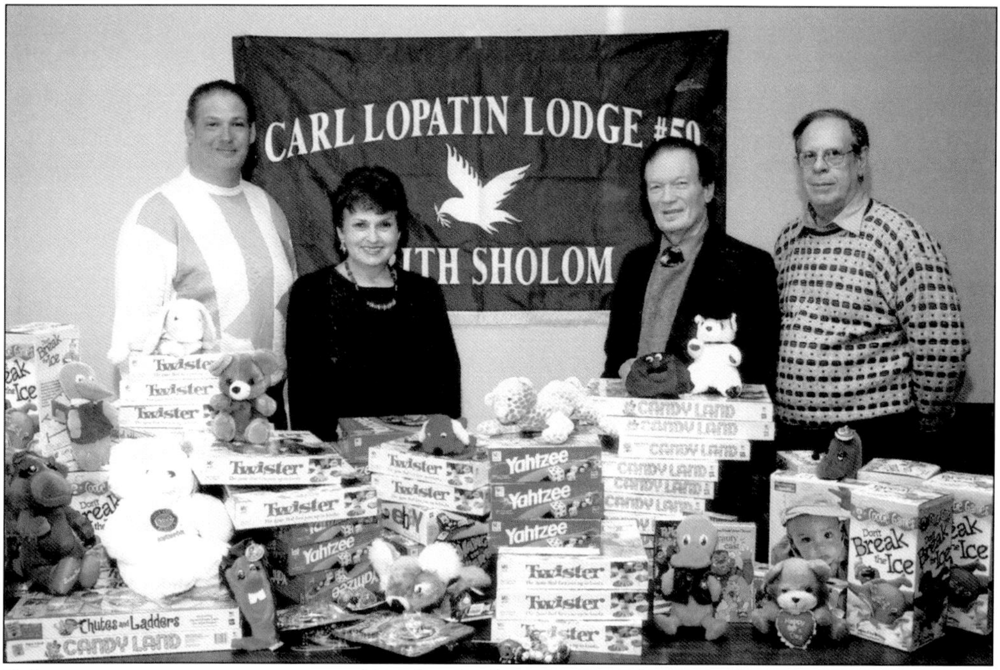

Other community organizations, like the Carl Lopatin Lodge No. 59 of B'rith Sholom and Toshiba Corporation, join in the caring spirit by donating to annual JFCS holiday toy drives. JFCS volunteer director Sandy Fryer is on hand to accept toys from a mitzvah project at the Carl Lopatin Lodge. Accepting the toys at a Toshiba Corporation presentation is JFCS director of operations Joan McCrane (bottom photograph, second from right). These gifts brighten the lives of scores of young JFCS clients. (Courtesy of JFCS.)

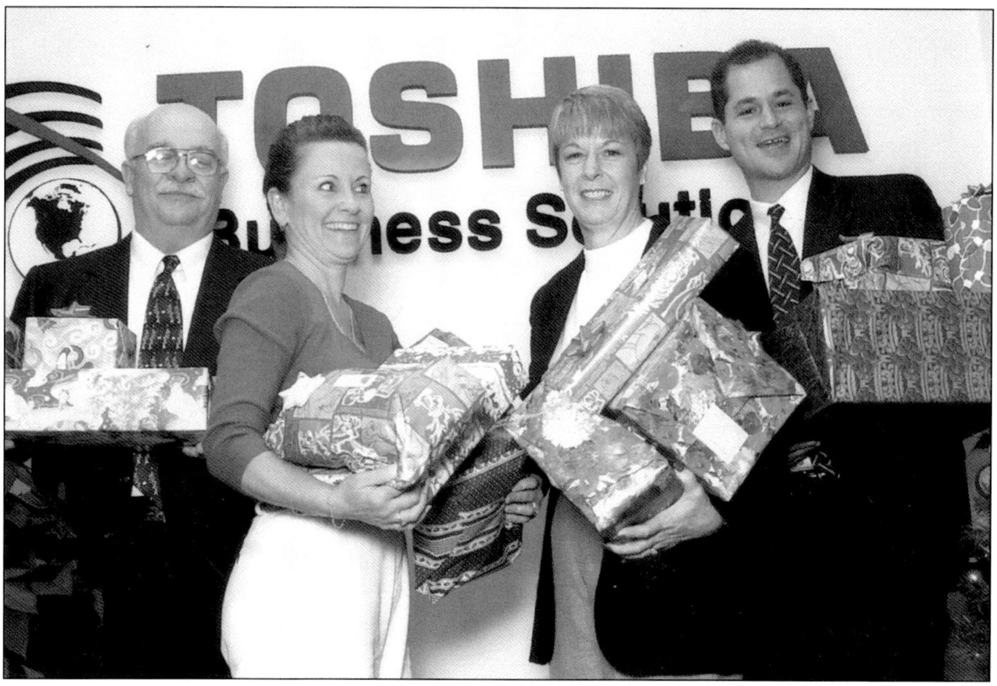

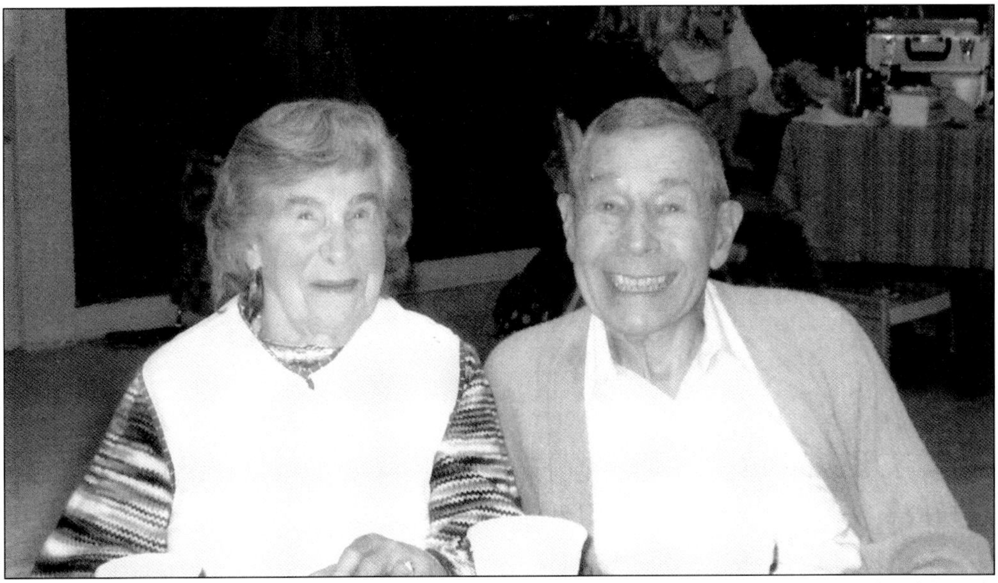

That famous smile is what JFCS volunteer Larry Kovnat is known for among his circle of friends and fellow volunteers. Kovnat grew up during the era of collecting funds in the familiar blue and white tin *pushkas*—banks for the Palestine Jewish National Fund for a Jewish homeland, pre-1948. That sense of communal responsibility motivates him to this very day. Pictured with him is fellow volunteer Elise Stern. (Courtesy of Larry Kovnat.)

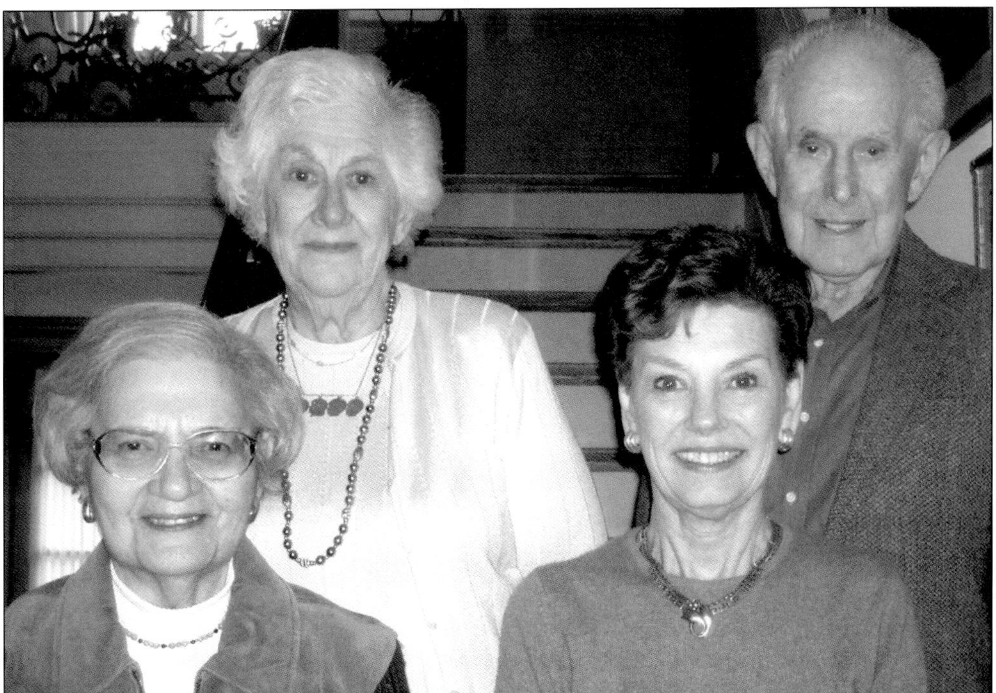

Cherishing strong bonds are longtime JFCS volunteers and members of the agency's Volunteer Steering Committee (first row) Florence Schwartz and Julie Greenbaum, immediate past chairman of the committee; (second row) Doris Pohl and Ernie Cohen. (Courtesy of JFCS.)

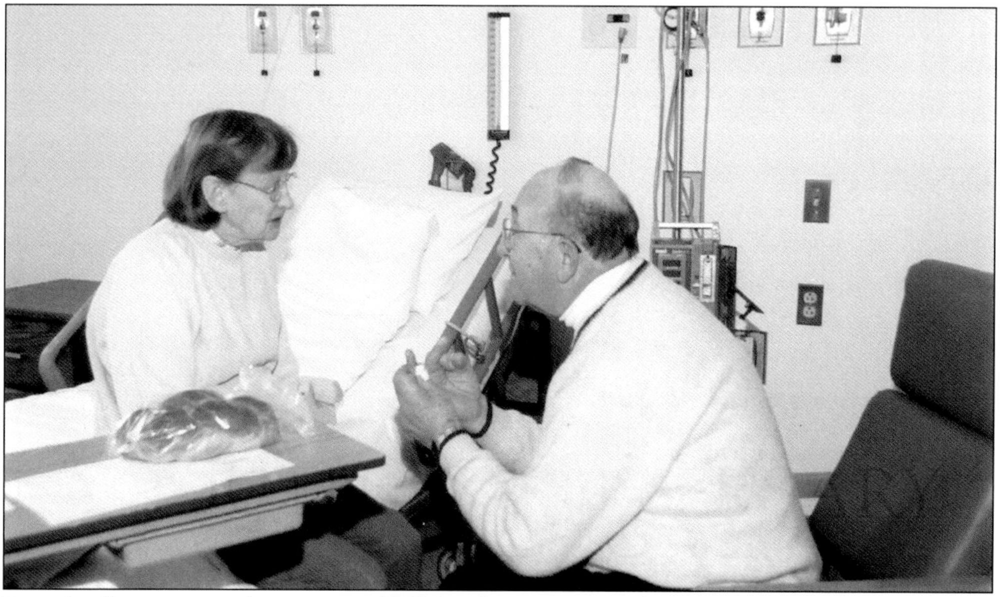

Para-chaplaincy is another aspect of JFCS volunteer outreach. Shown here, a hospital patient enjoys a Friday visit and personalized challah delivery by a volunteer para-chaplain from JFCS's Joan Grossman Center for Chaplaincy and Healing. The challah delivery program is one way JFCS reaches out to Jews with spiritual support during some of the most difficult moments in their lives. The Grossman Center also trains para-chaplains through its *Kesher* (Connections) program. (Courtesy of the Allen Meyers collection and JFCS.)

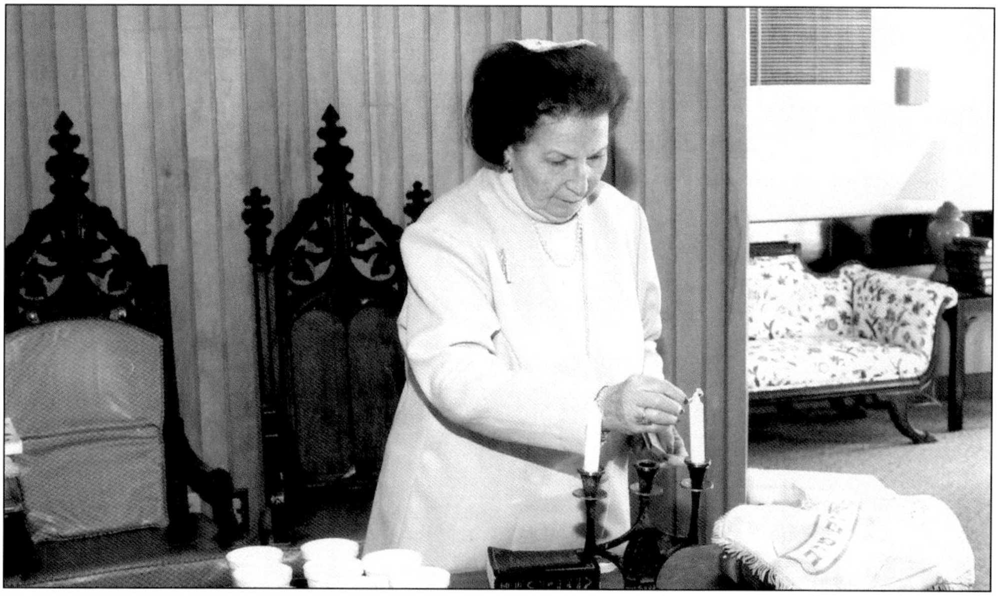

Doris Grossmann, a former public school and Hebrew teacher, is a volunteer para-chaplain with JFCS's Grossman Center. She has devoted decades as a para-chaplain in the Jewish community through the center and its forerunner, the Jewish Chaplaincy Service. Pictured here in 2005, she conducted a weekly Shabbat service at Saunders House, a long-term care center and nursing home in Wynnewood. Her dedication comes naturally. It is a matter of how good it feels to do good. (Courtesy of JFCS.)

Eleven

A 150th Anniversary Celebration

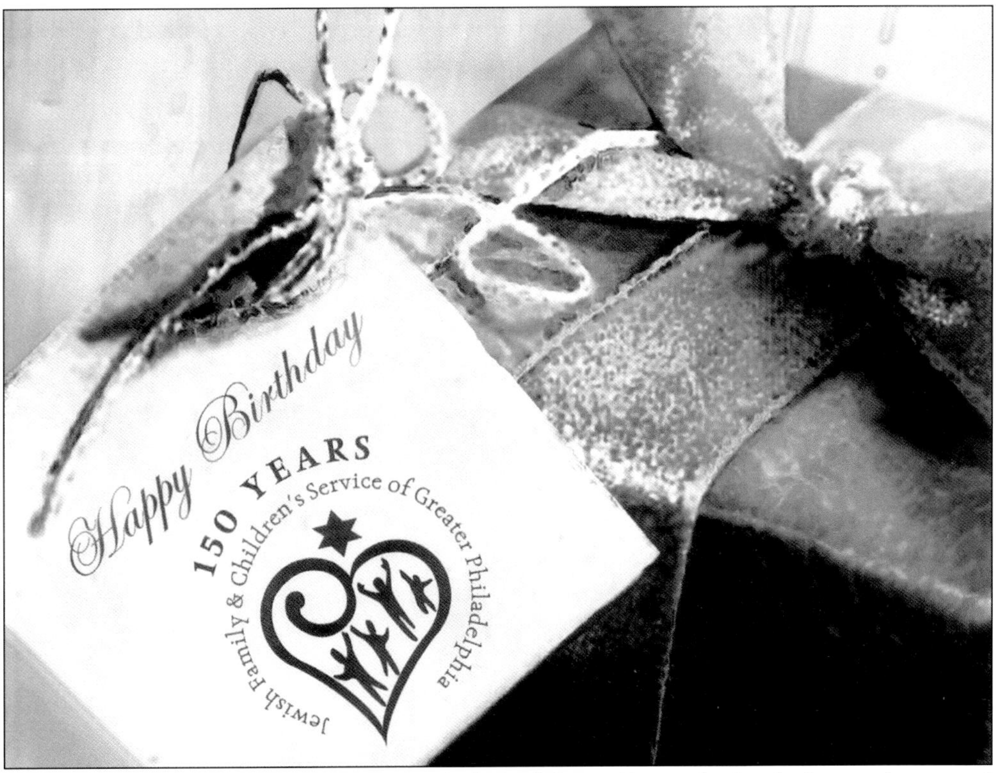

JFCS started celebrating early. A "JFCS 150th Birthday to Remember" gala dinner, dance, and auction on November 6, 2004, kicked off the agency's 150th anniversary and a yearlong series of events that continued through 2005. (Courtesy of JFCS.)

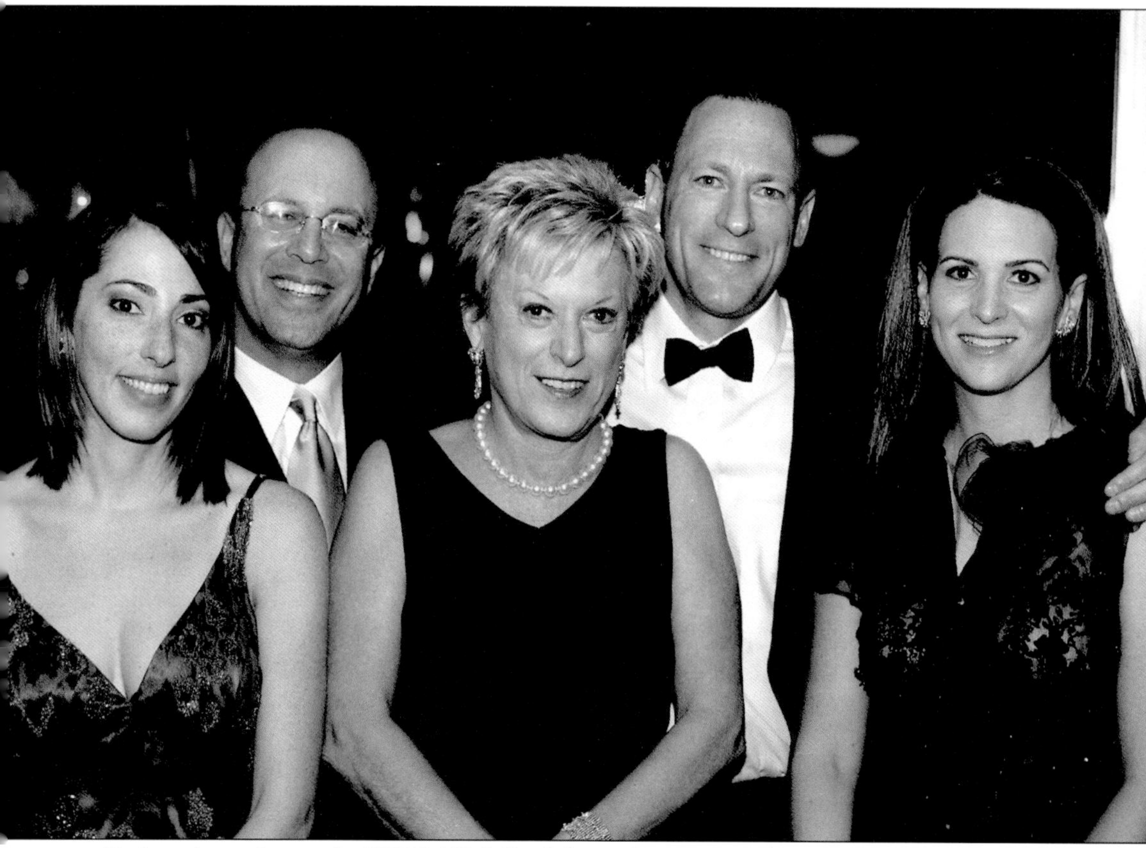

Gathered together at the "JFCS 150th Birthday to Remember" festivities are, from left to right, Carrie and Joel Shapiro, auction chairpersons; Carole Solomon, gala honoree; and David and Jessica Solomon, gala chairpersons. Carole Solomon, chairman of the Jewish Agency for Israel Board of Governors and a former leader in the Philadelphia Jewish community, was honored for her work of *tikkun olam* (repairing the world). In chairing the gala, her son David and daughter-in-law Jessica made it a real family affair. Held at the Loews Philadelphia Hotel in Center City, the event drew nearly 500 attendees and raised nearly $400,000 to support agency services. (Courtesy of JFCS.)

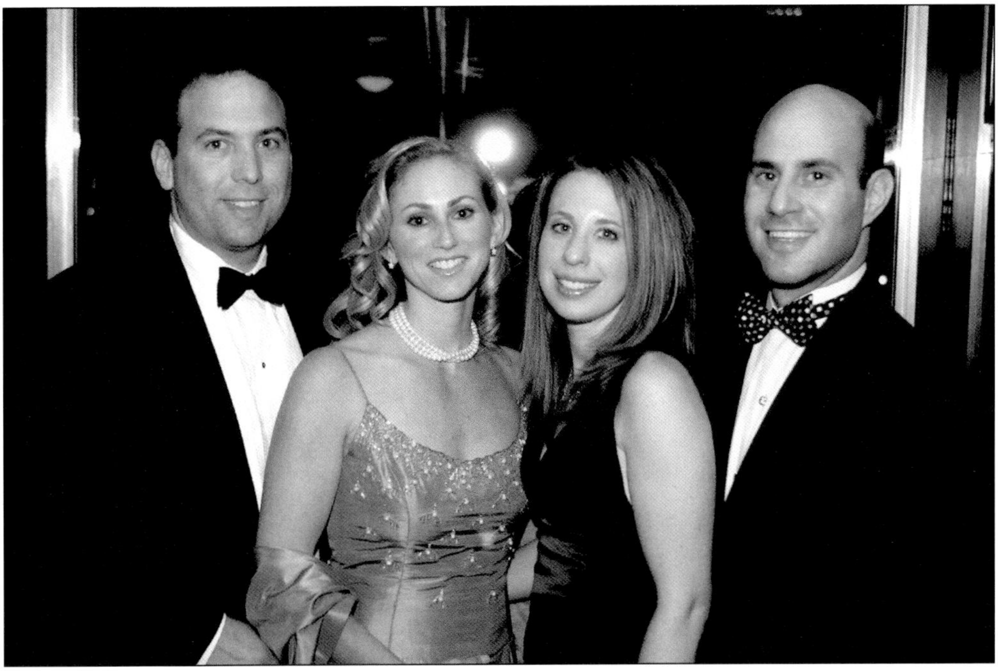

Adding to the evening's success were gala "under 39" chairpersons, from left to right, David and Lisa Newman and Suzy and Scott Goldstein, who helped make sure their contemporaries turned out in force for this event. (Courtesy of JFCS.)

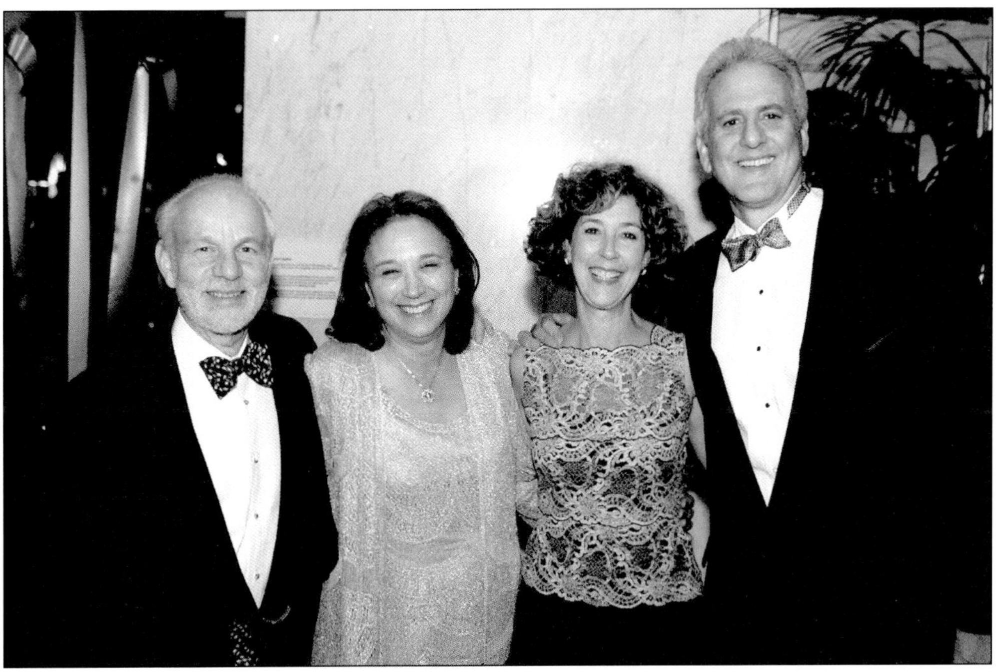

Pictured from left to right are Ed Brown and his wife Susan Garber and Bonnie and Bruce Marks. Ed and Bruce served as gala advertisement book chairmen. (Courtesy of JFCS.)

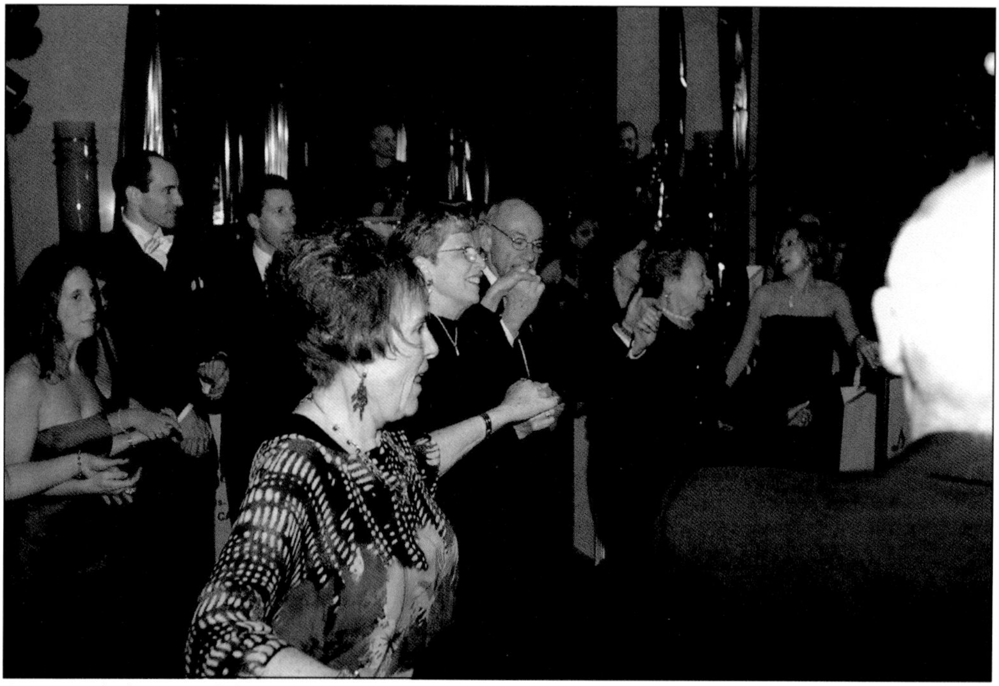

Few Jewish festive celebrations would be complete without a hora, and JFCS's birthday gala was no exception. (Courtesy of JFCS.)

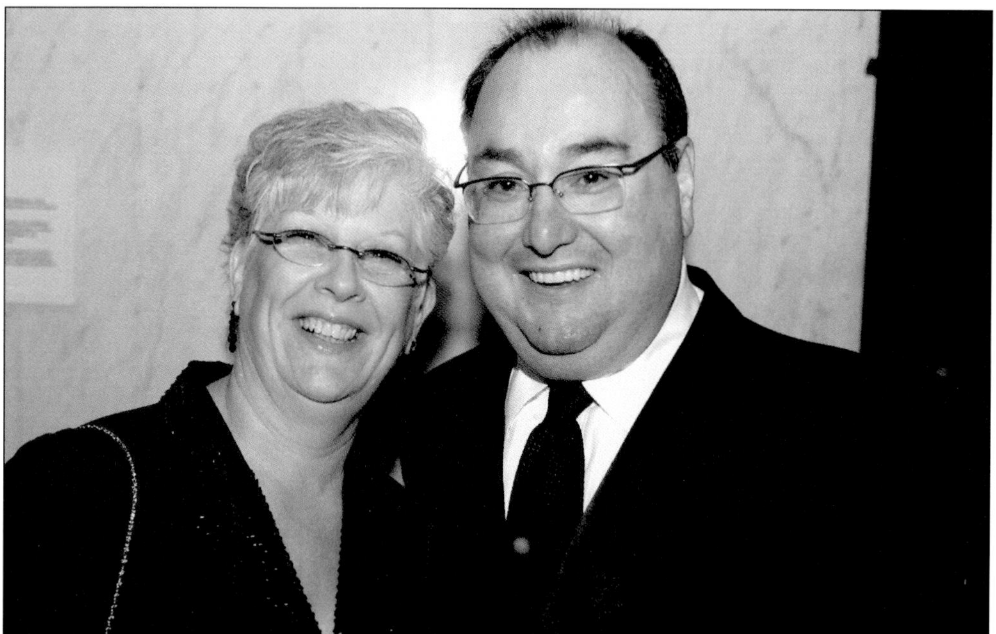

Enjoying the event are JFCS's then president and CEO Drew Staffenberg and his wife Ronnie. (Courtesy of JFCS.)

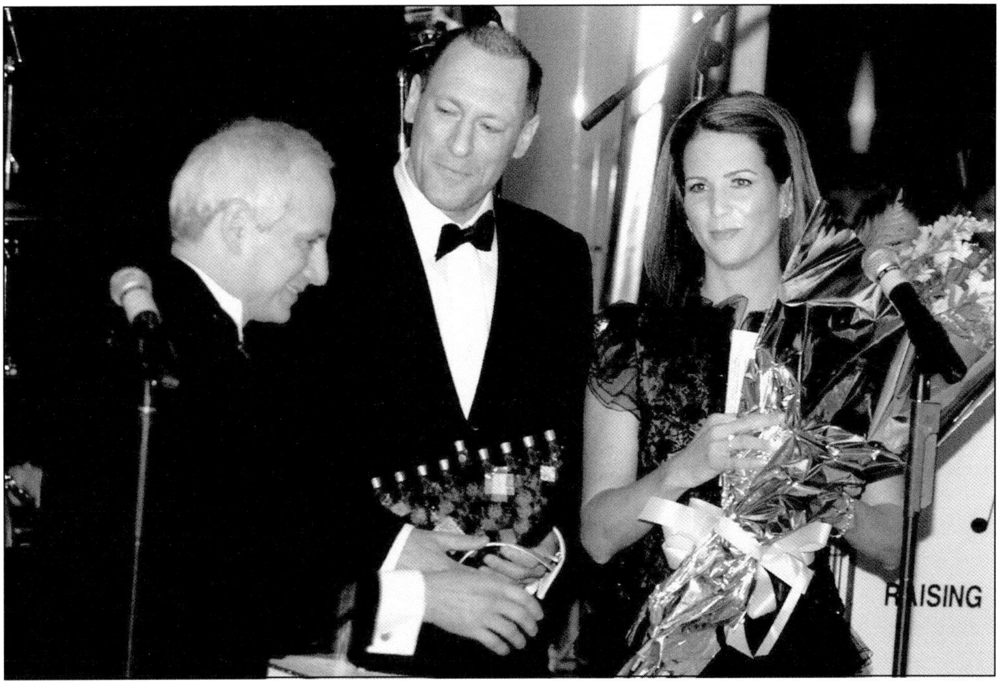

JFCS board chairman James Kahn presents gifts of appreciation to David and Jessica Solomon for their leadership of the 150th anniversary inaugural event. (Courtesy of JFCS.)

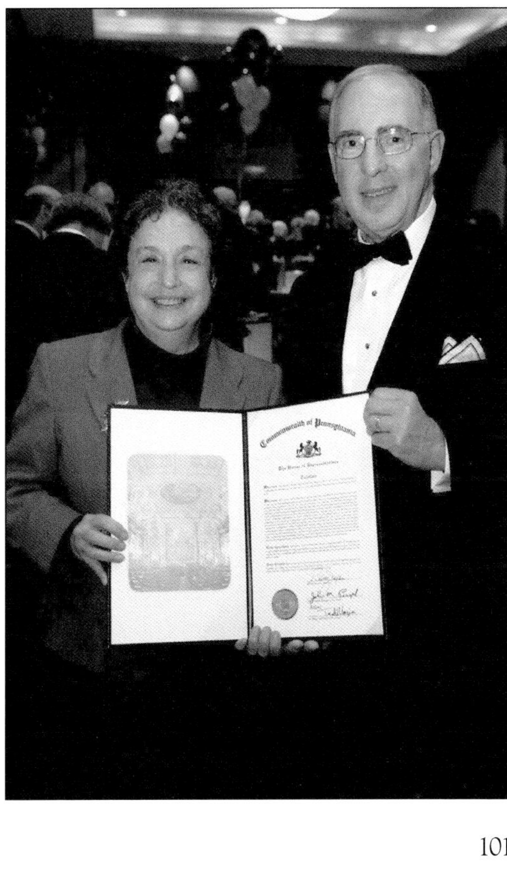

A proclamation from the Pennsylvania legislature honored JFCS on the occasion of its milestone anniversary. Pennsylvania state representative Babette Josephs (pictured with JFCS board vice chairman Robert Horen) personally presented it during the gala. (Courtesy of JFCS.)

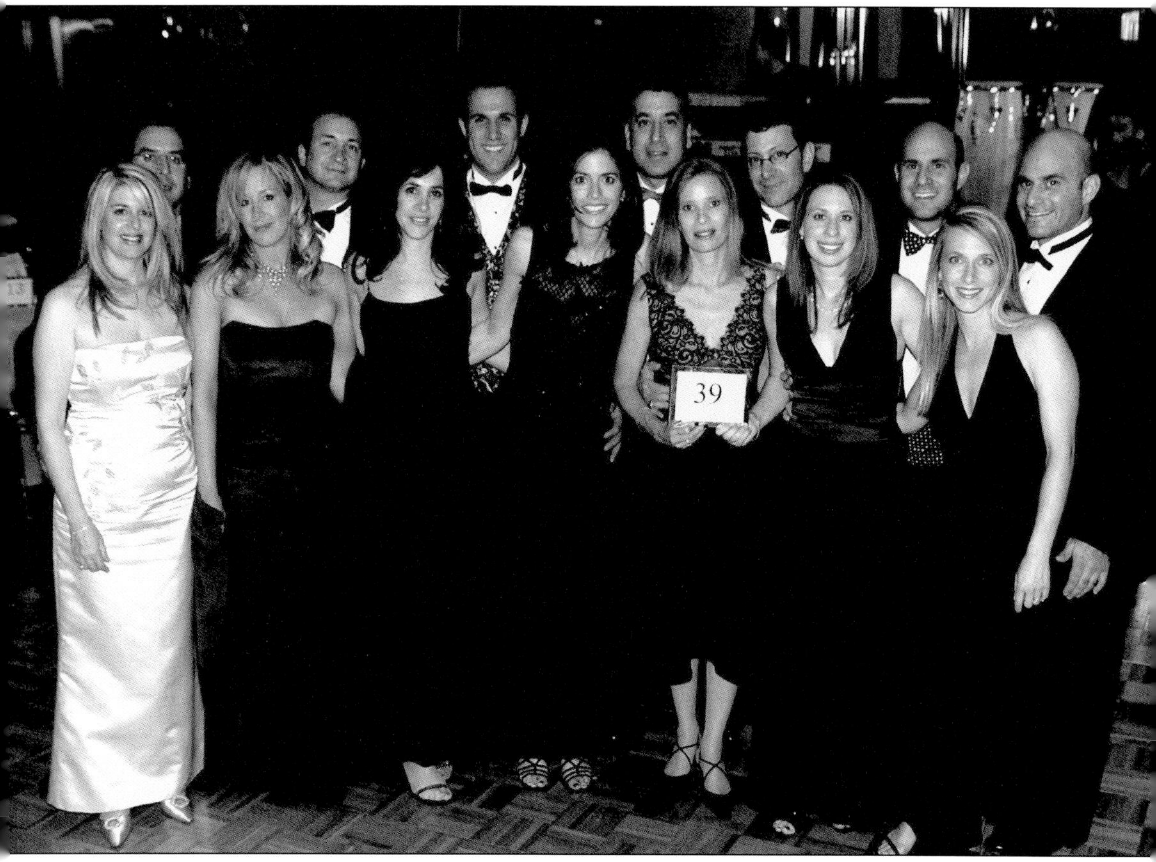

Members of the "under 39" crowd gather for a group picture. (Courtesy of JFCS.)

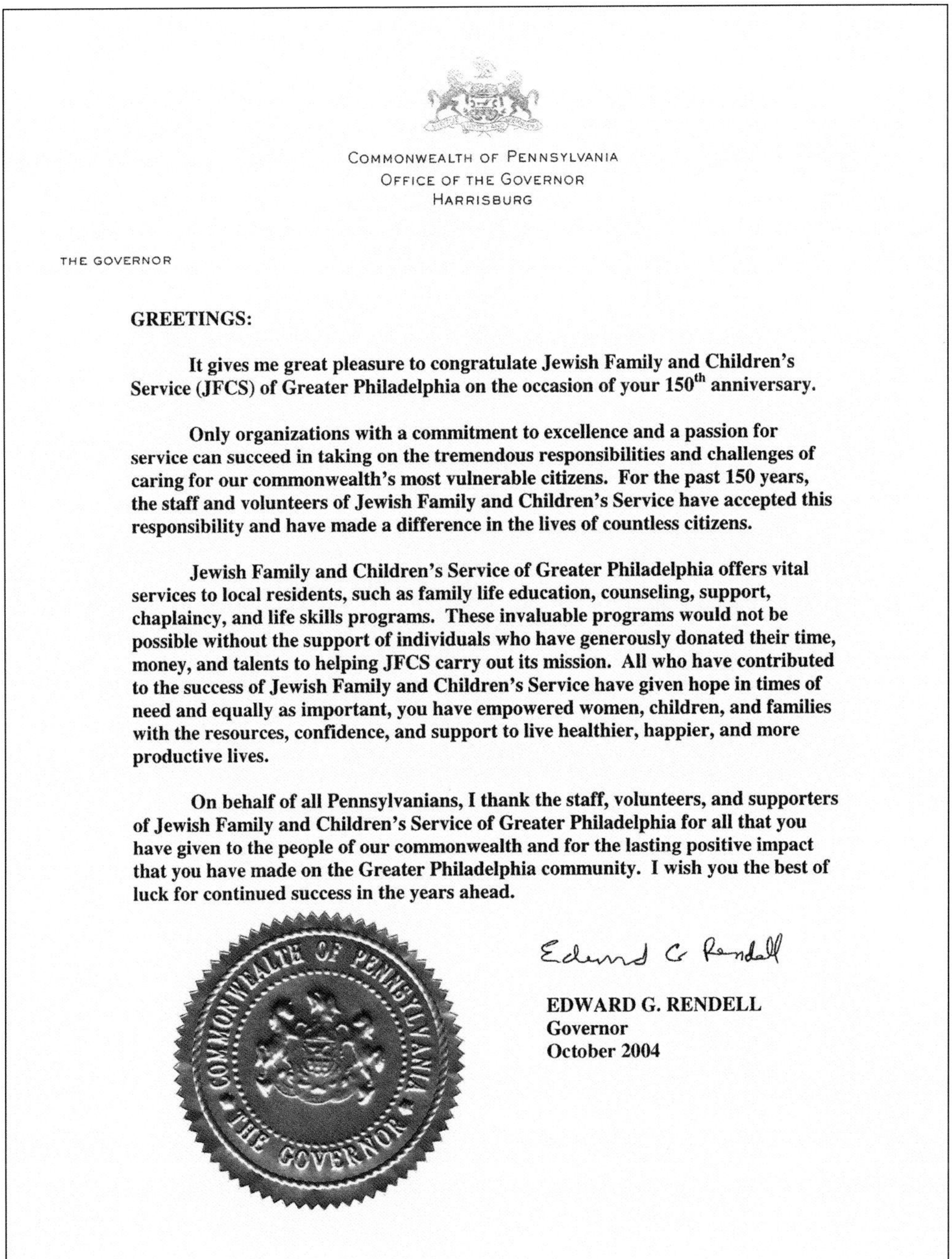

COMMONWEALTH OF PENNSYLVANIA
OFFICE OF THE GOVERNOR
HARRISBURG

THE GOVERNOR

GREETINGS:

It gives me great pleasure to congratulate Jewish Family and Children's Service (JFCS) of Greater Philadelphia on the occasion of your 150th anniversary.

Only organizations with a commitment to excellence and a passion for service can succeed in taking on the tremendous responsibilities and challenges of caring for our commonwealth's most vulnerable citizens. For the past 150 years, the staff and volunteers of Jewish Family and Children's Service have accepted this responsibility and have made a difference in the lives of countless citizens.

Jewish Family and Children's Service of Greater Philadelphia offers vital services to local residents, such as family life education, counseling, support, chaplaincy, and life skills programs. These invaluable programs would not be possible without the support of individuals who have generously donated their time, money, and talents to helping JFCS carry out its mission. All who have contributed to the success of Jewish Family and Children's Service have given hope in times of need and equally as important, you have empowered women, children, and families with the resources, confidence, and support to live healthier, happier, and more productive lives.

On behalf of all Pennsylvanians, I thank the staff, volunteers, and supporters of Jewish Family and Children's Service of Greater Philadelphia for all that you have given to the people of our commonwealth and for the lasting positive impact that you have made on the Greater Philadelphia community. I wish you the best of luck for continued success in the years ahead.

Edward G Rendell

EDWARD G. RENDELL
Governor
October 2004

A proclamation from the Commonwealth of Pennsylvania honored JFCS's "commitment to excellence and passion for service." (Courtesy of JFCS.)

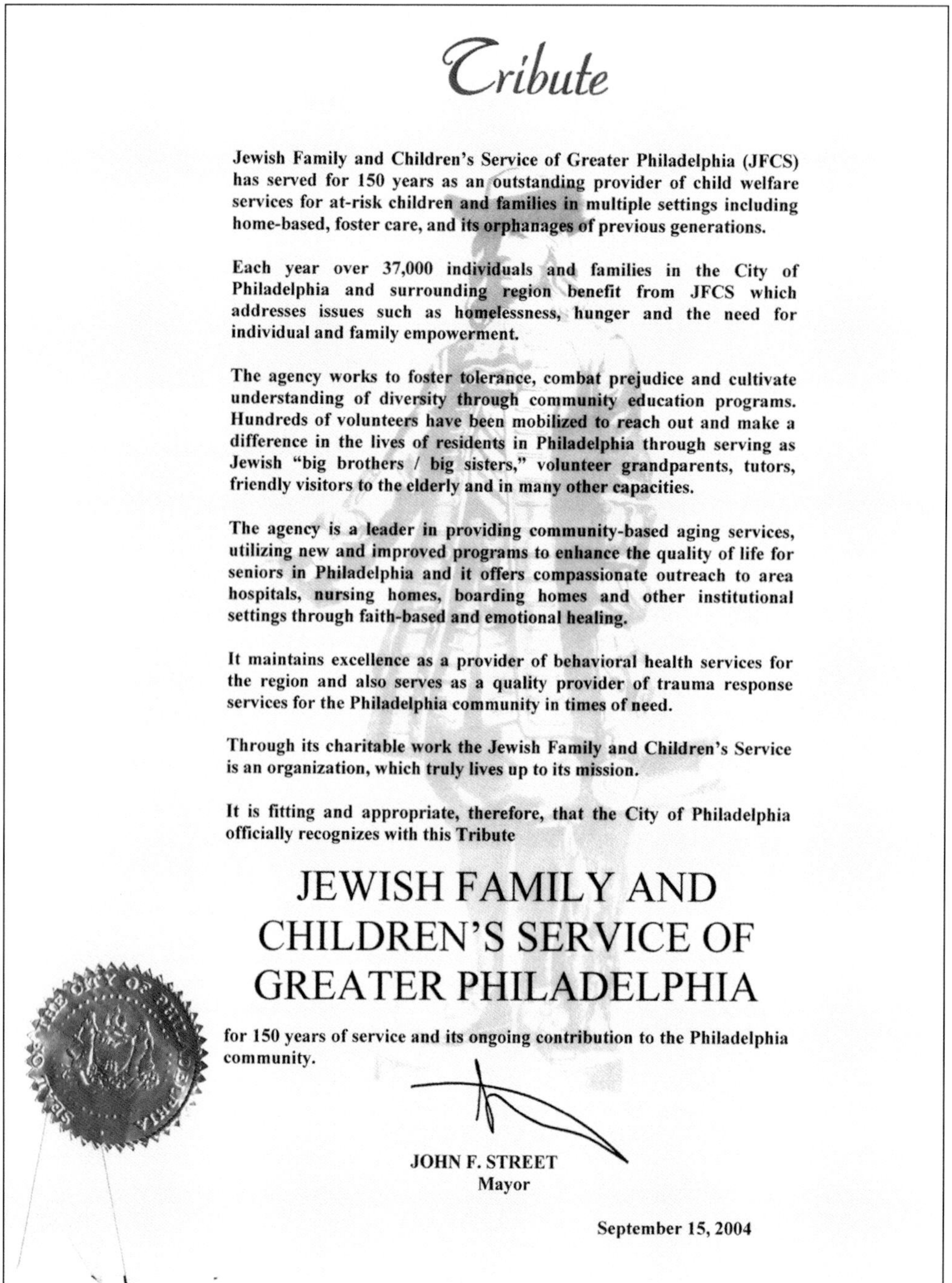

Tribute

Jewish Family and Children's Service of Greater Philadelphia (JFCS) has served for 150 years as an outstanding provider of child welfare services for at-risk children and families in multiple settings including home-based, foster care, and its orphanages of previous generations.

Each year over 37,000 individuals and families in the City of Philadelphia and surrounding region benefit from JFCS which addresses issues such as homelessness, hunger and the need for individual and family empowerment.

The agency works to foster tolerance, combat prejudice and cultivate understanding of diversity through community education programs. Hundreds of volunteers have been mobilized to reach out and make a difference in the lives of residents in Philadelphia through serving as Jewish "big brothers / big sisters," volunteer grandparents, tutors, friendly visitors to the elderly and in many other capacities.

The agency is a leader in providing community-based aging services, utilizing new and improved programs to enhance the quality of life for seniors in Philadelphia and it offers compassionate outreach to area hospitals, nursing homes, boarding homes and other institutional settings through faith-based and emotional healing.

It maintains excellence as a provider of behavioral health services for the region and also serves as a quality provider of trauma response services for the Philadelphia community in times of need.

Through its charitable work the Jewish Family and Children's Service is an organization, which truly lives up to its mission.

It is fitting and appropriate, therefore, that the City of Philadelphia officially recognizes with this Tribute

JEWISH FAMILY AND
CHILDREN'S SERVICE OF
GREATER PHILADELPHIA

for 150 years of service and its ongoing contribution to the Philadelphia community.

JOHN F. STREET
Mayor

September 15, 2004

SEAL OF THE CITY OF PHILADELPHIA

The City of Philadelphia also recognized JFCS for 150 years of leadership in providing vital human services. (Courtesy of JFCS.)

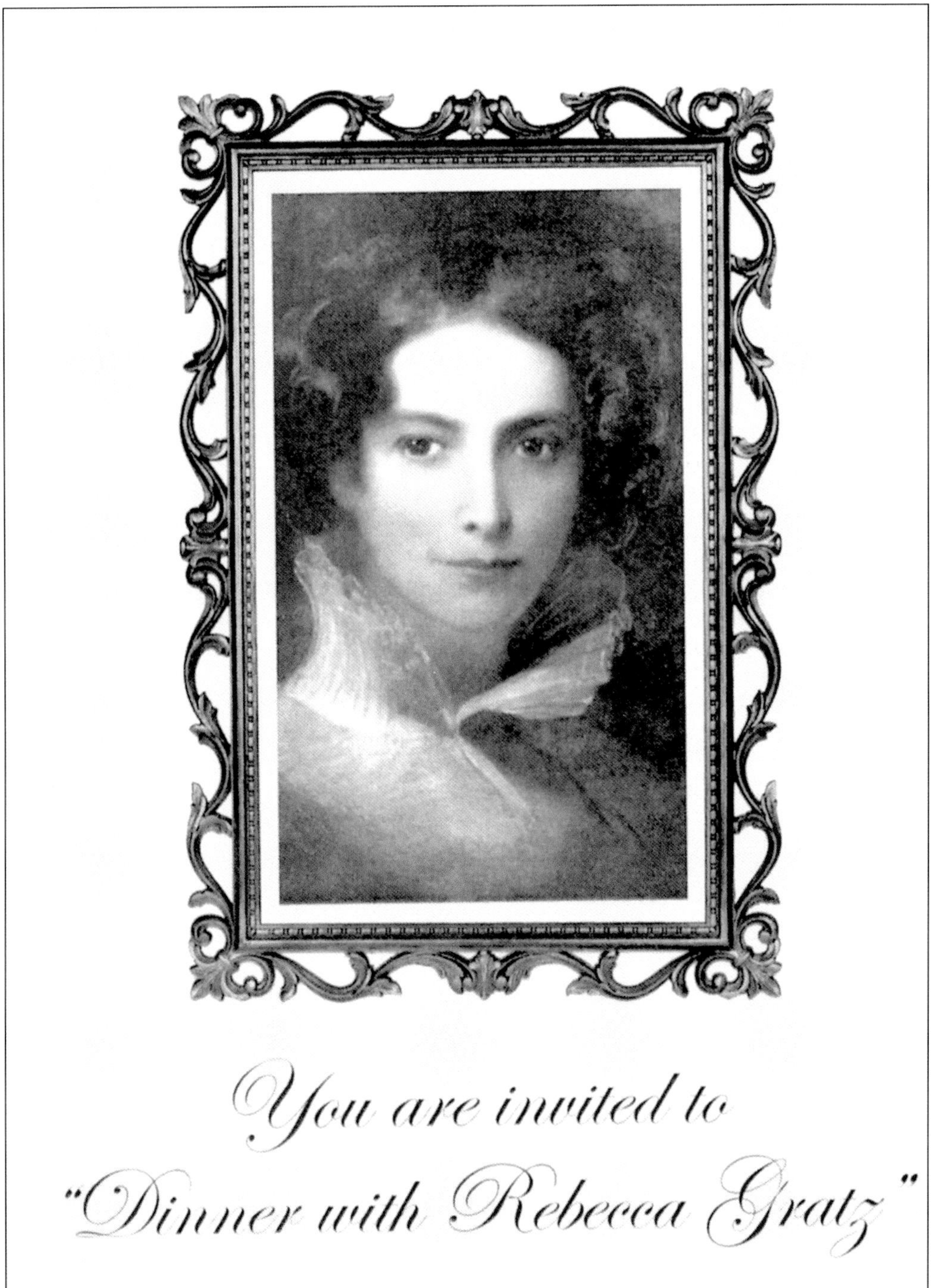

The series of 150th anniversary celebrations in 2005 began with the March 15th "Dinner with Rebecca Gratz," an event for board members and their families. Dianne Ashton, author of *Rebecca Gratz: Women and Judaism in Antebellum America*, spoke on the life, times, and legacy of JFCS's founder. The event took place at the Rosenbach Museum and Library in Center City, which features a number of famous paintings of the Gratz family. (Courtesy of JFCS.)

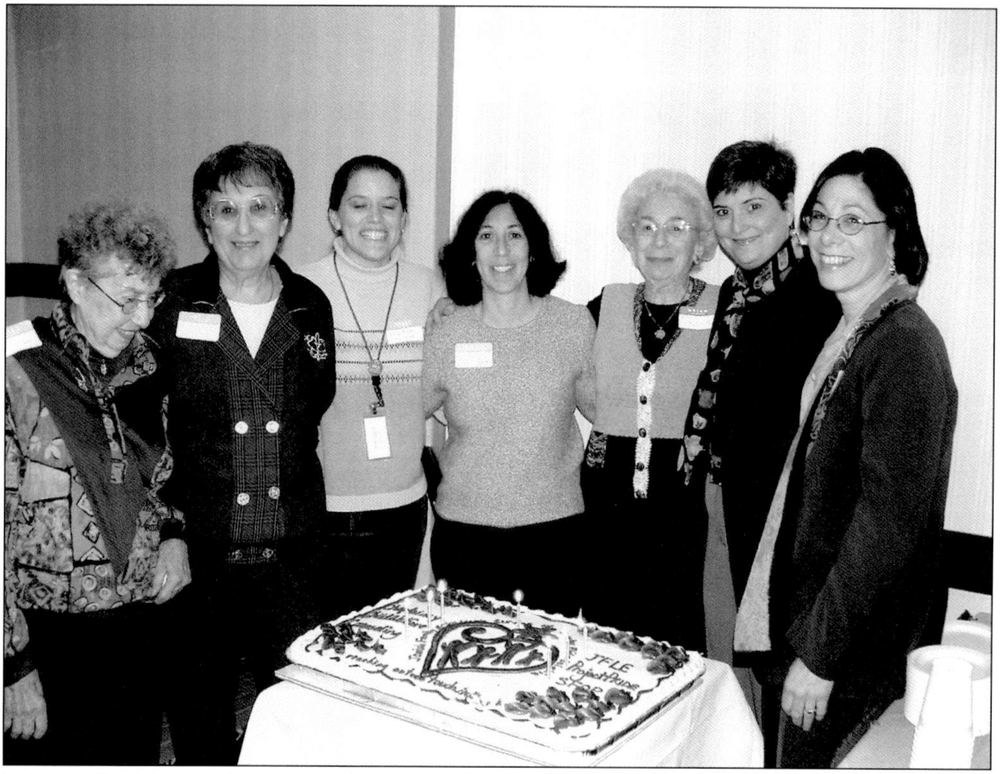

JFCS staff celebrated the agency's historic tradition of social work at an anniversary breakfast on April 4 sponsored by the board and trustees in their honor. Grouped around an agency birthday cake from left to right are staff members Kitty Sass, Dorothy Cohen, Renee Mezer, Margo Fine-Gabbay, Dene Bernstein (a JFCS trustee), Lonnie Beer, and Eleanor Bloch. (Courtesy of JFCS.)

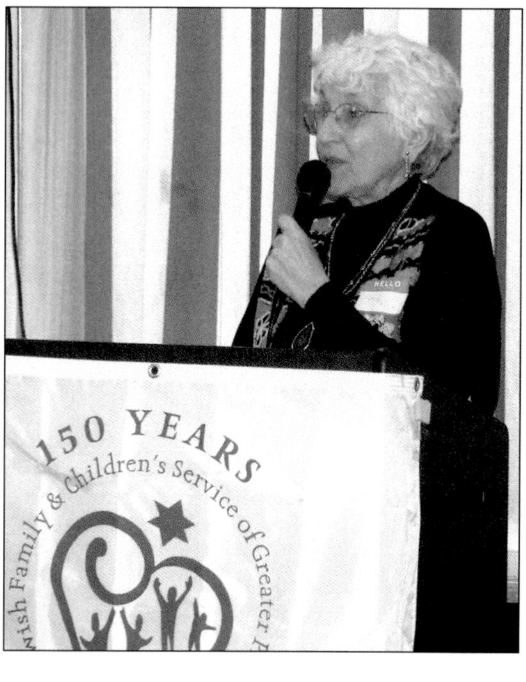

Adena Potok, a JFCS trustee and chairman of event, welcomes attendees. As a social work graduate student at the University of Pennsylvania years ago, she interned at JFCS's predecessor, JFS. (Courtesy of JFCS.)

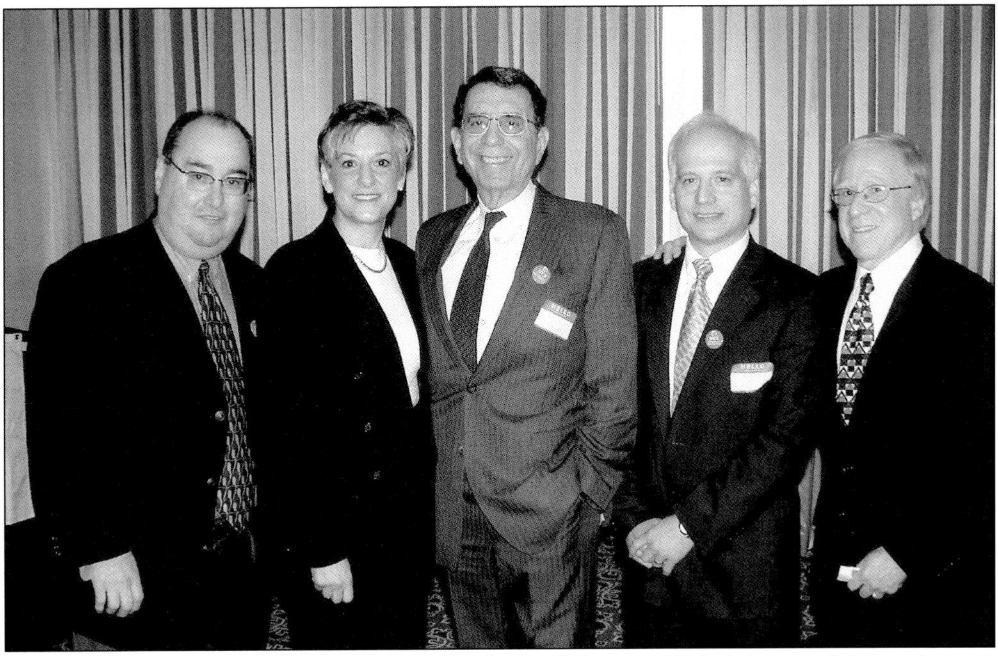

Keynoting the event was Congresswoman Allyson Schwartz (13th District of Pennsylvania), pictured here with, from left to right, Drew Staffenberg, then JFCS president and CEO; Carl Schneider, past JFCS board chairman; James Kahn, board chairman; and Leonard Cooper, JFCS 150th anniversary chairman and past board president. (Courtesy of JFCS.)

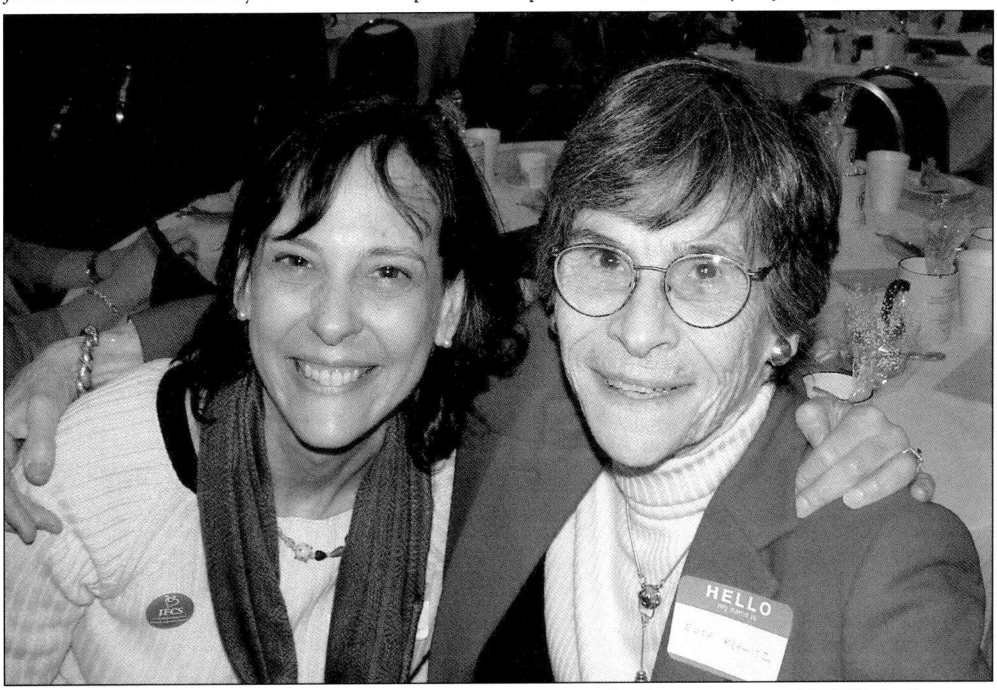

Sharing in the celebration and a smile are Sara Wenger (left), supervisor of JFCS's Lieberman Jewish Family Life Education and Group Services program, and Ruth Krawitz, JFCS trustee. (Courtesy of JFCS.)

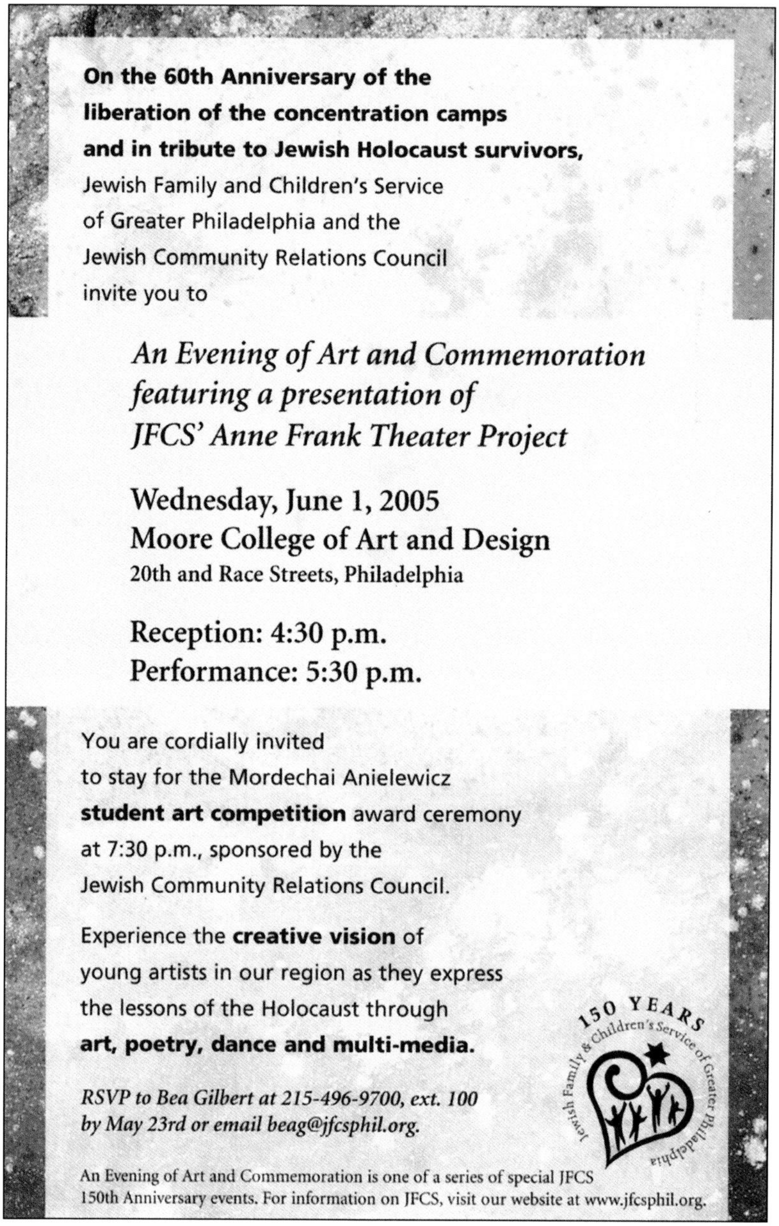

On the 60th Anniversary of the liberation of the concentration camps and in tribute to Jewish Holocaust survivors,
Jewish Family and Children's Service of Greater Philadelphia and the Jewish Community Relations Council invite you to

An Evening of Art and Commemoration featuring a presentation of JFCS' Anne Frank Theater Project

Wednesday, June 1, 2005
Moore College of Art and Design
20th and Race Streets, Philadelphia

Reception: 4:30 p.m.
Performance: 5:30 p.m.

You are cordially invited to stay for the Mordechai Anielewicz **student art competition** award ceremony at 7:30 p.m., sponsored by the Jewish Community Relations Council.

Experience the **creative vision** of young artists in our region as they express the lessons of the Holocaust through **art, poetry, dance and multi-media.**

RSVP to Bea Gilbert at 215-496-9700, ext. 100 by May 23rd or email beag@jfcsphil.org.

150 YEARS
Jewish Family & Children's Service of Greater Philadelphia

An Evening of Art and Commemoration is one of a series of special JFCS 150th Anniversary events. For information on JFCS, visit our website at www.jfcsphil.org.

JFCS and the Jewish Community Relations Council of the Jewish Federation of Greater Philadelphia sponsored "An Evening of Art and Commemoration," on June 1. Held at Moore College of Art, it honored survivors on the 60th anniversary of the liberation of the concentration camps. JFCS presented its Anne Frank Theater Project, an abridged version of *The Diary of Anne Frank* play, followed by an audience discussion of issues raised by the play. Many survivors participated in the discussion, making it especially memorable. The next event, the Mordechai Anielewicz Creative Arts Competition award ceremony, sponsored by federation's Jewish Community Relations Council in partnership with the Auerbach Central Agency for Jewish Education, honored award-winning student artwork on Holocaust themes. JFCS's ties to survivors are both historic, through resettlement and child welfare services, and current, through its Services for Older Persons Department. (Courtesy of JFCS.)

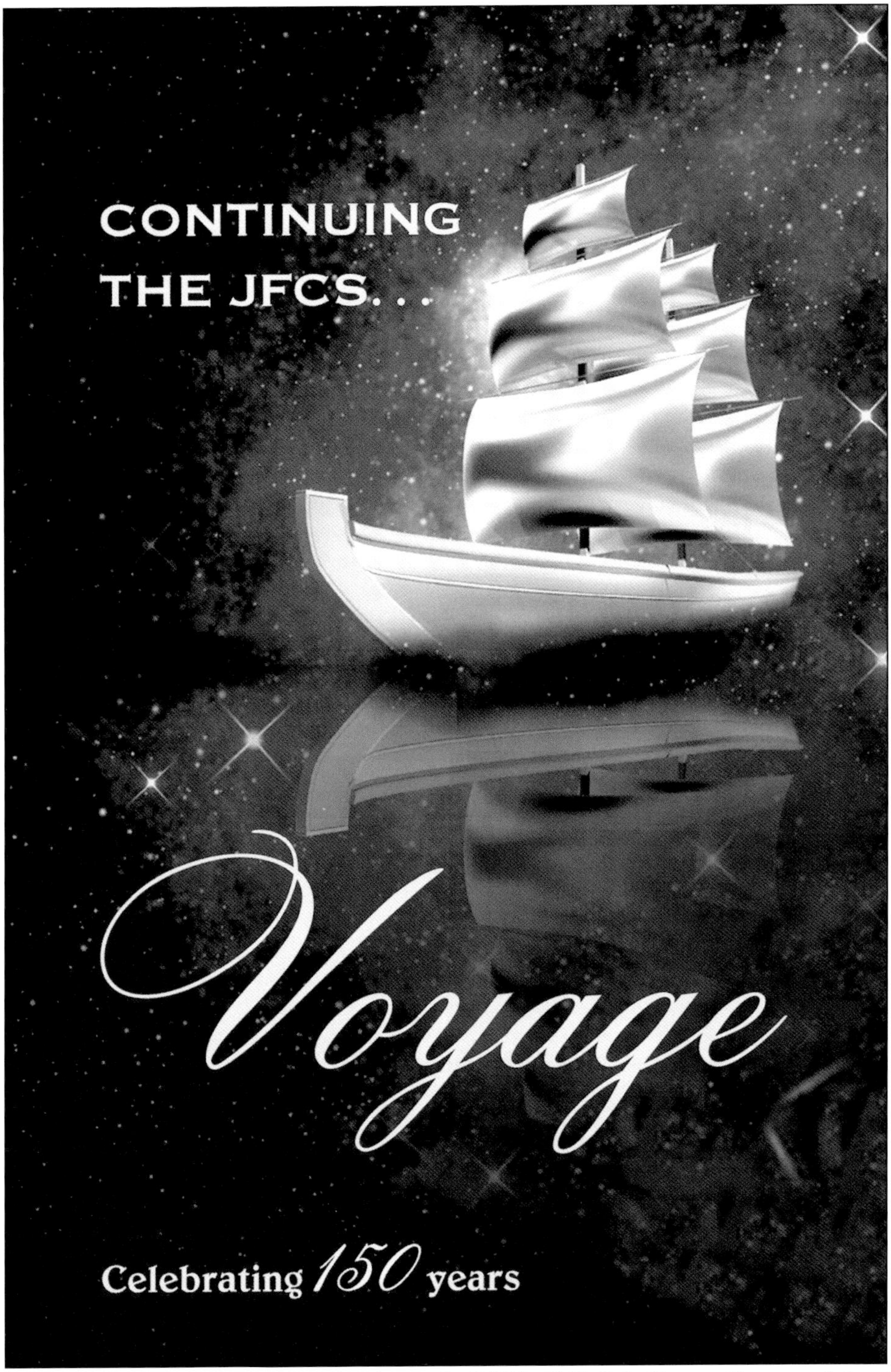

"Continuing the JFCS Voyage" was the theme for JFCS's 2005 Gala Dinner Dance and Auction on November 12. The black-tie event, held at Philadelphia's Independence Seaport Museum at Penn's Landing, featured nautical themes—an apt way of showcasing the agency's 150-year "journey." (Courtesy of JFCS.)

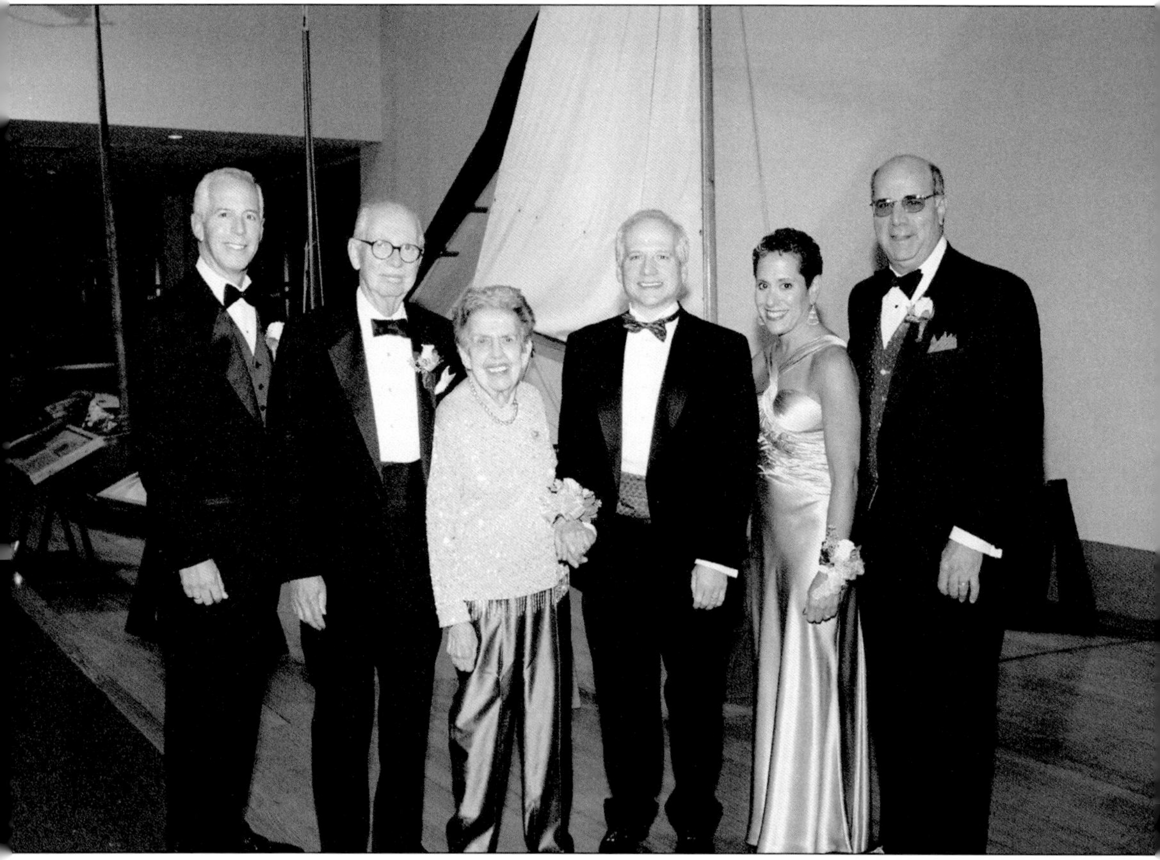

Pictured at the event (from left to right) are Jack Dembow, JFCS president and CEO; honorees Donald and Fahnya Bean; James Kahn, JFCS board chairman; and Susan and Daniel Behrend, gala chairpersons. Donald Bean, a JFCS honorary board member, has provided JFCS and its predecessor, JFS, with decades of dedicated leadership. In addition to securing key grants and endowments for the agency, he oversaw the purchase of JFCS's Verree Road office in Northeast Philadelphia. A past president of Rodeph Shalom Congregation, he is of counsel to the firm of Wolf, Block, Schorr and Solis-Cohen LLP. Fahnya Bean was celebrated for her community leadership in arts, educational, and civic activities. Fahnya's connection to JFCS started early. Her father was a president of the Homewood School, a predecessor agency of today's JFCS. (Courtesy of JFCS.)

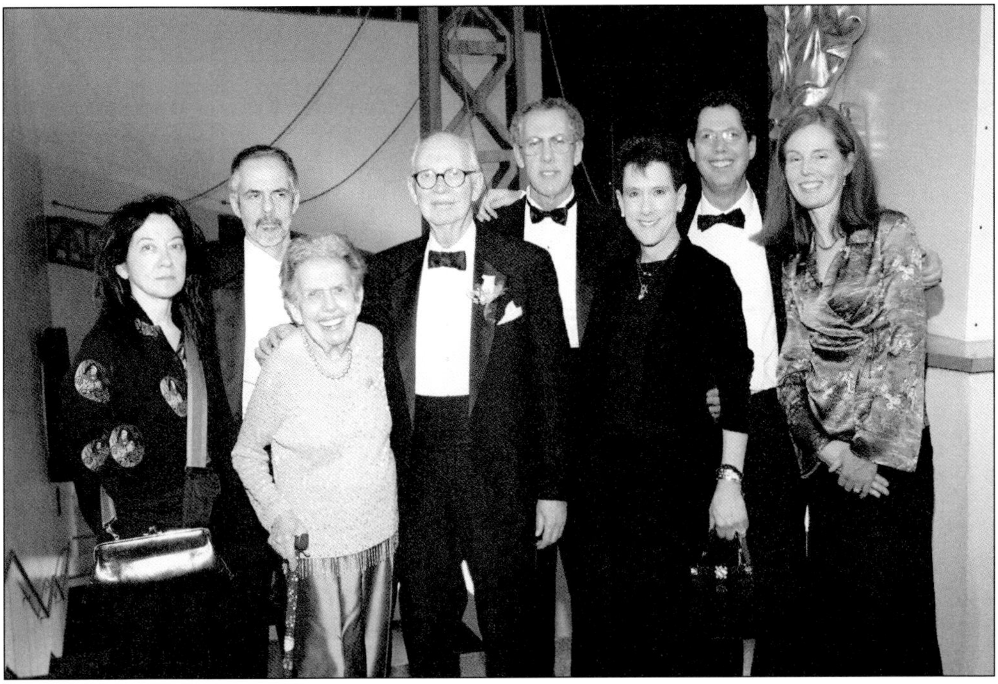

"Jewish family" is at the heart of JFCS. The Bean family is proof of it. With honorees Donald and Fahnya Bean are their sons and daughters-in-law. Seen from left to right are Leora, Barish, Fahnya, Donald, George, Jane, Skip, and Fionnala.

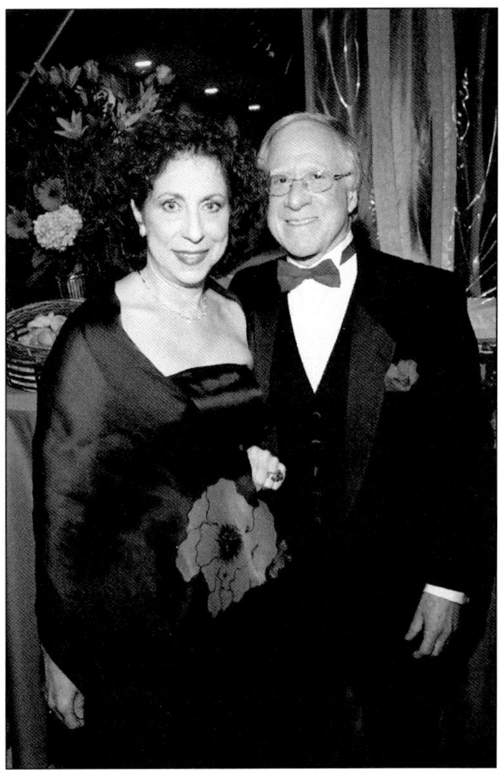

Pictured here are Leonard Cooper, 150th anniversary chairman, and his wife Wendy. The 150th anniversary celebration culminated with the 2005 gala and the JFCS family reunion event the next day. (Courtesy of JFCS.)

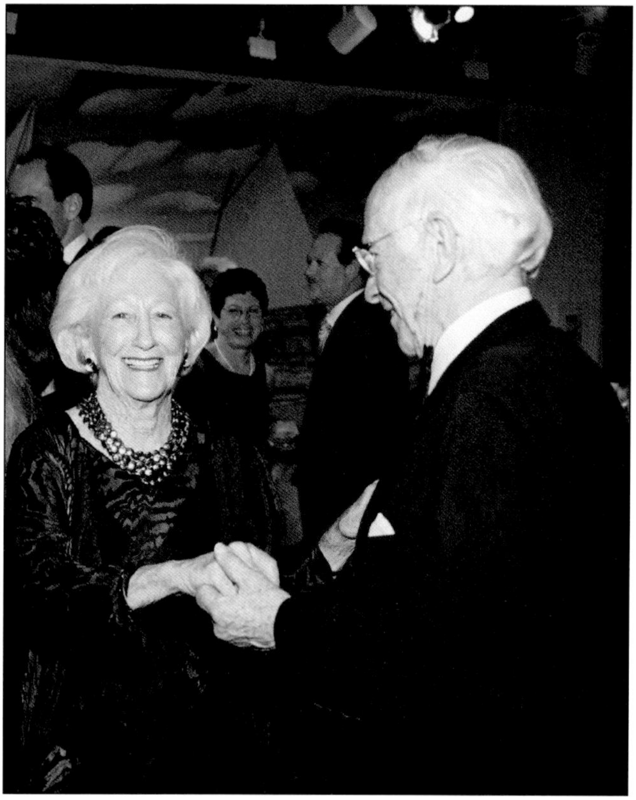

Past gala honoree Mary Bert Gutman and her husband Alvin join in the spirit and the dancing. Mary Bert's devotion to children's causes and the couple's community philanthropy is long-standing and renowned. At JFCS, the Mary Bert Gutman Children's Support Network helps to fund support services for children and their families in crisis and in need. (Courtesy of JFCS.)

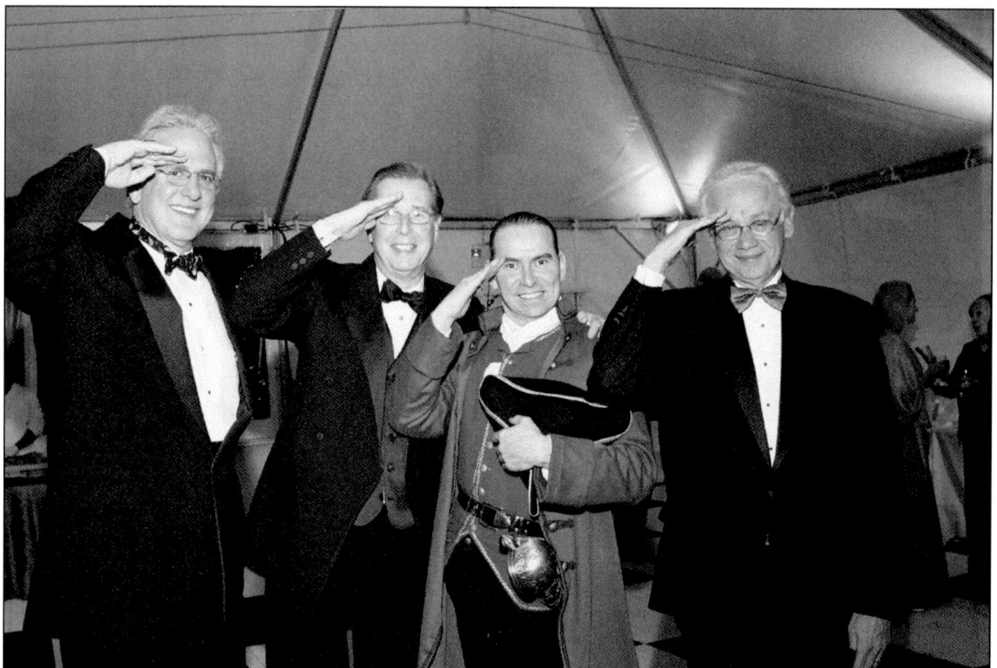

All aboard as the gala ship "sets sail." From left to right are Bruce Marks, Daniel Bacine, the "Captain," and Owen Knopping. (Courtesy of JFCS.)

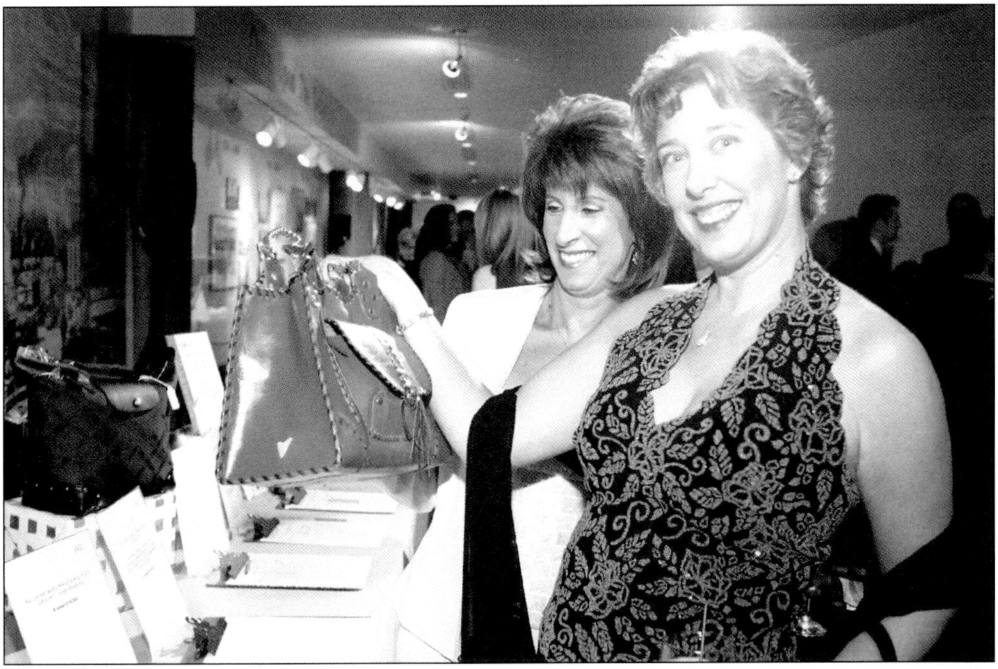

Enjoying the silent auction are Mara Brand (left) and Marcia Wasserman. (Courtesy of JFCS.)

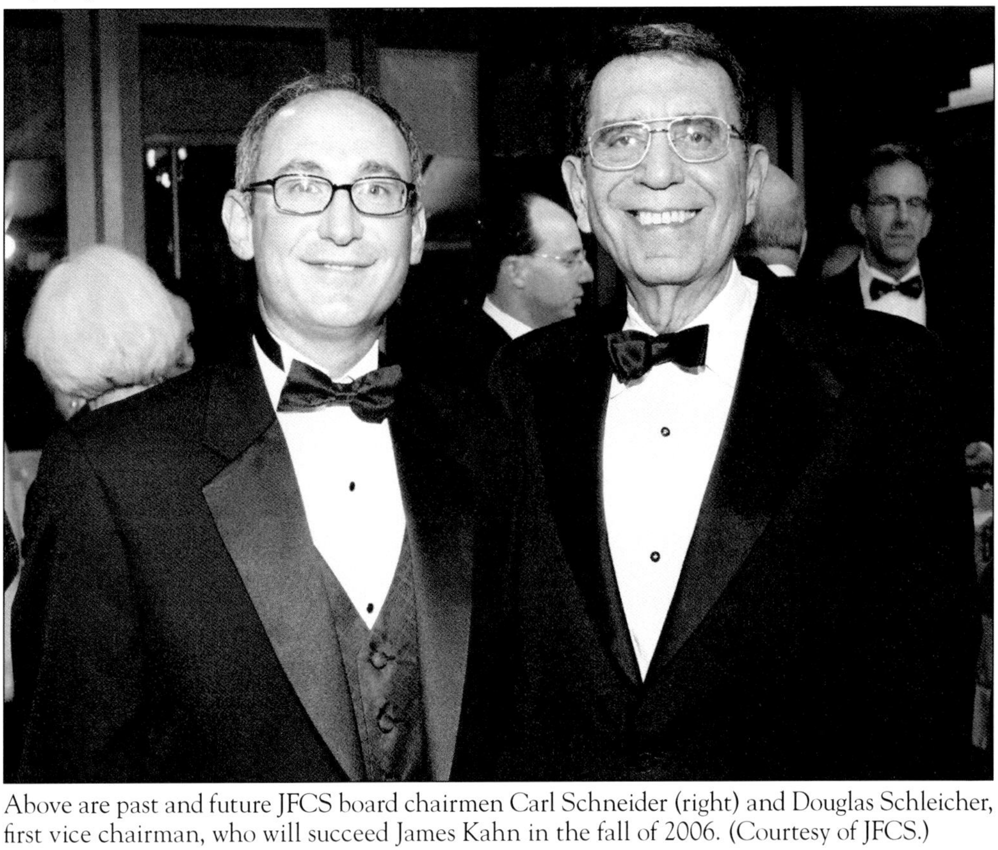

Above are past and future JFCS board chairmen Carl Schneider (right) and Douglas Schleicher, first vice chairman, who will succeed James Kahn in the fall of 2006. (Courtesy of JFCS.)

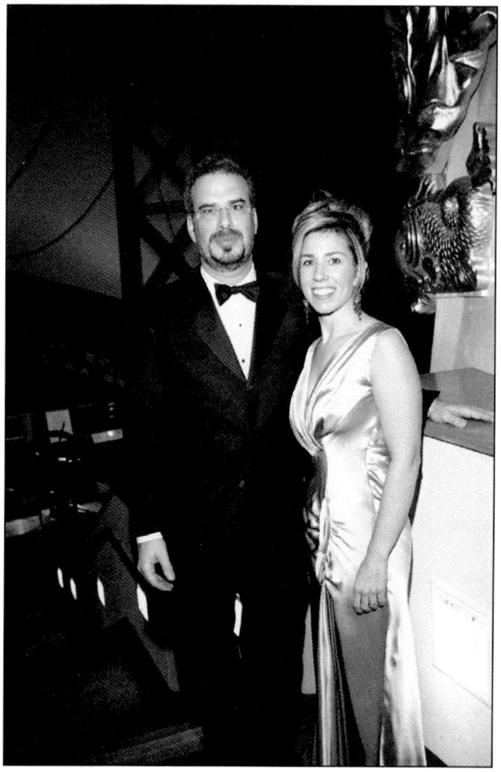

Advertisement book cochairs David Colman and Isa Welsch helped ensure the success of the gala event, which raised $350,000 to benefit JFCS and the clients it serves. (Courtesy of JFCS.)

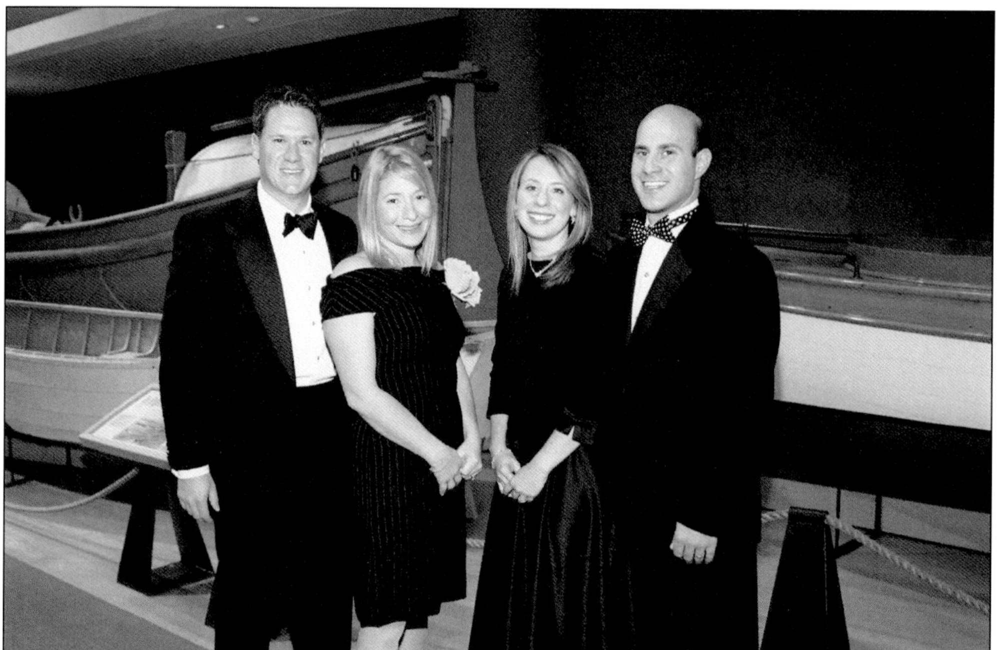

Cochairs of the silent auction are Lee Sussman (left) and Alison Erlbaum Sussman (second from left). Pictured with them are Suzy and Scott Goldstein, who chaired the Under 39 Committee. (Courtesy of JFCS.)

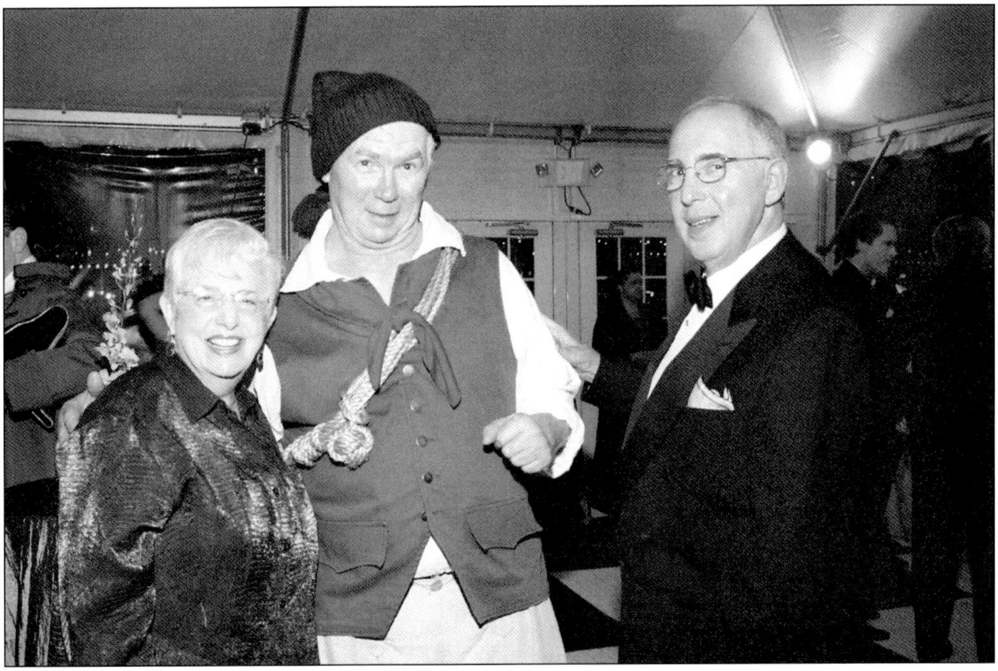

Betsy and Robert Horen pose with the "First Mate."

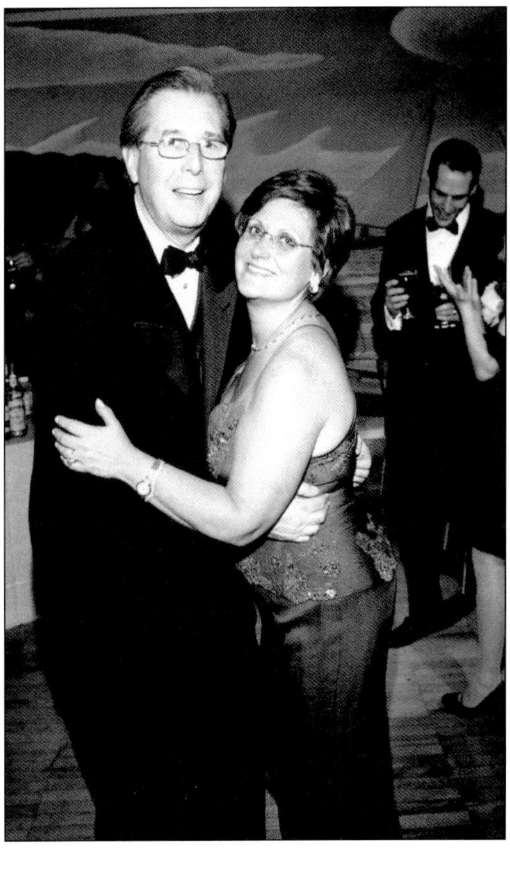

Joining in the action on the dance floor are Marci and Daniel Bacine.

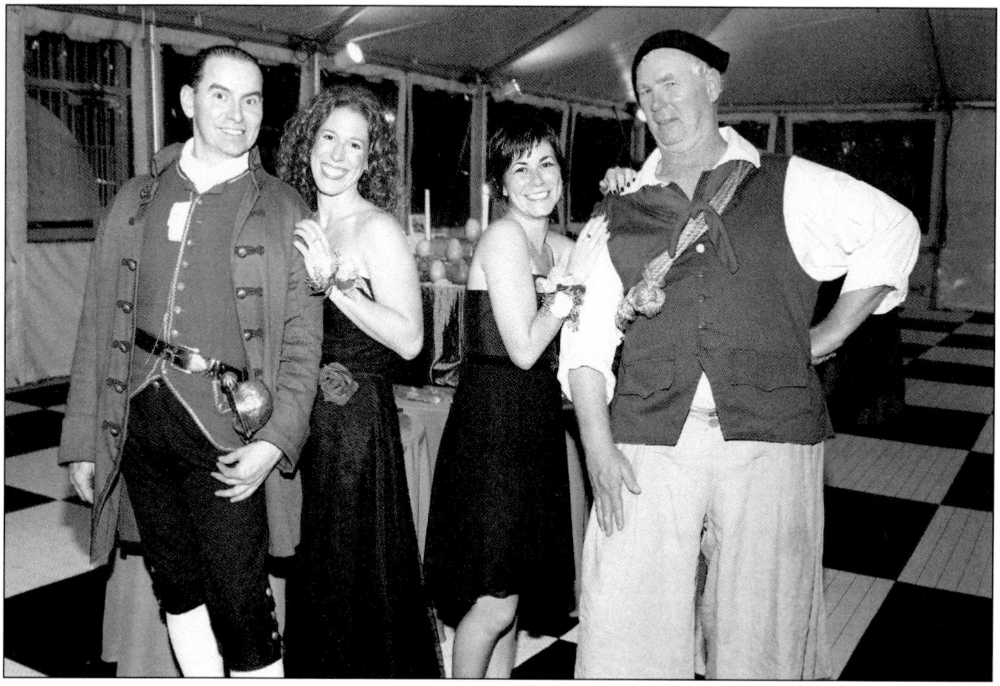

Moving from months working behind the scenes to being on the scene as they pose with the "crew" are Holli Elgart (second from left), JFCS marketing and public relations specialist, and Jaclyn Stephenson (second from right), JFCS marketing and public relations associate.

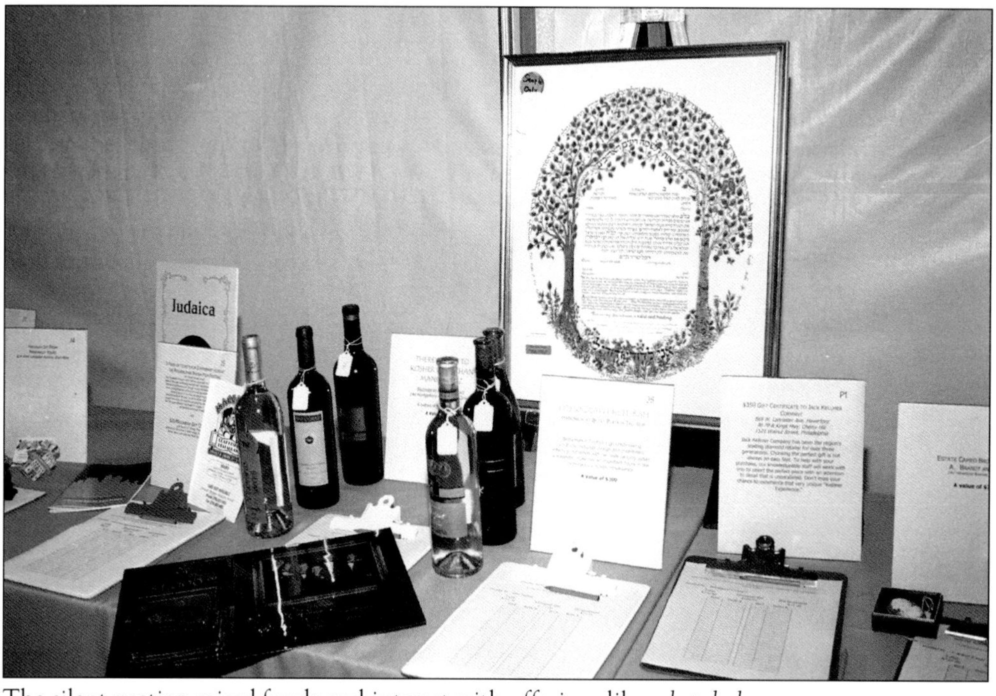

The silent auction raised funds and interest with offerings like a *ketubah*.

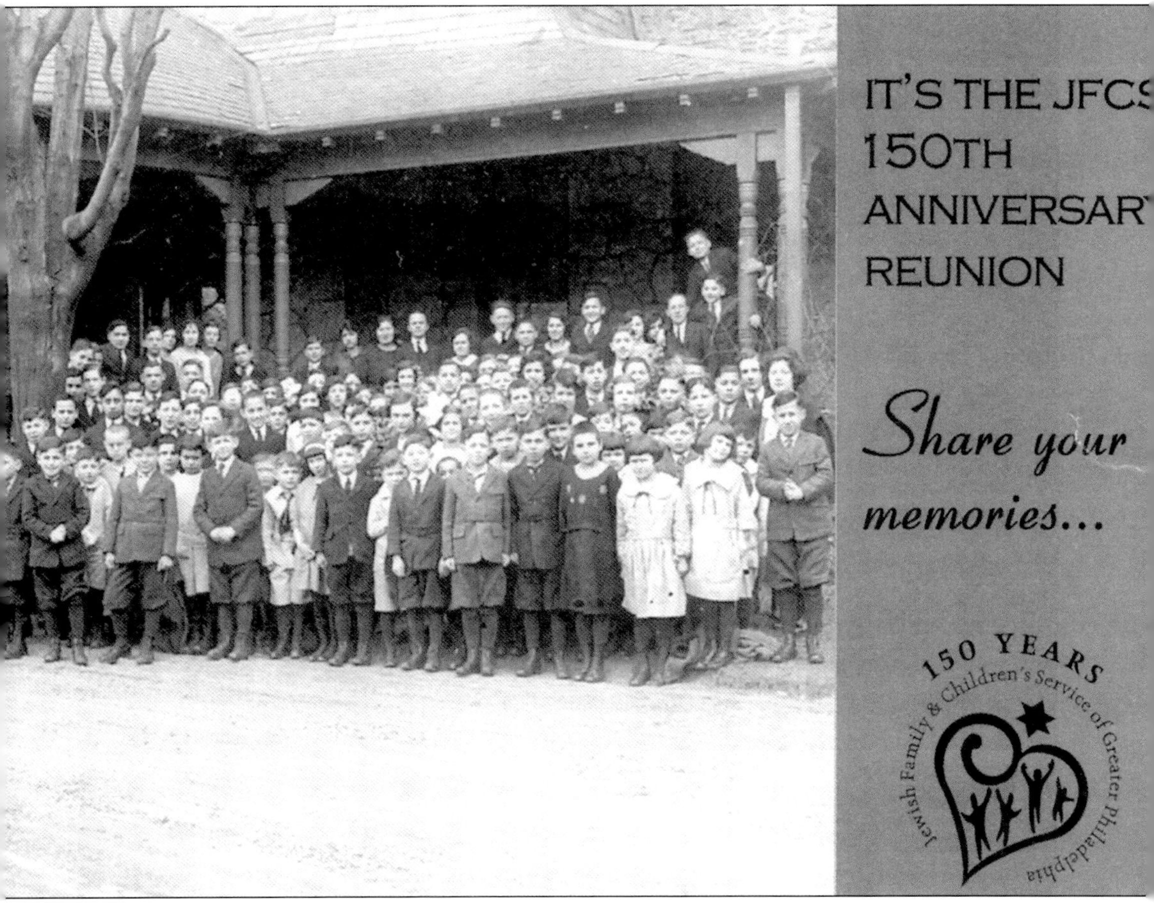

On November 13, a joyous "family reunion" brought together past and present staff, board members, volunteers, and those served by the agency for the final 150th anniversary event. Held at the University of Pennsylvania Museum of Anthropology and Archaeology in West Philadelphia, it was chaired by Curt Pontz. The reunion was sponsored by the law firm of Wolf, Block, Schorr and Solis-Cohen LLP, seven of whose attorneys have served as president/chairman of JFCS and its predecessors over the agency's history. Dozens gathered to mix, mingle, and share in the memories. (Courtesy of JFCS.)

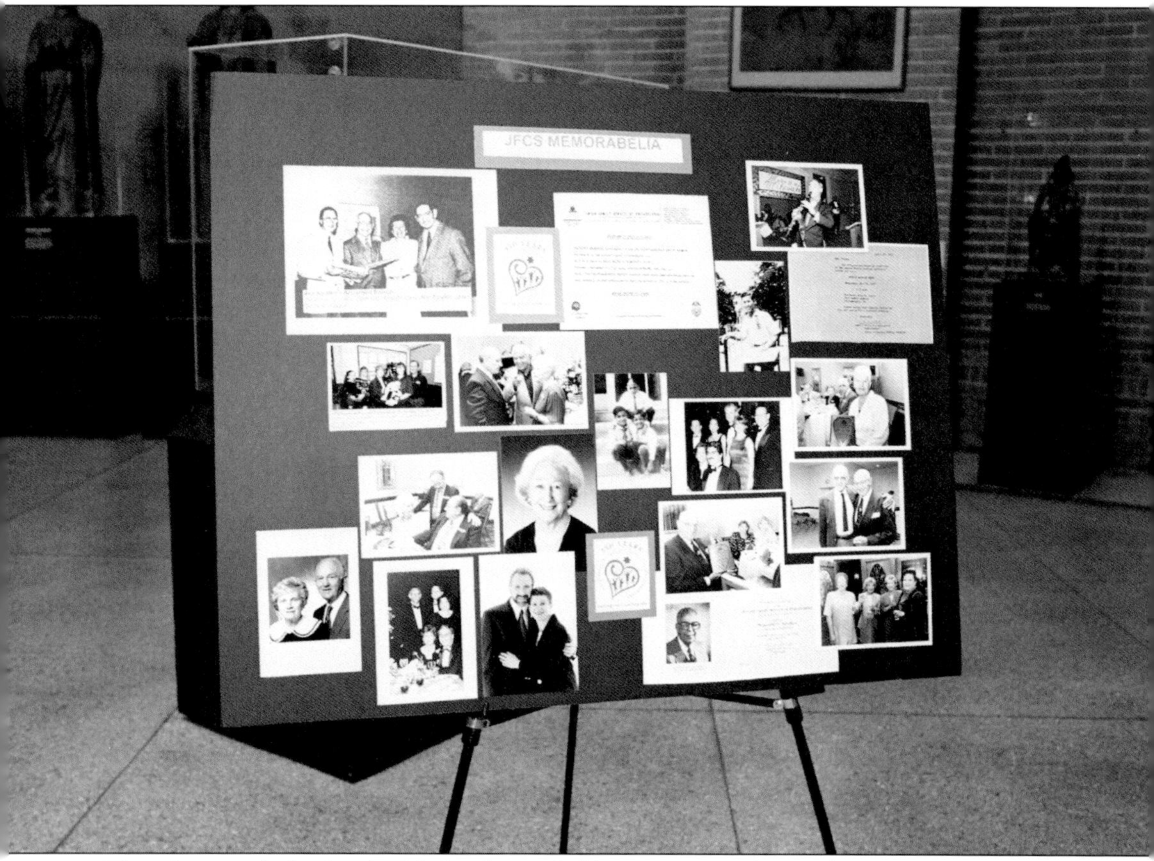

This photograph displays highlighted remarkable moments and remarkable people in the life of today's JFCS and its predecessors.

Pennsylvania governor Edward G. Rendell paid a surprise visit to congratulate JFCS on its 150th anniversary and its long tradition of caring.

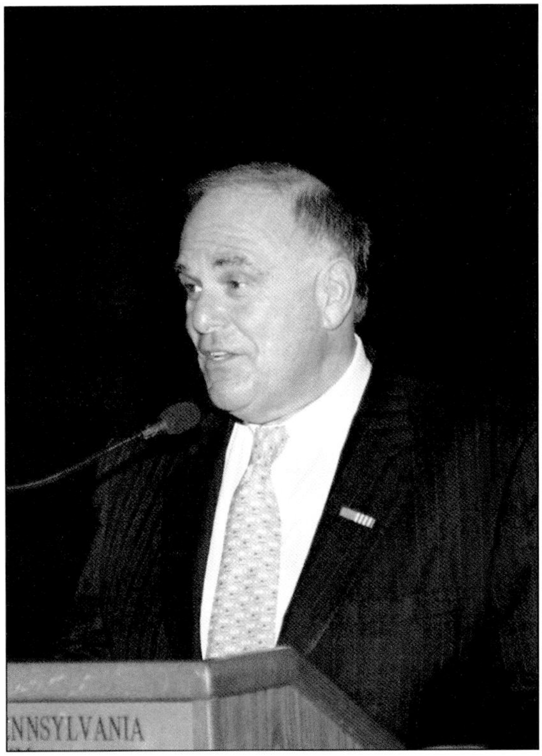

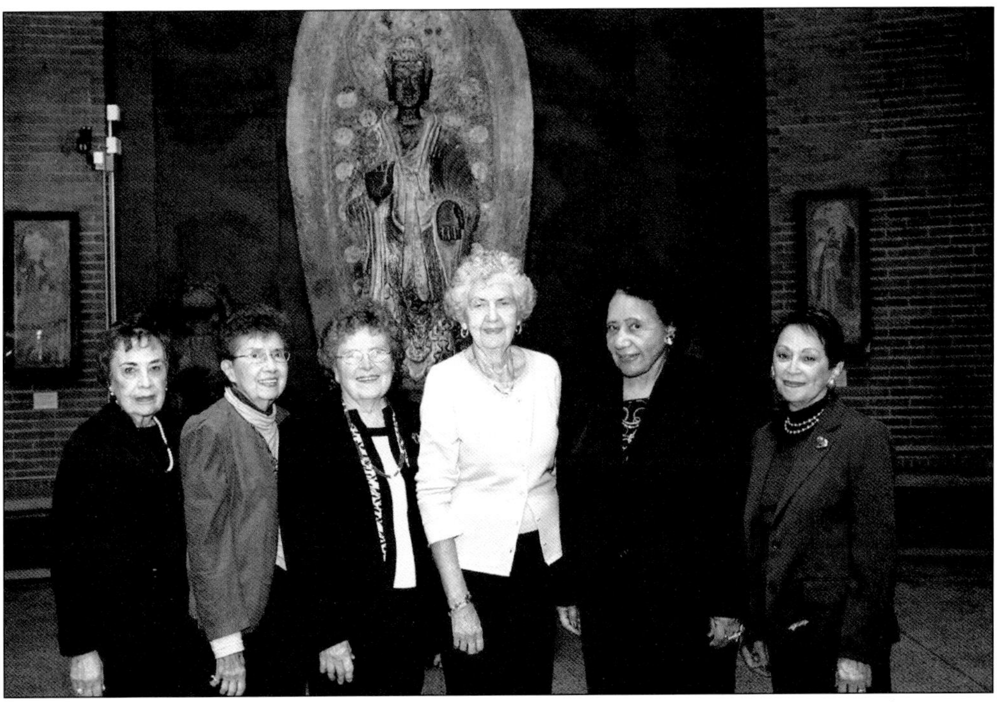

Among those representing the AJC at the event are, from left to right, Florence Silver, Kitty Sass, Marilyn Nepps, Edie Reiffnyder, Mildred Keeys, and Elaine Schwartz. The AJC and JFS merged in 1983, resulting in the modern-day JFCS. (Courtesy of JFCS.)

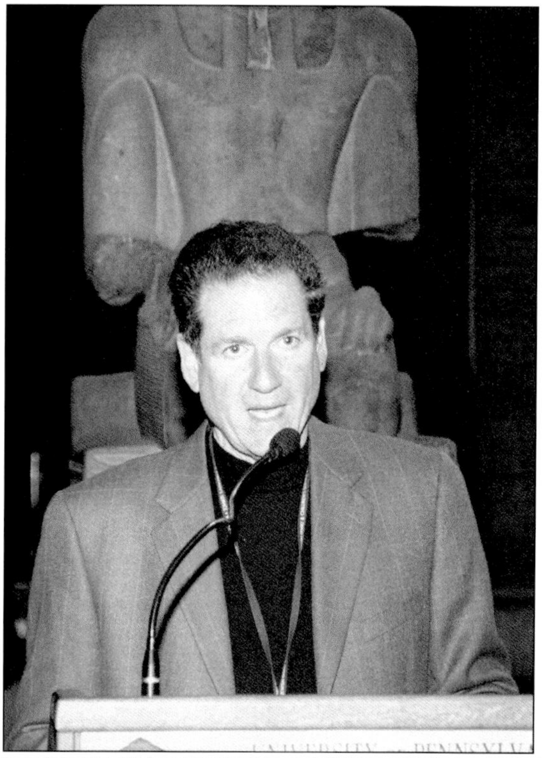

Family reunion chairman Curt Pontz welcomed the guests. He had envisioned a JFCS family reunion early on in the 150th anniversary planning to connect and reconnect those who had participated in the life of the agency. The gathering celebrated JFCS's past, present, and future, and the day's success would prove that bonds shared remained strong over the years in the JFCS family. (Courtesy of JFCS.)

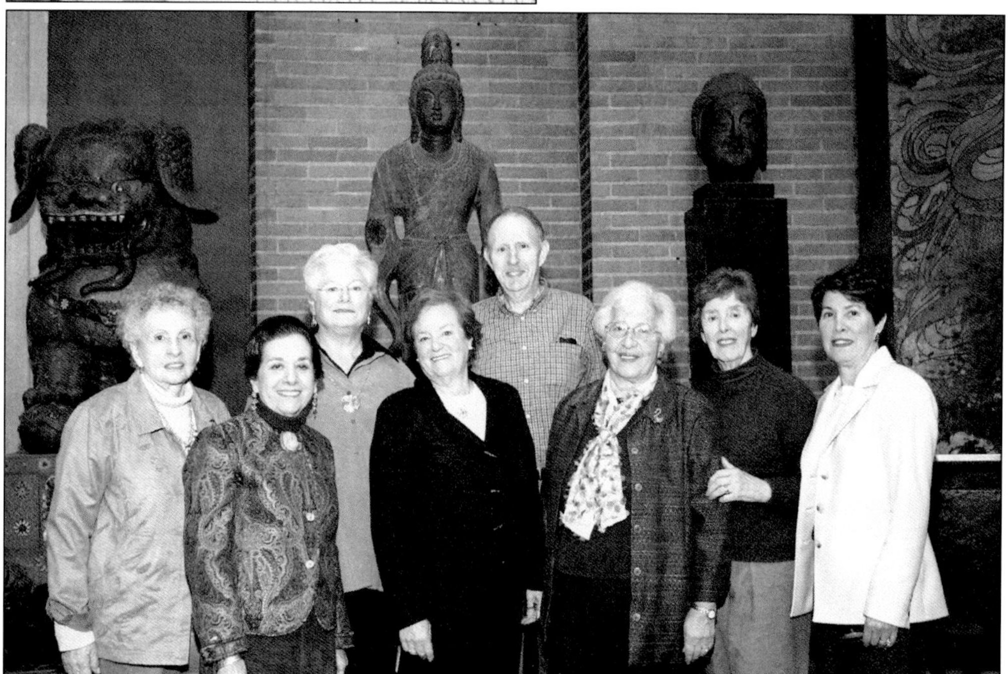

Among the attendees who had been on staff at JFS, an immediate JFCS predecessor agency, from left to right are Zipporah Segal, Deborah Shain, Linda Brunn, Myra Eskin, Steve Ramm, Sylvia Thomas, Mildred Weinles, and Susan Kershbaum. (Courtesy of JFCS.)

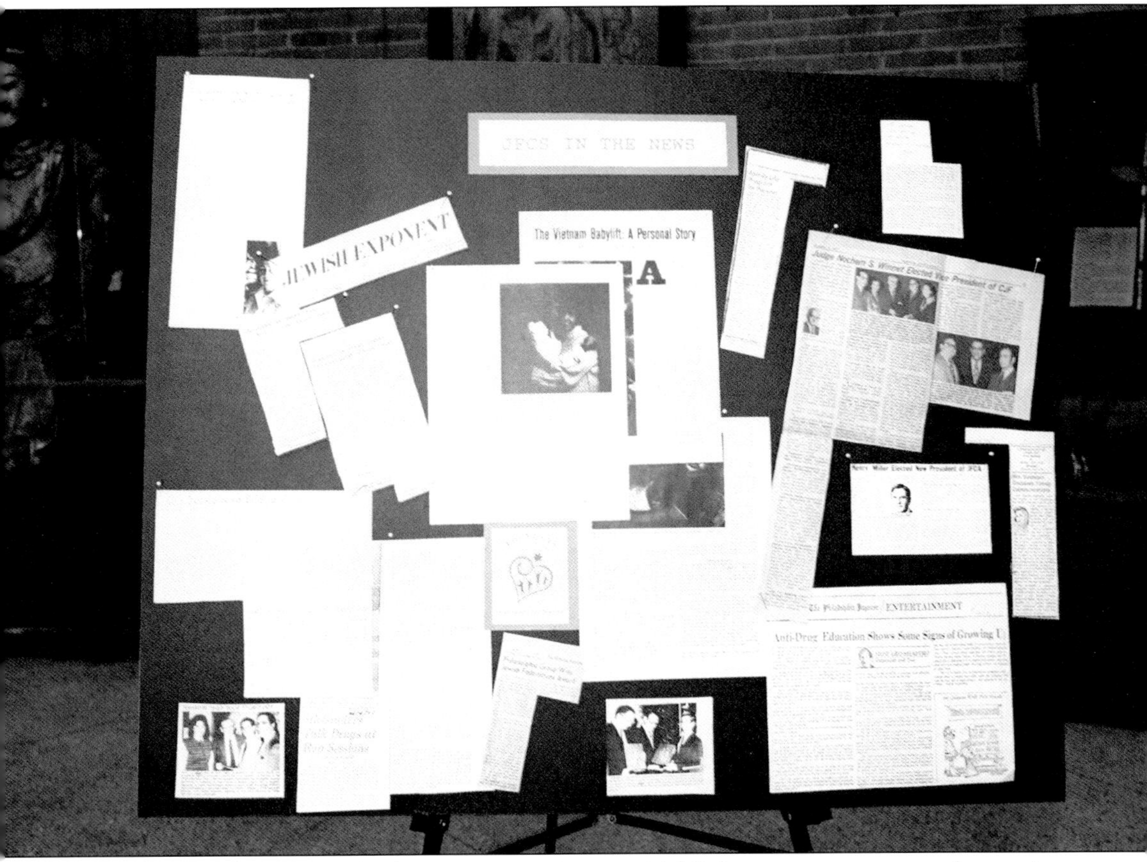

In another popular reunion display, newspaper clippings highlight agency programs and expertise and the stories of lives touched by JFCS and its predecessors.

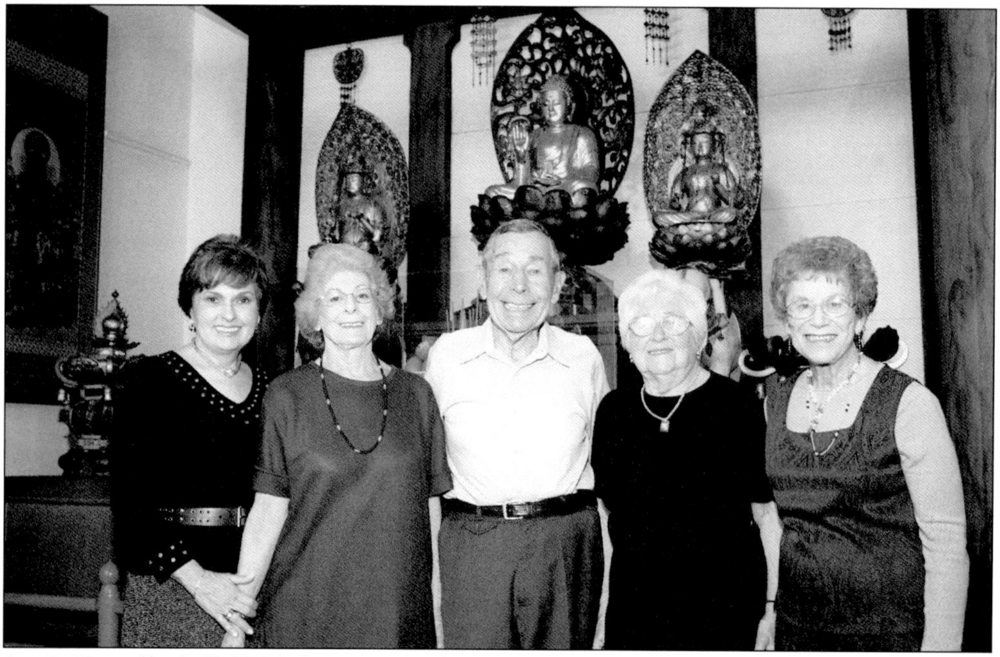

Sandy Fryer (far left), JFCS director of volunteer services, joins longtime volunteers (from left to right) Shirley Grayson, Larry Kovnat, Bertha Rabinowitch, and Anne Coben for this picture. These volunteers say they get even more than they give through the satisfaction of helping others and that it changes their own lives forever. (Courtesy of JFCS.)

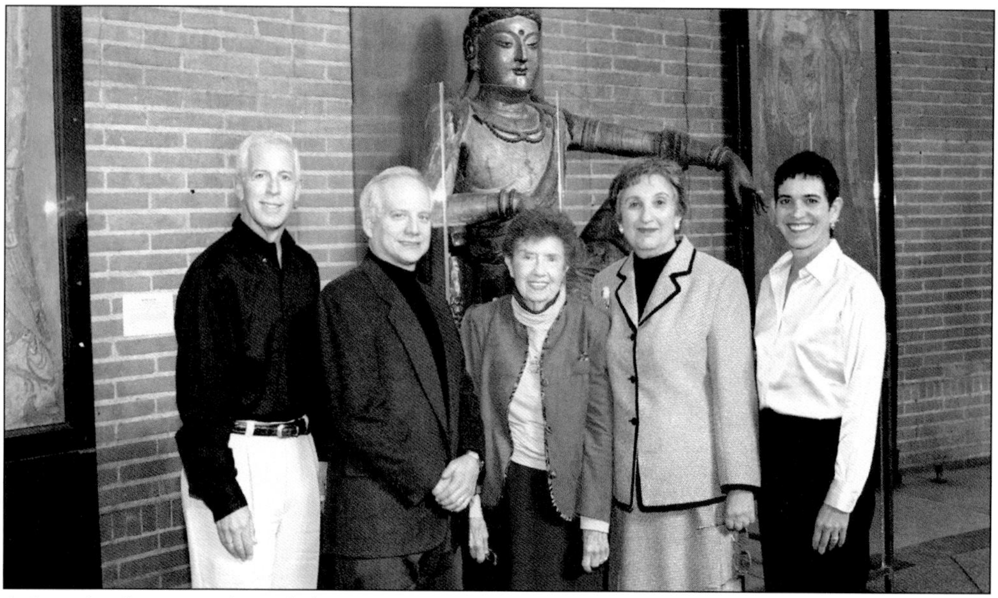

A love for the agency's work kept Kitty Sass and Dorothy Cohen (third and fourth from left) at JFCS and its predecessor, AJC, for decades. Sass worked in child welfare services recruiting foster parents. Cohen initially counseled children and now counsels seniors through JFCS's Services for Older Persons Department. Pictured with them at the reunion, from left to right, are Jack Dembow, JFCS president and CEO; James Kahn, JFCS board chairman; and (at far right) Lois Manowitz, JFCS executive vice president and COO. (Courtesy of JFCS.)

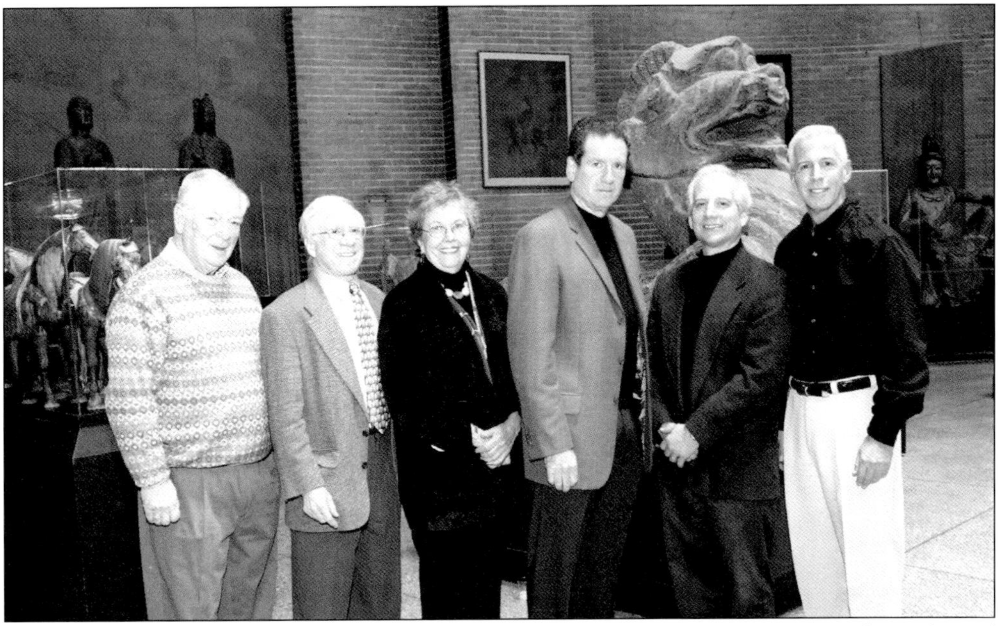

JFCS board leaders played a key role in planning for the reunion, helping JFCS reach out far and wide into the community. This image includes, from left to right, Michael Schwartz, Marketing Committee chairman; Leonard Cooper, 150th anniversary chairman; Miriam Finkel, agency vice chairman; Curt Pontz, reunion chairman; and James Kahn, JFCS chairman. Sharing in the planning was Jack Dembow, JFCS president and CEO (far right). (Courtesy of JFCS.)

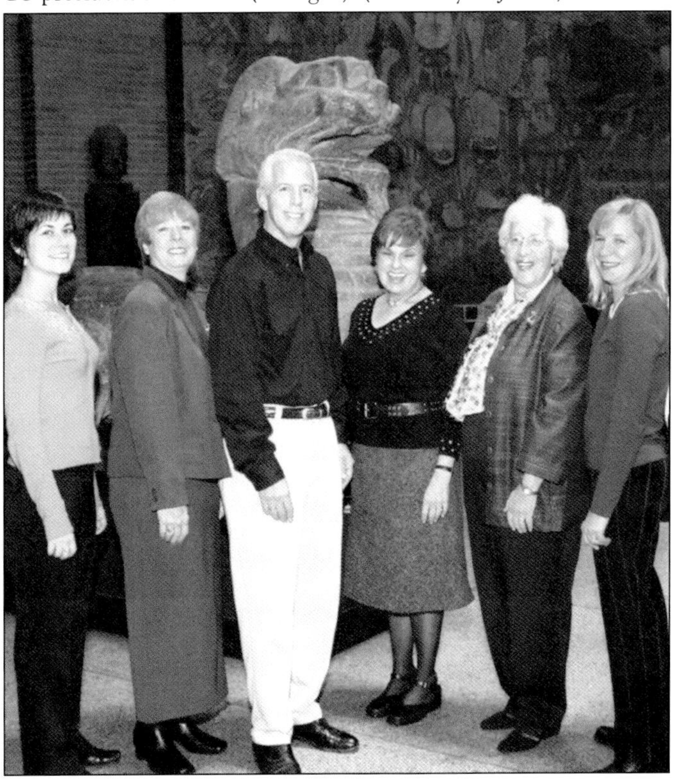

Among the JFCS staff serving on the reunion committee from left to right are Jaclyn Stephenson, marketing/public relations associate; Joan McCrane, operations director; Jack Dembow, JFCS president and CEO; Sandy Fryer, volunteer services director and coordinator of the family reunion event; Sylvia Thomas, former director of resettlement services; and Donna Miller, human resources director. (Courtesy of JFCS.)

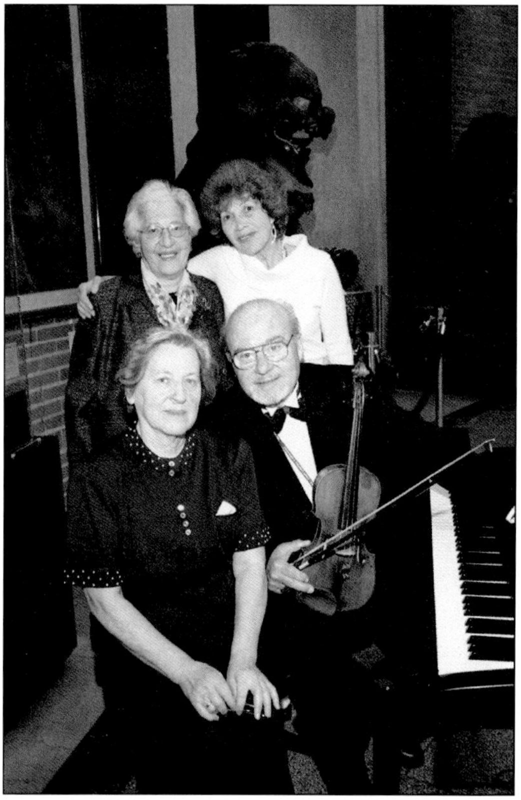

Providing entertainment at the reunion brunch are new Americans from the former Soviet Union who had been resettled by JFCS. From left to right are (first row) musicians Flora Lyudina and David Zaychik; (second row) Sylvia Thomas, former JFCS resettlement director, and Irma Simuni, former JFCS volunteer and resettlement coordinator. (Courtesy of JFCS.)

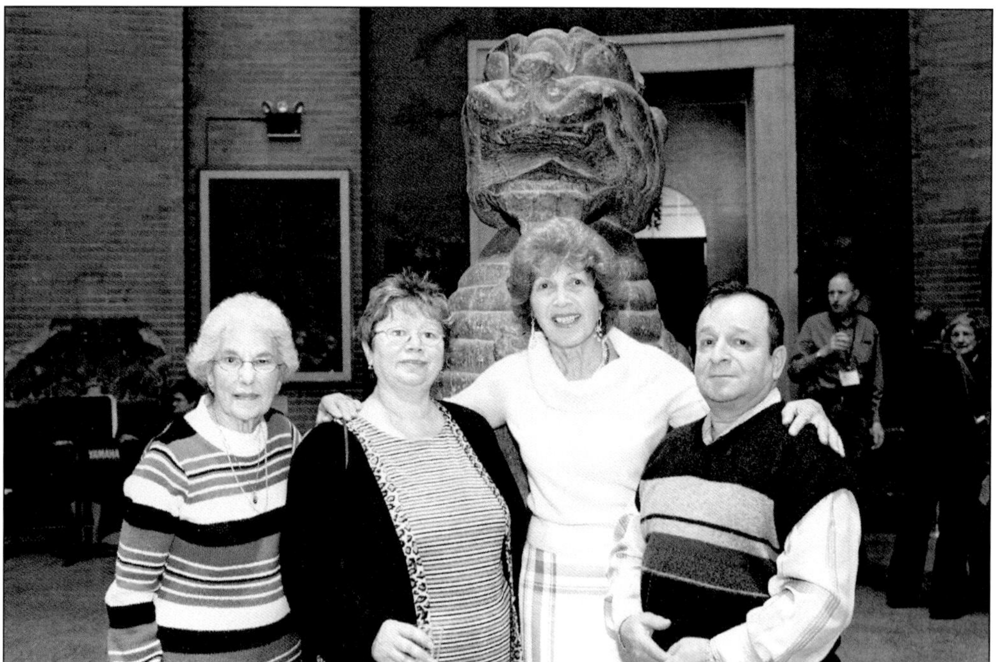

Enjoying the reunion event from left to right are Ilse Lindemeyer, Sofia Krivoruk, Irma Simuni, and Boris Minkovsky. (Courtesy of JFCS.)

For reunion participant Dr. Mickey Langsfeld, one of the first people to join JFCS's new membership society, the celebration of the agency's history was also personal. His mother, Anita Langsfeld, a past president of the AJC (1968–1969), had passed on her passion for the agency and its mission to him. His continuing connection to today's JFCS honors his mother and the work to which she was so dedicated. (Courtesy of JFCS.)

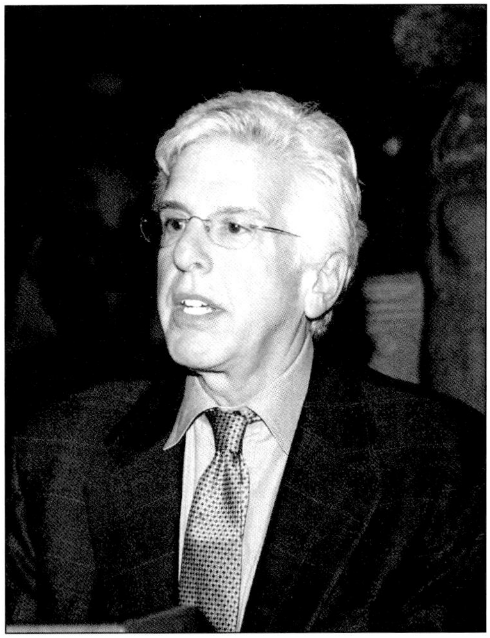

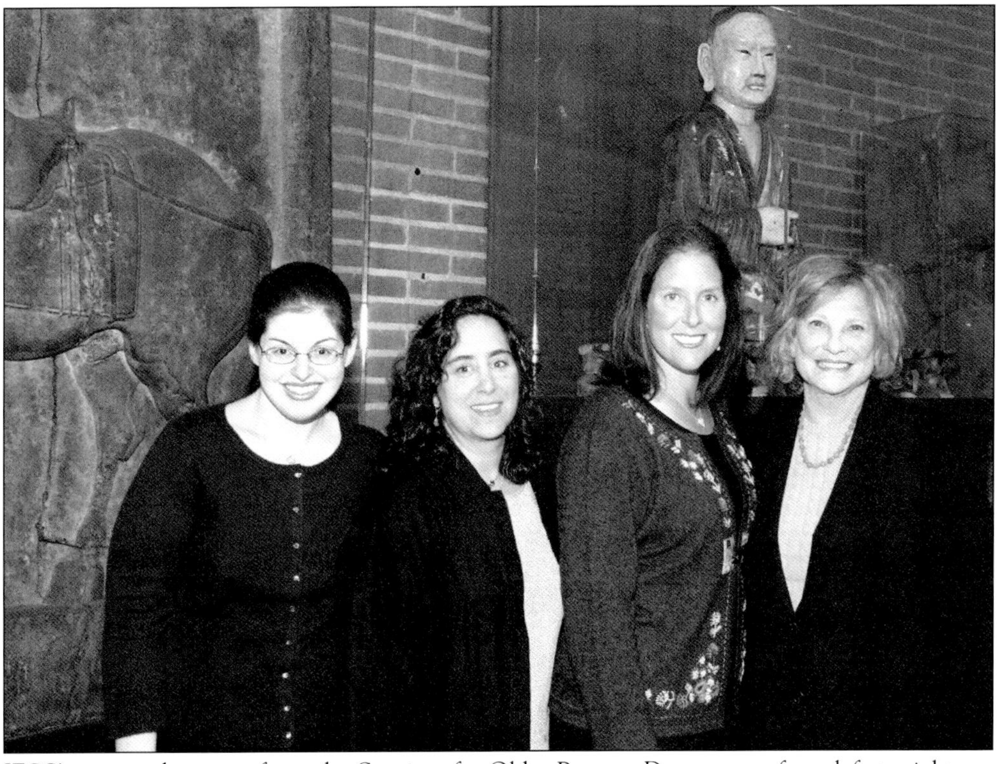

JFCS's past and present from the Services for Older Persons Department from left to right are Sara Popkin, former department social worker; Carrie Kanner, a current social worker who leads community outreach programming for the STAR (Services to Area Residents) program; Caren Comer-Fendrick, former Jewish Crisis Line manager; and Lenore Wasserman-Scola, department director, whose days with the agency began at JFCS's predecessor, JFS. (Courtesy of JFCS.)

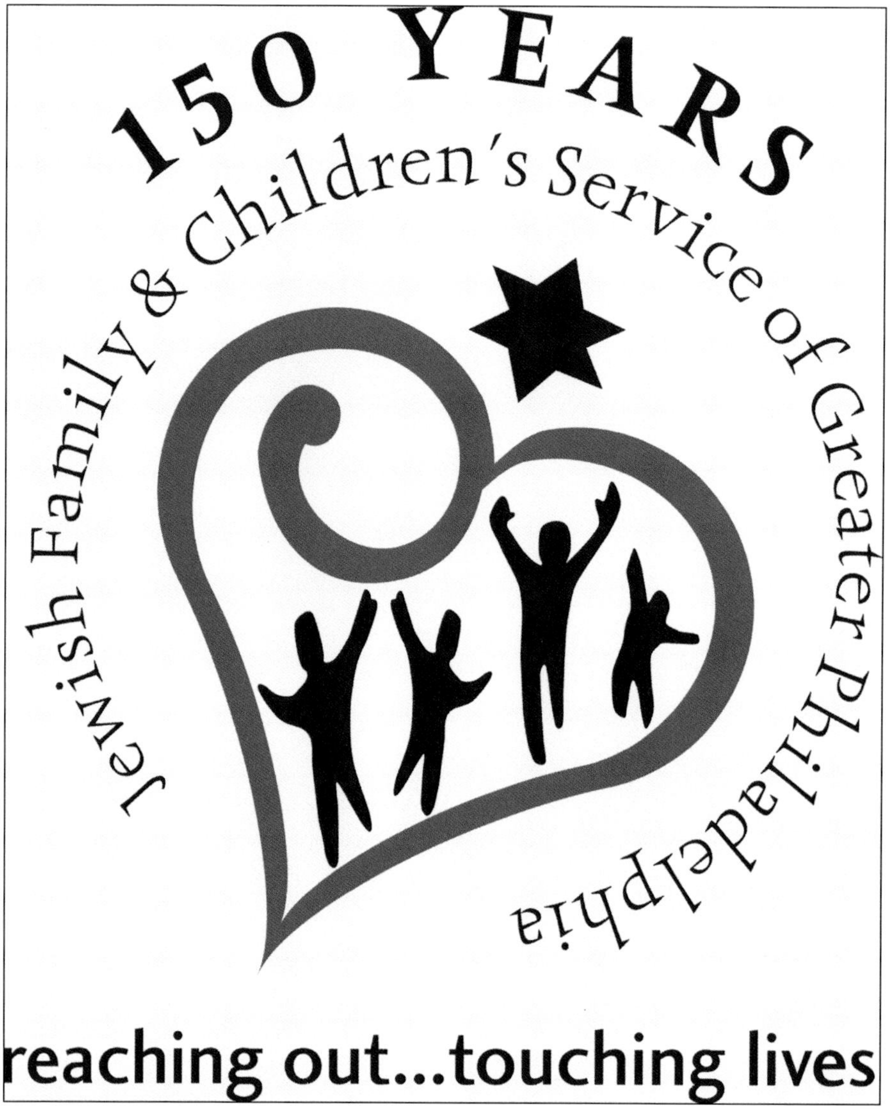

Jewish Family and Children's Service of Greater Philadelphia has undergone distinctive changes in its history. Founded to care for five Jewish children, today it serves 44,000 individuals and households each year and one in four households in the Jewish community. The 21st century is yet another era that brings new challenges to an agency that has celebrated not one but three jubilee anniversaries, with its 150th birthday in 2005. The 150th anniversary logo, shown here, did not feature a "traditional" family but a group of people of differing sizes to communicate that JFCS serves people of all ages—both individuals and families, including nontraditional families. The artwork reflects the aspirations of the agency in helping people "reach for the stars" and, as always, the Jewish values that guide its work. Jewish Family and Children's Service of Greater Philadelphia can be reached at:

2100 Arch Street, fifth floor, Philadelphia, PA 19103
Telephone: 215-496-9700
Help line: 1-866-JFCS-NOW
E-mail: info@jfcsphil.org
www.jfcsphil.org

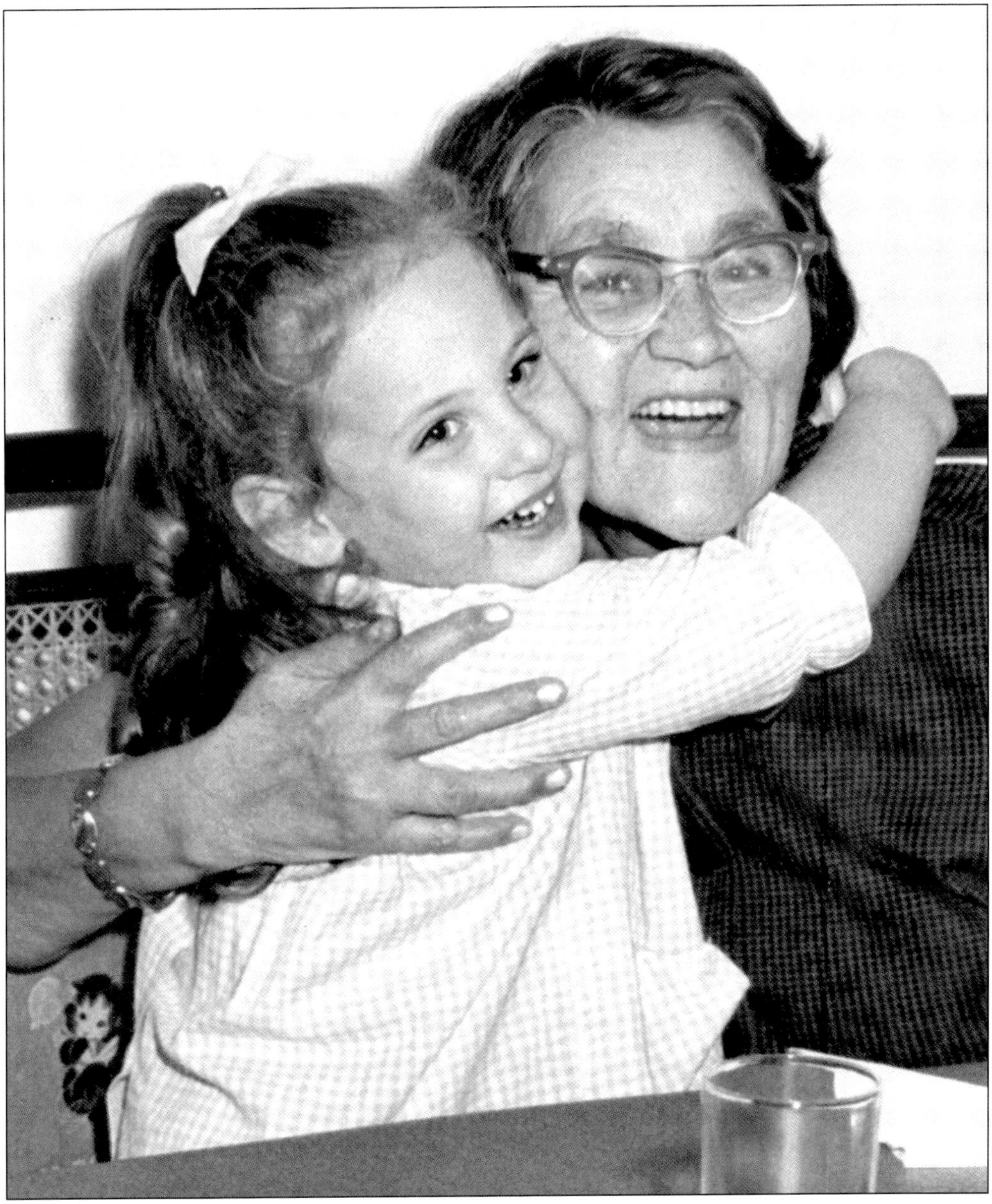

One hundred-fifty years, a million moments—the JFCS story continues.

AFTERWORD

I have had the honor of chairing the 150th anniversary celebration of our agency. It has certainly been a high point for me in my nearly 40 years of involvement with Jewish Family and Children's Service of Greater Philadelphia (JFCS) and one of its immediate predecessors, the Association for Jewish Children of Philadelphia (AJC)—years that include serving as JFCS board president and as solicitor for the merger of AJC with JFS. The 150th anniversary has given us the opportunity to recognize our staff, board of directors, volunteers, and clients with a series of events culminating in a wonderful reunion of people from all of these sectors and congratulations conveyed in person on that occasion by Pennsylvania governor Edward G. Rendell.

Throughout its existence, JFCS has raised the bar to help people in crisis and in need. It is truly the safety net for the Jewish community at all stages of the life cycle in providing services and programs that span birth through old age. In fact, even after my long years of involvement with the agency, I am still learning about the depth and breadth of our programs.

JFCS continues to be on the front lines of caring as a strong social service agency and advocate for people in need. Looking ahead, I feel confident of the continuing viability of our agency in its partnership with the Jewish Federation of Greater Philadelphia. The federation, in its strategic planning, has set forth certain priorities for funding, and I am confident that JFCS programs will continue to be a part of these priorities. For those programs that are not deemed to be a priority, the agency will look to our board and staff to raise the necessary funds to keep those programs going.

We really have much to celebrate from that time, over 150 years ago, when Rebecca Gratz started an orphanage for five Jewish children to our present agency, which serves more than 44,000 individuals and households a year. We have an outstanding staff, dedicated board leaders and volunteers, and a wide spectrum of clients who are all such an integral part of who we are and what we do. The theme of our anniversary gala in November 2005 was "Continuing the JFCS Voyage." What a voyage it has been for JFCS, and what a voyage I am sure it will continue to be for the next 150 years.

—Leonard Cooper